# Understanding
# CICS Internals

# J. Ranade IBM Series

| | | |
|---|---|---|
| 0-07-044129-4 | H. MURPHY | *ASSEMBLER for COBOL Programmers: MVS, VM* |
| 0-07-006533-0 | H. BOOKMAN | *COBOL II* |
| 0-07-051244-2 | J. RANADE | *VSAM: Concepts, Programming and Design* |
| 0-07-051245-0 | J. RANADE | *VSAM: Performance, Design and Fine Tuning* |
| 0-07-051143-8 | J. RANADE | *Advanced SNA Networking: A Professional's Guide for Using VTAM/NCP* |
| 0-07-051144-6 | J. RANADE | *Introduction to SNA Networking: A Guide to VTAM/NCP* |
| 0-07-051264-7 | J. RANADE | *DOS to OS/2: Conversion, Migration, and Application Design* |
| 0-07-051265-5 | J. RANADE | *DB2: Concepts, Programming, and Design* |
| 0-07-054594-4 | J. SANCHEZ | *IBM Microcomputers Handbook* |
| 0-07-054597-9 | J. SANCHEZ | *Programming Solutions Handbook for IBM Microcomputers* |
| 0-07-009816-6 | M. CARATHANASSIS | *Expert MVS/XA JCL: A Complete Guide to Advanced Techniques* |
| 0-07-009820-4 | M. CARATHANASSIS | *Expert MVS/ESA JCL: A Guide to Advanced Techniques* |
| 0-07-017606-X | P. DONOFRIO | *CICS: Debugging, Dump Reading and Problem Determination* |
| 0-07-017607-8 | P. DONOFRIO | *CICS: A Programmer's Reference* |
| 0-07-018966-8 | T. EDDOLLS | *VM Performance Management* |
| 0-07-033571-0 | P. KAVANAGH | *VS COBOL II for COBOL Programmers* |
| 0-07-040666-9 | T. MARTYN | *DB2/SQL: A Professional Programmer's Guide* |
| 0-07-050054-1 | S. PIGGOT | *CICS: A Practical Guide to System Fine Tuning* |
| 0-07-050686-8 | N. PRASAD | *IBM Mainframes: Architecture and Design* |
| 0-07-054528-6 | S. SAMSON | *MVS Performance Management* |
| 0-07-032673-8 | B. JOHNSON | *MVS: Concepts and Facilities* |
| 0-07-032674-6 | B. JOHNSON, D. JOHNSON | *DASD: IBM's Direct Access Storage Devices* |
| 0-07-071136-4 | A. WIPFLER | *Distributed Processing in the CICS Environment* |
| 0-07-071139-9 | A. WIPFLER | *CICS Application Development Programming* |
| 0-07-007252-3 | K. BRATHWAITE | *Relational DataBases: Concepts, Design, and Administration* |
| 0-07-028682-8 | G. GOLDBERG, I. SMITH | *The REXX Handbook* |
| 0-07-040763-0 | M. MARX, P. DAVIS | *MVS Power Programming* |
| 0-07-057553-3 | D. SILVERBERG | *DB2: Performance, Design, and Implementation* |
| 0-07-069460-5 | A. WERMAN | *DB2 Handbook for DBAs* |
| 0-07-002553-3 | G. HOUTEKAMER, P. ARTIS | *MVS I/O Subsystem: Configuration Management and Performance Analysis* |
| 0-07-033727-6 | A. KAPOOR | *SNA: Architecture, Protocols, and Implementation* |
| 0-07-014770-1 | R. CROWNITART | *IBM's Workstation CICS* |
| 0-07-015305-1 | C. DANEY | *Programming in REXX* |
| 0-07-037040-0 | J. KNEILING, R. LEFKON, P. SOMERS | *Understanding CICS Internals* |
| 0-07-022453-6 | A. FRIEND | *COBOL Application Debugging Under MVS: COBOL and COBOL II* |
| 0-07-008606-6 | L. BRUMBAUGH | *VSAM: Architecture, Theory, and Applications* |

# Understanding CICS Internals

John Kneiling

Richard Lefkon

Pamela Somers

**McGraw-Hill, Inc.**

New York   St. Louis   San Francisco   Auckland   Bogotá
Caracas   Lisbon   London   Madrid   Mexico   Milan
Montreal   New Delhi   Paris   San Juan   São Paulo
Singapore   Sydney   Tokyo   Toronto

**Library of Congress Cataloging-in-Publication Data**

Kneiling, John.
    Understanding CICS internals / John Kneiling, Pamela Somers,
Richard Lefkon.
       p.    cm. — (J. Ranade IBM series)
    Includes index.
    ISBN 0-07-037040-0
    1.  CICS (Computer system)   I.  Somers, Pamela.    II.  Lefkon,
Richard G.   III.  Title.   IV.  Series.
QA76.76.T45K64   1992
005.4'3—dc20                                        91–46305
                                                               CIP

Copyright © 1992 by McGraw-Hill, Inc. All rights reserved. Printed in the United States of America. Except as permitted under the United States Copyright Act of 1976, no part of this publication may be reproduced or distributed in any form or by any means, or stored in a database or retrieval system, without the prior written permission of the publisher.

1  2  3  4  5  6  7  8  9  0   DOC/DOC   9  7  6  5  4  3  2

**ISBN 0-07-037040-0**

*The sponsoring editor for this book was Jerry Papke, the editing supervisor was Joseph Bertuna, and the production supervisor was Pamela A. Pelton. It was set in Century Schoolbook by McGraw-Hill's Professional Book Group composition unit.*

*Printed and bound by R. R. Donnelley & Sons Company.*

---

Information contained in this work has been obtained by McGraw-Hill, Inc., from sources believed to be reliable. However, neither McGraw-Hill nor its authors guarantees the accuracy or completeness of any information published herein and neither McGraw-Hill nor its authors shall be responsible for any errors, omissions, or damages arising out of this information. This work is published with the understanding that McGraw-Hill and its authors are supplying information but are not attempting to render engineering or other professional services. If such services are required, the assistance of an appropriate professional should be sought.

*This book is dedicated to my wife Mescal
and my daughter Elizabeth*

— John

*This book is dedicated to my parents,
Arthur and Alice Somers*

— Pamela

# Contents

Preface    xi

## Chapter 1. Introduction    1

| | | |
|---|---|---:|
| 1.1 | CICS as a Multiprocessor | 1 |
| 1.2 | CICS Components | 1 |
| 1.3 | Control Modules | 2 |
| 1.4 | System Tables | 6 |
| 1.5 | Major Control Blocks | 7 |
| 1.6 | Application Programs | 8 |
| 1.7 | CICS Storage Layout | 9 |

## Chapter 2. Storage Control    15

| | | |
|---|---|---:|
| 2.1 | Introduction | 15 |
| 2.2 | DSA Organization | 16 |
| 2.3 | Storage Management Control Blocks | 19 |
| 2.4 | Storage Stress Conditions | 24 |

## Chapter 3. Task Control    27

| | | |
|---|---|---:|
| 3.1 | Introduction | 27 |
| 3.2 | Transactions and Tasks | 27 |
| 3.3 | The Task Control Area (TCA) | 28 |
| 3.4 | Attach and Dispatch | 31 |
| 3.5 | Dispatching Active Tasks | 34 |
| 3.6 | Suspend and Resume | 37 |
| 3.7 | Enqueue and Dequeue | 38 |
| 3.8 | End-of-Task Processing | 39 |

## Chapter 4. Program Control    41

| | | |
|---|---|---:|
| 4.1 | Introduction | 41 |
| 4.2 | DFHRPL and the PPT | 42 |
| 4.3 | Coding the PPT | 42 |

viii Contents

| | | |
|---|---|---|
| 4.4 | The PPT in Storage | 43 |
| 4.5 | Types of Programs | 44 |
| 4.6 | XA and Non-XA Flags | 48 |
| 4.7 | Programs in Core | 49 |
| 4.8 | SVA Program Counters | 51 |
| 4.9 | COBOL Fields | 51 |
| 4.10 | The Nucleus Load Table (NLT) | 52 |
| 4.11 | Interprogram Communication | 53 |
| 4.12 | LOAD and RELEASE | 56 |
| 4.13 | LINK, XCTL, and LOAD Logic | 58 |
| 4.14 | CICS Program Load Routine (OS) | 58 |
| 4.15 | RETURN Logic | 61 |
| 4.16 | Abend Processing | 61 |
| 4.17 | Postinitialization Processing | 62 |
| 4.18 | Shutdown Processing | 63 |
| 4.19 | The Command-Level Interface | 65 |
| 4.20 | The Assembler Language Interface | 72 |

## Chapter 5. Terminal Control 75

| | | |
|---|---|---|
| 5.1 | Introduction | 75 |
| 5.2 | Terminal Control Overview | 76 |
| 5.3 | BTAM Terminal Management | 78 |
| 5.4 | VTAM Terminal Management | 90 |
| 5.5 | Generating Terminal Control | 112 |
| 5.6 | NCP- and VTAM-Related Definitions | 116 |
| 5.7 | The TCAM ACB Interface | 117 |
| 5.8 | CICS VTAM Terminal Error Processing | 117 |
| 5.9 | Automatic Terminal Installation | 124 |

## Chapter 6. Terminal Hardware and Mapping Programs 129

| | | |
|---|---|---|
| 6.1 | Introduction | 129 |
| 6.2 | Basic Mapping Support (BMS) | 129 |
| 6.3 | Map Definition | 130 |
| 6.4 | BMS 3270 Feature Support | 131 |
| 6.5 | 3270 Device Support | 132 |
| 6.6 | CICS 3270 Data Streams | 138 |

## Chapter 7. File Control 145

| | | |
|---|---|---|
| 7.1 | Introduction | 145 |
| 7.2 | File Management Programs | 146 |
| 7.3 | The File Control Table (FCT) | 146 |
| 7.4 | BDAM Considerations | 147 |
| 7.5 | File Request Areas | 148 |
| 7.6 | Buffers and Strings | 150 |
| 7.7 | Local Shared Resources (LSR) | 151 |
| 7.8 | VSAM Subtasking | 153 |
| 7.9 | Alternate Indexes | 154 |
| 7.10 | Data Set States | 154 |

Contents ix

## Chapter 8. Database Management 157

| 8.1 | Introduction | 157 |
| 8.2 | Using CICS with a Database | 157 |
| 8.3 | The DB2–CICS Relationship | 160 |
| 8.4 | Two-Phase Commit Protocol (TPCP) | 168 |
| 8.5 | IMS and CICS | 169 |

## Chapter 9. Intercommunication Facilities 173

| 9.1 | Introduction | 173 |
| 9.2 | Overview | 173 |
| 9.3 | Connections | 174 |
| 9.4 | Why Use Intercommunication Facilities (ICF)? | 174 |
| 9.5 | Types of Intercommunication | 179 |
| 9.6 | Resource Definition | 182 |

## Chapter 10. Temporary Storage 183

| 10.1 | Introduction | 183 |
| 10.2 | Overview | 183 |
| 10.3 | Internal Uses of Temporary Storage | 184 |
| 10.4 | The Auxiliary Temporary Storage Data Set | 185 |
| 10.5 | Processing a WRITEQ TS Command | 187 |
| 10.6 | Auxiliary Temporary Storage Control Areas | 190 |
| 10.7 | Defining the Temporary Storage Table (TST) | 199 |

## Chapter 11. Interval Control 201

| 11.1 | Introduction | 201 |
| 11.2 | Time of Day | 201 |
| 11.3 | Task Synchronization | 202 |
| 11.4 | Task Initiation | 203 |
| 11.5 | Cancelling an Interval Control Request | 204 |
| 11.6 | Interval Control Data Areas | 204 |
| 11.7 | Request Handling Logic | 205 |
| 11.8 | ICE Expiration Analysis | 206 |

## Chapter 12. Transient Data 209

| 12.1 | Introduction | 209 |
| 12.2 | Transient Data Overview | 209 |
| 12.3 | Intrapartition Destinations | 210 |
| 12.4 | Extrapartition Destinations | 212 |
| 12.5 | Indirect Destinations | 212 |
| 12.6 | Automatic Task Initiation (ATI) | 213 |
| 12.7 | Transient Data Services Flow | 217 |
| 12.8 | Transient Data Facilities | 219 |
| 12.9 | Transient Data User Exits | 219 |

**x    Contents**

## Chapter 13.  Recovery/Restart Facilities    221

| | | |
|---|---|---|
| 13.1 | Introduction | 221 |
| 13.2 | A Recovery Philosophy | 221 |
| 13.3 | Types of Recovery | 223 |
| 13.4 | Error Analysis | 225 |
| 13.5 | LUWs and Sync Points | 226 |
| 13.6 | Logging and Journaling | 229 |
| 13.7 | Dynamic Transaction Backout (DTB) | 236 |
| 13.8 | User Recovery | 238 |
| 13.9 | Emergency Restart | 241 |
| 13.10 | File Control Resource Protection | 242 |

## Chapter 14.  Recovery/Restart Examples    245

| | | |
|---|---|---|
| 14.1 | Introduction | 245 |
| 14.2 | Transient Data Recovery | 245 |
| 14.3 | Main Storage Recovery Concepts | 254 |
| 14.4 | Temporary Storage Recovery | 258 |
| 14.5 | Interval Control Recovery | 262 |
| 14.6 | BMS Recovery and DTB (Page Building) | 265 |
| 14.7 | Terminal Control Error Handling | 267 |
| 14.8 | VTAM Message Protection Logging | 271 |
| 14.9 | Summary | 273 |

## Chapter 15.  Advanced Recovery Topics    275

| | | |
|---|---|---|
| 15.1 | Introduction | 275 |
| 15.2 | CICS/ESA | 275 |
| 15.3 | Extended Recovery Facility | 276 |
| 15.4 | XRF Configurations and Recovery Strategies | 281 |
| 15.5 | Forward Recovery with CICSVR | 282 |
| 15.6 | IMS/ESA with DBCTL | 285 |
| 15.7 | Recovery with DBCTL | 287 |
| 15.8 | XRF Support for DBCTL | 289 |

Index    291

# Preface

The purpose of this book is to present a detailed discussion of the architecture and internal processing of one of IBM's most widely used and successful products, Customer Information Control System (CICS). CICS is an online teleprocessing monitor that has enjoyed tremendous growth since its introduction in 1968, and it will continue to be a strategic product in the 1990s. This book is a first. There are quite a few books on the topic of CICS from an application programming viewpoint, and several devoted to various aspects of performance and tuning. But to date, a book on CICS internals has not been attempted. What you will find within is information that you might otherwise glean only by reading IBM licensed manuals or "going to the fiche." The book's ambition is to provide a type of knowledge and understanding that has been rather inaccessible to the wider audience within the CICS community.

### The Environment

The book covers CICS/DOS/VS version 1.7 and CICS/MVS version 2.1. There is a brief discussion of the new design of CICS that comes with CICS/ESA version 3, but it is only touched lightly, in the context of what is implied for the future of CICS. A treatment of version 2 is still of value today, as this version will exist into the mid-1990s and even beyond. Many applications, such as those written in Macro Level, will never be converted to version 3, and will simply remain running on version 2.

### Who the Book Is For

The book was written with various audiences in mind. Its most obvious appeal is to the systems programmer, who is either experienced in the field and wishes to fill in some gaps or who is just starting out and needs to acquire a broad base of knowledge. But, also, this book will appeal to a large group within the applications environment such as system designers, database administrators, and programmers, all of whom have a vested interest in understanding the underlying design and mechanics of the platform upon which they are implementing their own systems.

## What You Will Gain

After reading the book, you will have gained, on a general level, an understanding of why and how CICS is such an important offering, and what types of strategies will continue to ensure its future. With a fuller knowledge of the many CICS facilities, and the choices and tradeoffs available, the applications designer should be able to implement systems that take advantage of these. The systems programmer will become more cognizant of the range of options and parameters for tailoring CICS tables, and will be more knowledgeable of the key CICS resources that must be balanced and tuned for performance. You will learn about the major control programs and control blocks, their purposes, and how they interact in the performance of their functions. You will gain an understanding of the Macro underpinnings of CICS, which became all but transparent to the Command-level user with the advent of the High-Level Interface. By looking at details, you will gain an insight into the big picture of how CICS operates. You will be able to appreciate the theory behind this asynchronous, wait-driven, task-based software that is a mini-operating system onto itself.

## Required Background

Some basic knowledge of CICS is desirable as a prerequisite for comprehending the material, as this book positions itself from the outset on an advanced level. However, it is not necessary to be an expert in order to gain benefit. Backgrounds can range from extensive systems programming experience to some knowledge of Command Level application programming or to an overall understanding of CICS concepts and facilities.

## How the Book Is Structured

The material presented is based upon a two-semester course on CICS Internals given by John Kneiling at the New York University School of Continuing Education over the course of some years. It was the feedback from students concerning the topics of interest that helped fashion the course and refined it into the structure that is presented in this book. The first part of the book, which could be referred to as CICS internals I, devotes a separate chapter to each of the major management modules. The remaining chapters discuss advanced topics such as intersystem communication (ISC and MRO), restart and recovery concepts, and database management facilities (specifically IMS and DB2). Finally, there is a preview of some Version 3 features, focusing on enhancements to recovery and database management.

## Style of the Book

In order to explain some of the more arcane aspects of CICS, wording has deliberately been kept simple and conversational where possible, using the same informal classroom style in which the material was originally presented. Figures, diagrams, and coding examples are provided to supplement the text and provide elucidation where needed.

## Acknowledgments

I would like to acknowledge my students, whose interest provided the continual impetus for the development of the course, and, ultimately, this book.

*— John*

I would like to thank Henry Koeppel and Lynnette Lumbreyer, without whose generous help this book would not have been published.

*— Pamela*

We would like to thank Jerry Papke, our editor at McGraw-Hill, and other members of the editorial staff for their support and assistance in preparing this book for publication. We would also like to acknowledge Jay Ranade, our editor in chief, for his great patience in allowing this book to come to fruition. We are hoping that it will prove worth the wait.

*— The Authors*

# Understanding
# CICS Internals

Chapter

# 1

# Introduction

## 1.1. CICS as a Multiprocessor

All CICS processing is transaction-based. Just what is a transaction, and how does it differ from a task? There is always a little bit of confusion concerning the difference between a task and a transaction, because documentation will often use the two terms interchangeably. A task could be called the internal representation of a transaction: we might say that a transaction is a type of work, and a task is an iteration of that work. A transaction is invoked at a terminal, and CICS builds a task to execute that transaction. The major control block for a task is the Task Control area (TCA). The Program Control Table (PCT) contains the names of the different kinds of transactions. CICS can handle different pieces of work (tasks) at the same time by overlapping I/O with CPU, just as MVS manages jobs by balancing the two. When CICS was first developed, IBM could have designed a CICS that was hardware-based. Instead, CICS was developed as software, running as an on-line feature in what is essentially a batch machine. Ideally we would have a CPU and operating system dedicated to CICS; that is, CICS would be the operating system. We do not have that, so, as a result, we generally see CICS running at a high priority (sometimes higher than JES, in the MVS world). It is conceivable that the CICS of the future will be hardware-based, interacting with VTAM and NCP and the database, but for now it simply runs at a high priority, giving up control to the operating system when it has no work to do.

## 1.2. CICS Components

CICS can logically be divided into four areas: control modules, system tables, control blocks, and application programs.

## 2 Chapter One

### 1.2.1. Control modules

The control modules are programs running in the CICS region that handle requests from applications by implementing CICS macros and commands. They communicate with the outside world by issuing calls to the operating system. Although a control module is a system program to a CICS application, it is an application program in the eyes of the operating system. It implements a macro or command as a system program. It issues a request to the operating system as an application program.

### 1.2.2. System tables

How do we tell the control modules about the environment they control? We tell them, and also tailor our specific system to our needs, by coding CICS system tables. These tables form the basis of CICS.

### 1.2.3. Control blocks

Control blocks are very much like tables, but they contain information that changes as CICS runs. They have essentially dynamic information, as opposed to the system tables, which are fairly static. When CICS starts up, we have a certain finite environment in which certain things will change, for example the number of concurrent tasks. Those things that change are maintained in control blocks.

## 1.3. Control Modules

Now let us look at the functions performed by the different control modules, also referred to as management modules. We will not discuss specific management modules yet; we will just review the various functions.

### 1.3.1. Task Management

We said that CICS is transaction-based or task-based. Task Management, which is the heartbeat of CICS, is really nothing more than a dispatcher whose function it is to see if there is any work to be done, or if any pieces of work that are waiting (for example, on I/O) are able to continue. If they are, Task Control dispatches them.

### 1.3.2. Storage Management

The Storage Control module manages all storage in the CICS region. It manages the dynamic storage area (DSA) and performs all CICS storage allocation and deallocation. The major users of this facility are other CICS management modules, although CICS application programs use it when they explicitly request storage (by issuing a CICS GETMAIN).

### 1.3.3. Program Management

This facility manages the application programs. It controls the loading into storage, releasing from storage, and invocation of application programs. Invocation includes linking, returning, and transferring of control.

### 1.3.4. Terminal Management

Terminal Management handles all terminal I/O, in cooperation with the various terminal access methods (which today is primarily VTAM).

### 1.3.5. Time Management

This function keeps track of the time of day, and controls all time services. There are many time services within CICS. For example, a task can suspend itself for a period of time. Tasks time out occasionally. Also, we can request initiation of a task at a particular time of day or after a particular interval.

### 1.3.6. File Management

The File Management module is reponsible for access to all file and database requests used by applications running in the CICS region.

### 1.3.7. Transient Data Management

Transient Data is a queueing facility for data sent to and from user-defined destinations. It can be an internal or external facility; that is, we can define destinations to which data are sent both inside and outside CICS. We can also use this facility to send data from one application to another, and this was an early form of intersystem communication.

### 1.3.8. Temporary Storage Management

Temporary Storage is a scratchpad facility which uses either virtual storage or DASD. It is a kind of informal Transient Data which allows us to maintain small queues of data. Later, we will see how it differs from Transient Data.

### 1.3.9. Dump Management

This facility dumps a CICS task and, optionally, CICS tables in the event of a program abend. It also can produce a formatted dump for a system abend.

4 Chapter One

### 1.3.10. Journal Management

Journal Management allows creation, management, and retrieval of real-time sequential journals. CICS has journals that exist primarily for restart and recovery purposes, which we will cover in depth. Journals hold before-images of records so that changes can be backed out if they need to be (this is called backward recovery). They also hold after-images of records so that if we need to recover forward, we can take after-images and apply them (this is called forward recovery).

### 1.3.11. Trace Management

Trace Management allows application and control modules to trace their processing flow. CICS can produce a Trace Table which shows which control modules were entered and gives you a sketchy idea of what applications and control modules were doing in terms of requests to CICS. If we code an EXEC CICS command in our program, we issue a CICS request, and we get an entry in the Trace Table that says that our task asked CICS to service this request. We will also see a Trace entry if one control module asks another control module to do something. We can request an entry in the Trace Table ourselves at any point, which is useful for debugging. We might put something in a sensitive module or one that we are watching, so that we can see that it reached a certain point before crashing. For instance, we might put a Trace request in a terminal exit, so that if something occurred in production, we could see what it was. Trace Table debugging is particularly suited to a production environment, where we do not want to have a debugger running.

### 1.3.12. Basic Mapping Support

Basic Mapping Support (BMS) is another layer, or buffer, between the application and Terminal Management. It facilitates information display and allows device independence. It basically means that we can write to terminals without having to understand where to put all those hex fifteens and zero charlies. We do not have to understand 3270 data streams; we can let CICS map our output to a terminal or printer without actually having to format it ourselves. Instead of telling Terminal Management to send some data to a 3270, we tell BMS that we have some data, and request BMS to massage it into a format acceptable for the screen.

### 1.3.13. Intercommunication Management

Intercommuncication Management allows CICS to communicate with other CICS regions, other systems such as IMS or DB2, and other applications, CPUs, and operating systems. The two basic types of communication provided by CICS are interregion, or multiregion option (MRO), and intersystem communication (ISC).

### 1.3.14. On-line functions

Functions that happen on-line include CICS startup and shutdown, system initialization and termination, recovery from various types of errors, and Master Terminal Support, which is a way to vary the environment on-line via a command called CEMT. CICS also provides new facilities for defining resources on-line. Under the umbrella of Resource Definition On-line (RDO), we can define transactions, programs, and terminals on-line instead of coding macros and assembling system tables. For CICS/ESA, this is less an option and more a replacement for table definition.

### 1.3.15. Off-line functions

Off-line functions are those carried out when CICS is down, such as coding and assembling system tables, performing a system generation (SYSGEN), compiling application programs and maps, or processing CICS journals.

### 1.3.16. System generation

We do not really need to generate a system, as IBM gives us a pregenned tape. However, at least for releases of CICS prior to CICS/ESA, we have the ability to tailor the system to our needs. For instance, IBM gives us a Terminal Management function that supports every type of terminal, as IBM does not know what kind of terminals we have. But if everything in our shop is a 3270, we can use the system generation facility of CICS to tailor our Terminal Control Program to support only the 3270 devices and CICS printers that we need. Thus we can remove pounds and pounds of ugly fat from the CICS region.

### 1.3.17. Preparation of application programs

Any CICS application command-level program must go through a special processor called the Translator prior to compilation or assembly. The Translator translates EXEC CICS commands into either COBOL move statements and calls to the EXEC Interface program, or macros for assembler programs. The EXEC Interface program is the way command-level applications communicate with CICS. This will be discussed in detail in Chapter 4, "Program Control."

## 1.4. System Tables

The system tables are the mechanism by which we define our system and also tailor it to our particular environment. To illustrate how the various tables work, we will use an example of defining a sample inquiry transaction called INQY.

### 1.4.1. Terminal Control Table (TCT)

Since we need to access the transaction through a terminal, we will first define the terminal in the TCT. This is the mechanism by which we define the terminals, the printers, the lines, and links to other systems.

### 1.4.2. Program Control Table (PCT)

The next step is to define the transaction in the PCT. (This is really the Transaction Control Table, but the letters TCT were already taken by Terminal Control!) The PCT is a two-part table which contains the name of the transaction and the name of the first program associated with the transaction. This is the inquiry program INQYPGM that gets invoked when the transaction INQY is entered at the terminal.

### 1.4.3. Program Properties Table (PPT)

The PPT defines and contains information about the inquiry program INQYPGM and its associated mapset and map(s). The mapset contains the maps used by the program if it is using BMS mapping facilities. Each mapset is defined separately in the PPT.

### 1.4.4. File Control Table (FCT)

The FCT describes each file in the CICS region. In order to access a file from a CICS program, a request must be issued to File Control, which then gets the information it needs from the FCT. When we read or write to a file in CICS, we use the short name defined in the FCT.

### 1.4.5. Destination Control Table (DCT)

The DCT contains information about the Transient Data (TD) queues. TD destinations may be either within or outside of CICS, and must be defined in the DCT. Intrapartition destinations are those within CICS. You can associate an intrapartition destination with both a transaction and a printer, which is the traditional way of writing to a CICS printer. The application writes to destination ABC, which is associated in the DCT with printer ABC and transaction ABC. Transaction ABC gets initiated automatically when the program writes to the ABC queue. It reads the queue, and routes what was read to printer ABC. Extrapartition TD queues are outside the region. They might be QSAM files or the internal reader.

### 1.4.6. Journal Control Table (JCT)

The JCT works with the Journal Control function for defining system journals or logs. These may reside on tape or on disk.

### 1.4.7. Temporary Storage Table (TST)

This table is optional. Temporary Storage is a scratchpad queueing facility used by applications to save data. You can use the TST to define important Temporary Storage queues, thereby making them recoverable, but scratchpad queues are not normally defined in the TST. Temporary Storage can reside either in main storage or on auxiliary storage (DASD).

## 1.5. Major Control Blocks

### 1.5.1. Common System Area (CSA)

We have taken an overview of the CICS modules that control the environment, handle requests from CICS applications, and interface to the outside world. We have also looked at the system tables that define the environment to CICS. Now let us review the major control blocks within CICS. Control blocks, remember, contain changeable information about things that can happen on the fly, making them different from tables, which are static. The cornerstone control block in CICS is the CSA, which has all the baseline information about the CICS session for which it was built. There is one CSA per CICS region. It contains pointers to CICS management modules, system tables, the addresses of other control blocks, and some embedded system information and code. Everything is rooted in the CSA.

### 1.5.2. Task Control Area (TCA)

A TCA is built for each task when it is created. The TCA has pointers to the task's storage and to task-related information in other control blocks. It has information concerning what requests this task has made to CICS, and other task information such as the task's register save areas. For six iterations of the same transaction, six separate TCAs will exist.

### 1.5.3. Dispatch Control Area (DCA)

DCAs are chained off the TCA and used by Task Management to control task dispatching. The DCA is a logical extension of the TCA, and

## 8 Chapter One

for each TCA, there is a related DCA. The DCA contains information such as a task's priority and dispatching status. The DCA was created as a shorthand version of the TCA for performance reasons. All the Dispatcher really needs is a small amount of information, in contrast to the large size of the TCA. Use of a much smaller DCA can help optimize paging patterns: if all the DCAs can reside on one page, for example, chances are that dispatching will go a lot faster.

### 1.5.4. Terminal Input-Output Area (TIOA)

The TIOA is the vehicle of communication between the application and CICS Terminal Management. If an application wants to send data out to a terminal, it does not need to know anything about the terminal. It simply asks CICS to send some data. The data are placed in a buffer, where they will be read by Terminal Management, which communicates with VTAM. VTAM actually sends the data to the terminal.

### 1.6. Application Programs

CICS applications can be written in the Assembler, COBOL, PL/I, or RPG II (DOS only) language. When an application needs something, it asks CICS to intercede on its behalf. Figure 1.1 lists some of the services an application can ask for. This is by no means a comprehensive

| Service | Macro | Command |
|---|---|---|
| Task | DFHKC | DEQ, ENQ, SUSPEND |
| Storage | DFHSC | GETMAIN, FREEMAIN |
| Program | DFHPC | LINK, LOAD, XCTL |
| Terminal | DFHTC | SEND, RECEIVE |
| Time | DFHIC | START, ASKTIME |
| File | DFHFC | READ, WRITE |
| Transient data | DFHTD | WRITEQ TD, READQ TD |
| Temporary storage | DFHTS | WRITEQ TS, READQ TS |
| Dump | DFHDC | DUMP |
| Journal | DFHJC | JOURNAL |
| Trace | DFHTR | ENTER, TRACE ON |
| Basic mapping support | DFHBMS | SEND MAP, RECEIVE MAP |

**Figure 1.1** Some CICS service requests.

listing of the commands (and the corresponding macros) that can be issued. Management modules use macros to request services from one another. Originally CICS was a macro-level system. You coded a macro, and that macro generated code to put the request in the TCA. It loaded an address—for instance, the address of the File Control module—from the CSA into register 14, then issued a branch to this address. CICS is still macro-driven, but now we have an interface built on top of the existing structure, called the EXEC Interface (DFHEIS). We essentially branch to a piece of code that issues a CICS macro. In Fig. 1.1 we see that each macro starts with DFH, followed by the two-letter designation for the management module the macro corresponds to. For instance, DFHKC is a call to DFHKCP, the Task Control module. File Control has a counterpart within the EXEC Interface, in a program called DFHEFC. All DFHEFC does, besides some validity checking and internal table management, is issue a macro to DFHFCP. Once out of the interface, CICS is macro-based. An application WRITE may pass through a DFHJC macro if the file is protected, for example, to perhaps issue an enqueue. It might then pass through DFHSC to get some file buffer storage. Everything is modular, in a real sense, within CICS. Each function is insulated, has a particular job to do, and does not duplicate what another module is doing. CICS is very clean this way. When we type in INQY at the terminal, Terminal Management's function is twofold: it first reads the input into a buffer, and then asks Task Control to get the task going by issuing a request to the Task Control program (DFHKC TYPE=ATTACH). Reasons for not using macro-level CICS? Macro-level support is now frozen by IBM, and is on its way out the door. Many parameters for macros are not documented, the reason being that IBM did not wish to commit to supporting those parameters. What they were saying was that they might change their internal architecture, so do not use this particular parameter (which is exactly what IBM has done with CICS/ESA).

## 1.7. CICS Storage Layout

The CICS region is functionally divided into three main areas: the nucleus, the DSA, and the operating system storage (OSCOR for MVS or GETVIS for DOS). In general, it can be said that the nucleus belongs to the system, and contains management information, while the DSA belongs to the application, and contains task information. The third area is used for CICS communication with the operating system. At initialization, CICS allocates the nucleus and the OSCOR/GETVIS areas first. The remainder is used for the DSA. Therefore, DSA size is largely a function of region size. Figure 1.2 shows diagrams of the CICS regions under MVS and DOS/VSE.

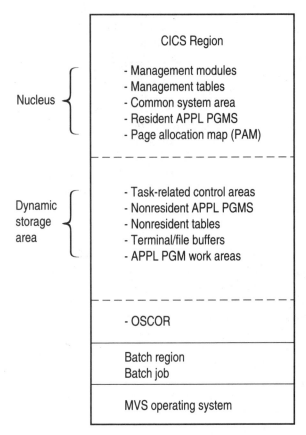

**Figure 1.2(a)** CICS storage in MVS.

### 1.7.1. The nucleus

The nucleus consists primarily of system modules, tables, and control areas used to maintain systemwide status information. However, user-written application programs may be designated to reside in the CICS nucleus. The nucleus is built during system initialization and is fairly static, changing very little during execution. We may have a control block that changes, but that control block is built at initialization and stays there for the duration of CICS.

### 1.7.2. CICS control block characteristics

Control blocks are used by CICS management modules to hold control information, as opposed to environmental information. For example, environmental information might be a list of terminals or files, as contained in a table, while control information would be the address of a

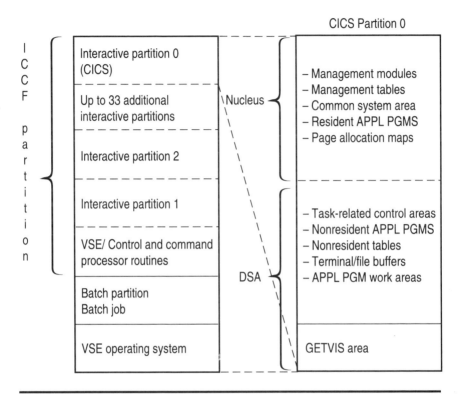

**Figure 1. 2(b)** CICS storage in VSE.

management module. Control blocks are built during initialization, and may be large or small, static or dynamic. The control block is generally in the nucleus, but can also be in the DSA. In the DSA there is a logical pool of pages called the Control subpool, a special subpool that contains control blocks. Two key control blocks in the nucleus are the CSA, which contains the environmental information, and the Page Allocation Map (PAM), which contains data used by CICS storage management to handle dynamic allocation and deallocation of DSA storage. Figure 1.3 shows a depiction of the CSA and its adjacent areas.

### 1.7.3. The common system area (CSA)

The CSA resides in the nucleus, and exists from initialization until shutdown. It has three parts: the CSA system area, the common work area (CWA), and the optional features list (OFL). The CSA system area contains pointers to management modules, tables, control blocks, exception handling routines, and active task information.

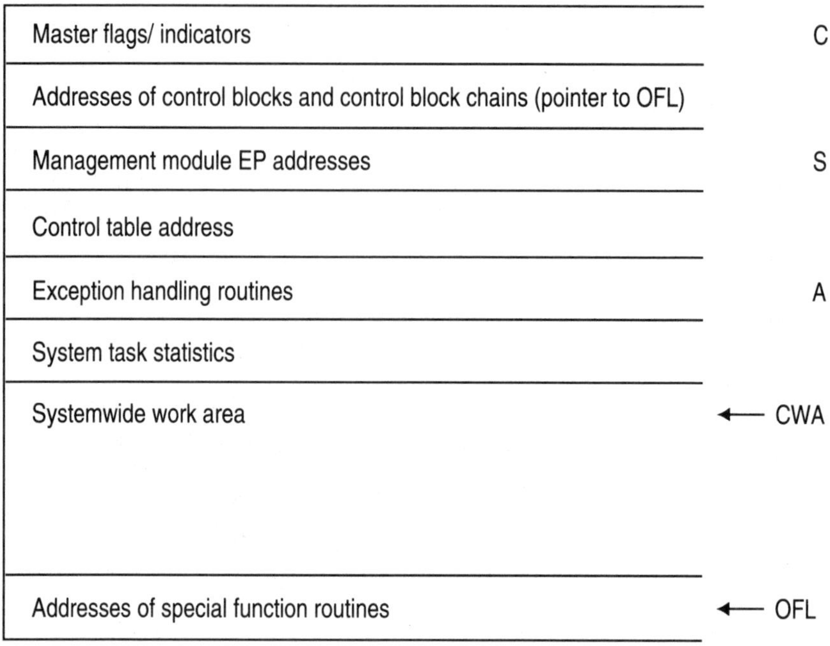

**12    Chapter One**

| | |
|---|---|
| Master flags/ indicators | C |
| Addresses of control blocks and control block chains (pointer to OFL) | |
| Management module EP addresses | S |
| Control table address | |
| Exception handling routines | A |
| System task statistics | |
| Systemwide work area | ← CWA |
| | |
| Addresses of special function routines | ← OFL |

**Figure 1.3**  The CSA, CWA, and OFL.

### 1.7.4.  Common work area (CWA)

The CWA, which is optional, can be used by applications to contain systemwide information. It provides a way to store information, perhaps table addresses, a date, or a switch setting, in a central location which can be accessed by all applications, analogous to what IBM does on the system level, but for applications. The CWA can be any size, but is guaranteed to start adjacent to the end of the CSA. Since it is not a system area, it is called a work area. To access the CWA, you must first establish addressability to the CSA, then determine the offset, based on CSA size, which is fixed.

### 1.7.5.  Optional features list (OFL)

The OFL was created to accommodate some new features that had been added to CICS, such as BMS, the DL/I interface, recovery routines, the EXEC Interface program, and more. IBM needed to enlarge the CSA, but the CWA was in the way. To avoid forcing users to recompile/reassemble all their existing programs, IBM created an extension to the CSA called the OFL, having it start at the end of the CSA, or the CWA if it exists.

### 1.7.6. Dynamic storage area (DSA)

The DSA is a pool of storage pages that is used as needed by transactions executing in CICS. It is a single contiguous block of virtual storage, logically divided into subpools, which satisfies all requests for dynamic storage, either for transaction processing or for resource management. The reason for having different logical (not necessarily contiguous) subpools is so that different types of storage can be grouped together based on similar characteristics, such as size, frequency of use, type of use, or length of use, to better take advantage of MVS paging algorithms. The DSA is managed by the Storage Control Program (DFHSCP), which uses a PAM and associated byte maps to account for DSA pages. A GETMAIN or FREEMAIN request is directed to DFHSCP rather than to the operating system. DSA storage is allocated for non-resident programs, data areas, and task management areas. Storage is acquired and released dynamically. The DSA is not static, and changes constantly: One second, a piece of the storage may be used for terminal input-output, and the next, it may contain a copy of an application program.

CICS uses the DSA to manage some system resources, such as Temporary Storage and BMS. The DSA is divided into virtual storage increments, determined by the SIT PGSIZE operand. DSA pages are normally either 2 or 4 Kbytes, and are not necessarily the same size as operating system pages but can correspond, as this is usually the most efficient size. Control blocks that reside in the DSA are primarily task-related, such as:

- File, Terminal, TD, and TS areas
- CICS internal control blocks
- Task Control areas (TCAs)
- Journal Control areas (JCAs)

### 1.7.7. Operating system storage

OSCOR (in MVS) or GETVIS (in DOS) is used primarily for access methods and work areas. It exists at the low end of the address space, and contains access method programs, VSAM buffers and strings, and channel programs built by the access methods. OSCOR in MVS is created in the following manner:

CICS issues a conditional/variable GETMAIN for 16 Mbytes.

OSCOR gets all the remaining storage in the region for CICS.

CICS FREEMAINs 10 Kbytes from the high end and 8 Kbytes from the low end to allow room for control blocks used during initialization.

CICS does a conditional `GETMAIN` for the SIT OSCOR value.

If it succeeds, the area is freed immediately and is available for OSCOR `GETMAIN`s.

If it fails, the OSCOR value is freed from the future DSA area.

So how much OSCOR is there? It is a function of the following formula:

The OSCOR value specified in the SIT + the IEALIMIT exit routine. The default is 64 Kbytes + the 18 Kbytes freed during initialization + any remaining unallocated storage in the region.

Figure 1.4 shows a graphic illustration.

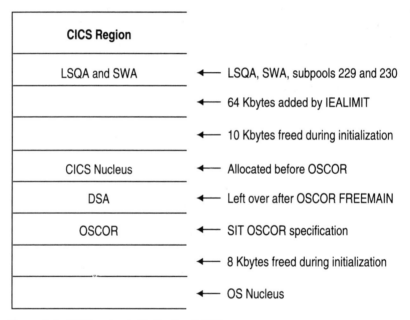

**Figure 1.4**  CICS region initialization (MVS).

Chapter

# 2

# Storage Control

## 2.1. Introduction

This chapter explains the balancing of dynamic storage against the other CICS areas, and a step-by-step description shows just how CICS responds to storage shortages. The reasoning behind the six dynamic storage subpools is discussed, as are the indicators associated with every page of this storage. The features of storage accounting areas and free area queue elements are compared.

At the end of the chapter you will know:

- How the dynamic storage area (DSA) is organized
- What the CICS subpools are used for, and how to locate them
- How to follow free and allocated storage area chains
- How transaction storage is chained
- How to interpret the contents of the Page Allocation Map (PAM)
- The relationship between byte maps and the DSA
- How program compression recycles DSA storage pages
- What happens during the Short-on-Storage (SOS) condition
- How CICS recovers from a storage violation

The Storage Control Program (SCP) manages all storage in the DSA. When an application or system module needs main core for a control block or work area, the SCP will find an available area, allocate it, and pass it to the requesting module. Later, when the storage is no longer needed, SCP will deallocate it. An application program can request storage explicitly by using the EXEC CICS GETMAIN command. Often,

16    Chapter Two

however, storage is requested by CICS management modules to facilitate processing an application request. When an application issues an `EXEC CICS READ DATASET` command, for instance, the File Control Program (FCP) issues the storage control macro on its behalf.

## 2.2. DSA Organization

The DSA is divided into blocks of virtual storage called pages (see Fig. 2.1). A page is usually 2 or 4 Kbytes, depending on the `PGSIZE` value in the System Initialization Table (SIT). The DSA itself is allocated by the System Initialization Program after it initializes the CICS nucleus and either OSCOR (OS) or GETVIS (DOS).

### 2.2.1. Subpools

The DSA is used to satisfy a variety of storage requests, and it contains many different types of control blocks and work areas. To keep similar storage areas together, the SCP groups them by size and duration into logical areas of the DSA called subpools (see Fig. 2.2). A subpool is a logical (not necessarily contiguous) collection of DSA pages. These pages may be clustered or scattered within the DSA. Although a subpool may own more than one page, two subpools may not share pages. The size of a subpool at any given time is dynamic and is a function of the number of requests issued for that type of storage.

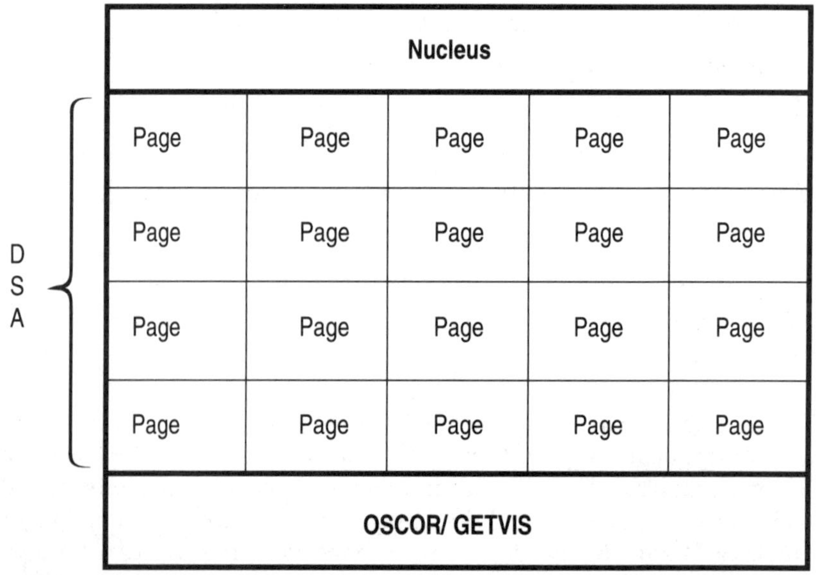

| Nucleus | | | | |
|---|---|---|---|---|
| Page | Page | Page | Page | Page |
| Page | Page | Page | Page | Page |
| Page | Page | Page | Page | Page |
| Page | Page | Page | Page | Page |
| OSCOR/ GETVIS | | | | |

D S A

**Figure 2.1**  Dynamic storage area.

## Storage Control    17

| Code | Name | Subpool | Description |
|------|------|---------|-------------|
| 80 | 1 WD | 05 | Undocumented; used by CICS mgt modules |
| 81 | DCA | 01 | Used by KCP to chain and dispatch tasks |
| 82 | QEA | 01 | Used by KCP to control resources |
| 83 | Reserved | | |
| 84 | Line | 02 | LIOA; BTAM line storage |
| 85 | Terminal | 02 | TIOA; Terminal I/O storage |
| 86 | ICE | 01 | Unexpired time-ordered event |
| 87 | AID | 01 | Expired ICE waiting for a terminal |
| 88 | Program | 08 | Nonresident application program |
| 89 | RSA | 04 | Saves registers between LINK and RETURN |
| 8A | TCA | 04 | Central control block for each task |
| 8B | LLA | 04 | Acquired for programs LOADed by a task |
| 8C | User | 04 | General purpose transaction storage |
| 8D | TRANSDATA | 04 | TDIA and TDIO; Transient Data requests |
| 8E | TEMPSTRG | 04 | TSIOA; Temporary Storage requests |
| 8F | File | 04 | File request storage |
| 90 | RPL | 06 | VTAM Request Parameter List storage |
| 91 | BCA | 05 | Asynchronous batched control area |
| 92 | WRE | 05 | Asynchronous batched transaction area |
| 93 | Shared | 05 | Various infrequently referenced areas |
| 94 | Control | 01 | Management module long-term storage |
| 95 | Reserved | | |
| 96 | TACLE | 05 | BTAM out-of-service line entry |
| 97 | TSMAIN | 05 | MAIN Temporary Storage |
| 98 | TSTABLE | 05 | Temporary Storage maps |
| 99 | Map | 05 | Used by BMS for map processing |
| 9A | Reserved | | |
| 9B | JCA | 04 | Used for Journal Control requests |
| 9C | Reserved | | |
| 9D | DWE | 04 | Work deferred until a syncpoint |
| 9E | Mapcopy | 04 | BMS maps |
| 9F | DL/I | 06 | DL/I Interface Scheduling Block (ISB) |

**Figure 2.2**  Subpools.

The three main reasons for having subpools are to eliminate as many page faults as possible, to avoid storage fragmentation, and to provide a mechanism for recovery. The DSA contains six subpools. Each subpool has a name, and a number from 01 to 08. Subpool 07 does not exist, and subpool 03 support was dropped in CICS release 1.7. Application programs do not make direct use of subpools 01, 05, and 06.

The Control subpool (01) contains CICS system control blocks used by management modules only. These areas are small, of long duration,

18    Chapter Two

and frequently referenced, and tend to remain paged in. Dispatch control areas (DCAs) requested by the Task Control Program (DFHKCP) are allocated from this subpool when a task is created. (See Chap. 3.)

The RPL subpool (06) is used only for VTAM Request Parameter Lists. The CICS VTAM Terminal Control Program (DFHZCP) requests RPL storage when it issues a VTAM command to satisfy an application's terminal I/O request.

The Shared subpool (05) holds Temporary Storage control blocks, main storage data, DL/I control blocks, and other infrequently referenced control blocks. In XA versions of CICS, all DSA storage above the 16-Mbyte line belongs to this subpool.

The Teleprocessing (TP) subpool (02) holds line and terminal I/O areas. When a task requests CICS Terminal Control services, it places the data in a Terminal Input-Output Area (TIOA) satisfied from this subpool.

The Isolated subpool (04) holds non-terminal-oriented task storage. All of this storage is chained from the task's main control block, the TCA (task control area).

Nonresident application programs are loaded in the Program subpool (08). These pages are usually contiguous, and can be found at the high address end of the DSA. Programs do not share pages with one another. If a program is larger than a page, SCP will place it on adjacent pages within the DSA. SCP tries to keep these pages separate from all other subpool pages by allocating program and nonprogram storage from opposite ends of the DSA.

### 2.2.2. Storage classes

Storage Control allocation requests specify a particular type of storage by name. When SCP fulfills the request, it tags the area with a code corresponding to the name. There are 32 possible types of DSA storage in CICS. Each type is assigned to a storage class with a hexadecimal code between 80 and 9F. Each of these classes is in turn assigned to a particular subpool.

### 2.2.3. Summary

Storage Control requests are satisfied out of the DSA. The DSA is divided physically into 2- or 4-Kbyte pages, and logically into subpools. Each subpool is a collection of DSA pages that hold similar classes of storage. System-related areas are allocated from the Control, Shared, and VTAM RPL subpools (01, 05, and 06, respectively). Task-related storage uses the Isolated and Teleprocessing subpools (04 and 02). Nonresident programs use the Program subpool. Pages from this subpool are allocated from the high end of the DSA; all others, from the low end.

## 2.3. Storage Management Control Blocks

The SCP uses several control blocks to manage the DSA. The PAM and its associated byte maps keep track of each page. Storage accounting areas (SAAs) prefix each area allocated within a DSA page. The free area queue element (FAQE) accounts for unallocated storage within most (but not all) pages.

### 2.3.1. The Page Allocation Map (PAM)

Storage Control uses a PAM while processing `GETMAIN` and `FREEMAIN` requests (see Fig. 2.3). The PAM is in the nucleus, and is addressed by the CSAPAMA at offset CSA + X'98'.

The PAM contains a subpool header for each subpool (see Fig. 2.4). Each 16-byte header contains information about allocated and free areas for that subpool.

The PAM area after the subpool headers contains more information about the DSA in general (see Fig. 2.5).

SCP uses the remainder of the PAM as a program work area to hold miscellaneous values that it needs during request processing. (Note

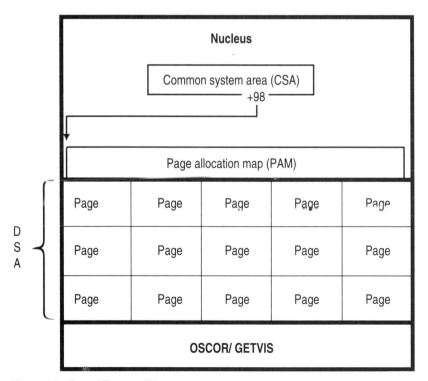

**Figure 2.3** Page Allocation Map.

20   Chapter Two

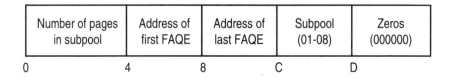

Figure 2.4   Subpool header.

| Page size (PGSIZE) | Number pages in DSA | Address of DSA | Address of byte map 1 |
|---|---|---|---|
| 70 | 74 | 78 | 7C |

Figure 2.5   PAM information area.

that although it is still indicated, subpool 03 is no longer supported.) The total PAM then, looks like Fig. 2.6.

### 2.3.2. Byte maps

The PAM points to a pair of byte maps from hex offset X'7C'. Each byte in the maps corresponds to a page in the DSA. The first byte map shows which subpool (if any) each DSA page is allocated to. (See Fig. 2.7.) If

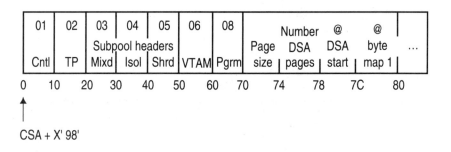

Figure 2.6   Page Allocation Map.

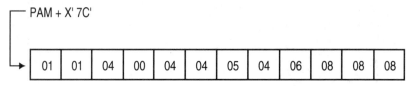

Figure 2.7   Byte map 1.

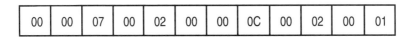

**Figure 2.8** Byte map 2 (find by adding PAM + X'74' to byte map 1 address).

the second byte of byte map 1 contains the number 01, for instance, the second DSA page is owned by subpool 01. Hex zeros in a byte indicate that the corresponding DSA page is not yet allocated to a subpool.

The number of bytes in each byte map is the same as the number of pages in the DSA. That number can be found at PAM+X'74'. The address of any given DSA page can be found by multiplying the DSA page size (PAM+70) by the relative byte address of byte map 1, then adding that number to the address of the DSA (PAM+78), or @DSA_PAGE = @DSA + (PGSIZE * RBA).

The second byte map is contiguous to the first. (See Fig. 2.8.) Its address can be calculated by adding the number of DSA pages to the address of the first byte map (at PAM+7C). Each byte in map 2 contains a number which gives more specific information about each DSA page, depending on the subpool, requested against it before the page is freed. If the byte corresponds to an Isolated (04) subpool page, this number shows the number of pages originally allocated to the transaction which owns the page. Similarly, bytes which map Program subpool pages tell how many pages are allocated to hold that program.

### 2.3.3. The storage accounting area (SAA)

When SCP acquires storage, it starts it with an SAA (see Fig. 2.9). The SAA tells us what type of storage has been allocated (storage class), the bit configuration it was initialized to (initial image), its length (including the SAA), and, in some cases, the address of the next piece of associated storage. There are different types of SAAs for different types of storage.

The SAA for transaction storage (see Fig. 2.10) is 8 bytes long. For these subpools only, there is a duplicate SAA at the end of the storage

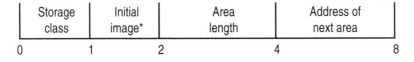

* Task control areas (TCAs) have their subpool ID (04) here instead.

**Figure 2.9** Transaction storage (subpools 02 and 04).

## 22 Chapter Two

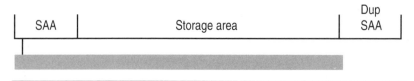

**Figure 2.10** Storage accounting areas.

area used for recovery. The length of the duplicate is not included in the area length field.

Storage for each transaction is chained together through the last 4 bytes of the SAA (see Fig. 2.11). The last storage acquired points back to the first storage, always the TCA. Terminal storage is chained from the task's Terminal Control Table Terminal Entry (TCTTE), which is also addressed by the TCA.

**Transaction storage chaining.** SAAs for system storage (see Fig. 2.12) do not contain chaining information, and are only 4 bytes long. An excep-

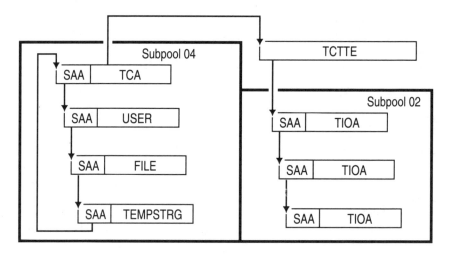

**Figure 2.11** Transaction storage chaining

**Figure 2.12** System storage (subpools 01, 05, 06, and 08).

## Storage Control 23

|   | Reserved (unused) | Length of free area | Address of next FAQE | Address of previous FAQE |
|---|---|---|---|---|
| 0 | | 2 | 4 | 8 |

**Figure 2.13** Free area queue element.

tion to this is the Program storage subpool. Because programs must be loaded on a doubleword boundary, the SAA is "padded out" to 8 bytes. The last 4 bytes contain no useful information.

### 2.3.4. The free area queue element (FAQE)

When an allocated area is freed, its SAA is destroyed and an FAQE is created there instead (see Fig. 2.13). The SCP uses FAQEs to keep track of unallocated space on pages assigned to a subpool. Program subpool pages do not have FAQEs because the remaining free space on their pages can never be used.

### 2.3.5. Free area chaining

Free DSA areas in the Control, Teleprocessing, Shared, and VTAM RPL subpools (01, 02, 05, and 06) are chained from the PAM. The anchors occupy the second and third fullwords of their respective subpool headers, as shown in Fig. 2.4. Isolated subpool free areas are chained from pointers in the TCA of the task owning that storage (see Fig. 2.14). (As mentioned, program pages neither use nor account for free storage.)

### 2.3.6. Summary

The SCP maps the DSA with a PAM and two associated byte maps. Each time a piece of storage is allocated, it is prefixed by an SAA. Transaction storage (subpools 02 and 04) is chained together by SAA address pointers. When storage is freed, the SAA is replaced with a FAQE. These FAQEs are chained from either a subpool header of the

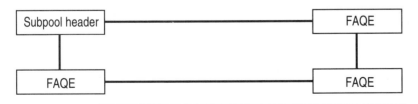

**Figure 2.14** FAQE chain.

## 24   Chapter Two

PAM or an Isolated subpool TCA. The Program (08) subpool does not chain free areas.

## 2.4.  Storage Stress Conditions

The DSA is often subject to excessive demands for storage, because it is used by many applications and control modules for many purposes, and, after all, its size is limited. CICS uses an "available page" threshold called the storage cushion to determine whether the number of storage requests is becoming a problem. If the number of pages in the DSA falls below this threshold, CICS takes action to alleviate the situation. The storage cushion might be envisioned as an unoccupied "no man's land" in the DSA between subpool 08 in high DSA storage and all other pages in lower storage. Actually, the vacant pages are often more dispersed than this, and everything about the storage cushion is hypothetical except its size. The system programmer enters the storage cushion size as the SCS parameter of the System Initialization Table (DFHSIT).

### 2.4.1.  Program compression

When the DSA has too many pages allocated, CICS tries to solve the problem by using the program compression routine to logically delete programs (subpool 08) which are not being used. This routine is invoked whenever the storage cushion has been breached, CICS is Short-on-Storage (see below), or a Program subpool page has been allocated below another subpool's page. Remember that SCP allocates non-Program pages from the low end of the DSA and Program pages from the high end. If they cross in the middle, CICS assumes that the DSA must be running out of free pages.

Program compression deletes programs which are not being used. It takes place only if a PAM flag (PAMCMPRS) has been set by the Program Control Program (PCP), showing that at least one program's use count went to zero since the last compression—even though it may have gone up again by the time SCP checks it.

If a program is being used, however, SCP flags it for deletion on a later pass by changing its byte map entry from X'08' to X'18'. Program compression is intended to cause a rotation of Program subpool pages so that they remain concentrated at the high end of the DSA. If it never occurred, programs could remain loaded indefinitely.

In compression, Storage Control scans sequentially through the DSA, flagging programs for deletion until it reaches the high address end or the "ideal packing point." This is the point in the DSA where there are just enough pages to hold all current non-Program storage, plus enough to satisfy the storage cushion. After compression, programs will get pushed up toward the high address end of the DSA, where they will not mix in with other pages.

Program compression is effective as a buffer against the Short-on-Storage condition only if there are many Program storage pages. A highly used program can interfere with the program compression routine because if its use count never drops to zero, it cannot be deleted. It will remain in the DSA, possibly below a non-Program page.

One way to avoid this problem is to make the program resident in the nucleus instead of the DSA by coding RES=YES in its PPT entry or adding it to the ALT (Alternate Load Table). But because every byte gained by the nucleus is a byte lost to the DSA, performance will actually be degraded by making programs resident if they are not particularly active. Program compression has a large effect on performance, but a certain amount is inevitable and even desirable.

### 2.4.2. The Short-on-Storage condition (SOS)

If the program compression routine reclaims enough pages of unused storage to reinstate the storage cushion, the problem is over, and processing continues as usual. If it is not successful, however, CICS sets the SOS flag in the CSA (CSASOSI) and sends a SYSTEM UNDER STRESS message to the console. Tasks requesting storage are suspended, and will not be resumed until the storage problem has been solved.

If the system goes into a stall, CICS takes extreme action and frees storage by abending suspended tasks (see Chap. 3). The stall time is coded as the ICVS parameter of the System Initialization Table (DFH-SIT). During a stall purge, SCP scans upward from the end of the suspended task chain, examining each task. If the transaction has been coded with SPURGE=YES in its PCT entry, it is moved to the active task chain. The Task Control Program (KCP) can then dispatch the task for abend processing.

A potential problem exists when dynamic transaction backout (DTB=YES) has also been coded in the same transaction's PCT entry. DTB itself issues GETMAINs for DSA storage, and will make the problem worse. PCT entries which contain DTB=YES should be coded with SPURGE=NO.

SOS is an extreme situation. While it is in effect, terminal polling and transaction initiation stop. The program compression routine is entered for every GETMAIN request. On each FREEMAIN, SCP checks for tasks waiting for storage and checks the number of free pages in the DSA. If any tasks are waiting for storage, the PAMREQQI flag is set, and SCP scans the entire chain of suspended tasks, looking for ones which have the "waiting for storage" bit set. For each of those tasks, the

**26 Chapter Two**

GETMAIN is retried, even if the retry for tasks already waiting has failed. All of this is very expensive in terms of CPU cycles. The queued storage requests are processed on a "last-in first-out" (LIFO) basis, as explained in Chap. 3.

### 2.4.3. Storage recovery

The Storage Control Recovery Program (SCR) can intervene when DSA storage becomes corrupted. Such a storage violation occurs when an application moves data in a way that damages an FAQE or an SAA. CICS discovers storage violations when it tries to free or allocate data. A damaged FAQE is discovered during a GETMAIN for that DSA space, and a bad SAA is detected when a request is made to FREEMAIN its area.

The Teleprocessing, Mixed, and Isolated subpools are most vulnerable to damage because they are directly involved in application storage requests. For this reason, their SAAs are duplicated. CICS cannot recover damaged SAAs in other subpools. To recover a damaged storage area, SCR replaces the damaged SAA with the valid duplicate copy. Note that SCR can recover only the SAA, not the data in the allocated area, so the program probably sees garbage anyway.

If an FAQE chain is invalid, SCR tries to correct the chain by using the backward FAQE chain pointers. If an FAQE itself is corrupted, SCR takes it out of circulation, either by changing its length field to a very small number or by simply chaining around it. In either case, the entire page will never be returned to the DSA.

Storage recovery is set by the SVD parameter of the SIT. Storage violation dumps can be requested by specifing SVD=(NO|YES|nn). The "nn" subparameter tells how many storage violations CICS will dump. A value of 99, for instance, means that CICS will dump the first 99 violations. Storage violations are very costly in terms of CPU overhead incurred during dumping and SCR code executions. If CICS cannot solve a storage violation, it terminates itself with a U503 abend.

### 2.4.4. Summary

A storage violation occurs when an SAA or FAQE is damaged. CICS does not detect the violation until it attempts to process a GETMAIN or FREEMAIN against the area. Transaction storage subpools (02 and 04) have a trailing duplicate SAA which SCR can use if the original is damaged. CICS tries to recover FAQE chains by going through the backward pointers, or by putting an FAQE out of service. The decision to implement storage recovery is made by using the SVD parameter of the System Initialization Table (DFHSIT).

Chapter

# 3

# Task Control

## 3.1. Introduction

The fit of various indicator fields in the task control area (TCA) is explored in depth in this chapter, as is the purpose of its junior partner, the dispatch control area (DCA). The concepts of work and resource synchronization are also introduced here. At the end of this chapter you will know:

- The difference between a transaction and a task
- The difference between system and user tasks
- How CICS creates, dispatches, and terminates tasks
- How tasks are arranged on the active and suspend chains
- How to interpret the contents of the TCA, DCA, and other task-related control blocks
- The relationship between tasks and enqueued resources
- How Task Control synchronizes tasks and resources
- What happens when CICS cannot find a task to dispatch

## 3.2. Transactions and Tasks

A transaction is an external request for processing. To the application designer, a transaction defines a business function. In short, it is a type of user work and is named by a transaction code (TRANSID) up to four characters long which is placed in the Program Control Table (PCT) by the system programmer, either directly or via Resource Definition Online (RDO).

## 28   Chapter Three

In CICS, each execution of a transaction is called a task. If three operators enter the same TRANSID called INQY, there will be three tasks associated with INQY within CICS. When a task is attached, it is represented by a TCA. Each time a task is created, it is given a new sequential number, which is stored in the TCA allocated for that task. When the system shuts down at the end of the day, the last TASKID is also the number of tasks that executed that day.

There are two types of tasks in CICS: user tasks and three major system tasks. User tasks are created to process application transactions. The system tasks, on the other hand, are used by CICS to control its environment. They handle terminal I/O, journaling, and task dispatching, and are identified respectively as TC, JJJ, and KC. A special transaction, DSNC, is used to control the DB2 attachment.

CICS handles multiple tasks by overlapping I/O and CPU processing. A task executes until it needs to wait for a resource, such as a record from a file. While it is waiting for this external event to complete, CICS allows another task to run. When that task waits, yet another task is dispatched. Eventually, a task's waited-for event will complete, and it will control the CPU again in turn. The overall architecture of the task dispatching mechanism is based on the simple fact that each task is either running or waiting, active or suspended.

The Task Control Program (DFHKCP) creates, dispatches, and terminates tasks. In addition, KCP synchronizes internal and external resources used by different tasks. Temporary Storage and Transient Data (see Chaps. 10 and 12) are examples of internal resources, which can be accessed without any help from non-CICS system software. A file record is a type of external resource controlled by access method software, such as VSAM. Because external resources are not directly controlled by CICS, KCP periodically gives up control to the operating system to allow requests for these resources to complete.

A transaction is a type of user work represented by a TRANSID in the PCT, and is usually declared via RDO. When a known TRANSID is input, CICS creates a task, gives it a unique number, and allocates a TCA.

User tasks perform application processing, whereas system tasks control terminal I/O (TC), journaling (JJJ), and dispatching (KC). "Dispatcher" code in KCP synchronizes tasks, resources, and communication with the operating system.

### 3.3.  The Task Control Area (TCA)

KCP acquires a TCA for each task (see Fig. 3.1). This area exists for the duration of the task, and is the major control block for the task. Just as the CICS region has its own CSA, each task has its own TCA. This area

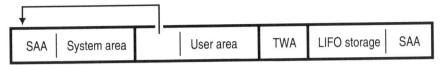

**Figure 3.1** Task control area.

is the primary communication vehicle between CICS and the applications used to process a task.

The TCA is divided into four parts: a system area, a user area, a transaction work area (TWA), and LIFO storage (see Fig. 3.1). When CICS refers to a task's TCA, it usually points to the user area, which in turn addresses the system area (the actual start of the TCA).

The TCA system area contains addresses and data used by CICS to control the task, such as pointers to the PCT and the task's current PPT entries (respectively the sixth and fourteenth fullwords). It holds the sequential user task ID at TCAKCTTA (TCA + 11), a 3-byte packed number. For system tasks, however, this field contains the name of the task (KC, TC, or JJJ) instead. Access to this part of the TCA should be limited to management modules.

The system area itself begins with a fullword SAA. Explained more fully in Chap. 2, this SAA points to the chain of storage owned by the task.

The TCA's user area (see Fig. 3.3) facilitates communication by CICS with application programs: it is accessed by both user and control pro-

| SAA | @ 1st task storage | @ 1st free area | @ last free area | Unique packed taskid | @ PCT entry | @ DCA | ... | @ PPT entry | ... | @ Initial LIFO segment |
|---|---|---|---|---|---|---|---|---|---|---|
| 0 | +04 | +08 | +0C | +11 | +14 | +18 | | +34 | | +94 |

**Figure 3.2** TCA system area (see Fig. 3.8).

| @ TCA system area | @ task TCTTE if any | ... | KCP's RSA 14-11 | @ SCP storage area | SCP's RSA 14-5 | Common control area | Common RSA 14-11 |
|---|---|---|---|---|---|---|---|
| 0 | +08 | | +20 | +5C | +60 | +80 | +A0 |

**Figure 3.3** TCA user area.

## 30  Chapter Three

gram code. The first word addresses the TCA system area just discussed. The next important field is the TCAFCAAA at offset X'08'. If this byte is X'01', the task is being run from a terminal, and the next 3 bytes give the address of that terminal's TCTTE entry.

Starting at offset X'20' is a register save area (RSA) used by KCP to save the application's registers 14 through 11 while KCP is running. There is a similar RSA at offset X'60' for Storage Control, although it holds only registers 14 through 5. In a Storage Control request, such as a GETMAIN or FREEMAIN, the address of the storage area being processed is held at offset X'5C'.

Starting at offset X'80', and continuing all the way to X'E0', is an area used by various CICS control modules while they process application requests. If a task makes a request to the Program Control Program (PCP), for instance, this area is used by PCP to hold the request code, the name and address of the program involved, and other pertinent information. Although bytes X'80' through X'A0' can vary, X'A0' is always a save area for registers 14 through 11. The remainder of the user area contains trace and miscellaneous information.

After the TCA's user area comes an optional transaction work area (TWA) at offset X'100'. This area is used mainly by user macro-level programs and some CICS management modules. The TWASIZE is specified during RDO in that transaction's entry on the PCT.

At the end of the TCA is a last-in first-out (LIFO) storage area for use by CICS management modules (see Fig. 3.4). Many of them need special transaction storage because they execute as read-only (without work areas) and have no way of allocating storage for variables. When a read-only module is called, the caller's registers are saved in an entry within a LIFO segment (a segment is a stack of entries.) These entries are variable in length and are dynamically allocated (stacked) within a segment as room permits. The first 60 bytes of each stack entry are common to all entries.

In addition to the RSA, the stack entry contains forward and backward pointers and the address of the next available free space within the LIFO segment. At offset X'50', the module ID tells us which pro-

| Control info | @ prev stack entry | @ next stack entry | Appl reg 14-12 | @ next free LIFO | Module ID | Submod ID | @ parm list | Variable data |
|---|---|---|---|---|---|---|---|---|
| 0    +4 | +8 | +C | +4C | +50 | +51 | +54 | +60 | |

**Figure.3.4**  TCA LIFO stack entry.

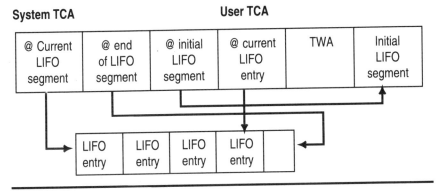

**Figure 3.5** System TCA.

gram owns the entry. Some very large modules use the next byte to identify a submodule ID.

The first LIFO stack entry belongs to KCP and begins with the embedded doubleword `LIFOSTOR`. As shown in Fig. 3.2, this is pointed to by the address at offset X'94' of the TCA's system area.

If any LIFO segment is not large enough, overflow segments of 1 Kbyte are allocated from user storage (storage class X'8C') as needed, and they remain allocated until the task ends. The system TCA (see Fig. 3.5) maintains pointers to the current LIFO segment start and end addresses at offsets X'88' and X'8C', respectively. A pointer in the user TCA at offset X'10' addresses the LIFO stack entry currently in use. The size of the initial LIFO segment is in the transaction's PCT entry. This value is dynamically updated based upon the overflow of the last execution of the transaction.

KCP gives each task a four-part TCA for communication between CICS and the application programs. The TCA's system area is used by management modules to control the task. The user area facilitates task requests to management programs and addresses the three register save areas. An optional user-defined TWA is appended to the TCA for macro-level programs. Finally, LIFO storage is allocated for use by read-only management modules when a task is ATTACHed, and KCP can allocate additional segments as needed. Each LIFO stack contains the module ID of the CICS management program which owns it.

## 3.4. Attach and Dispatch

A task is created and terminated only once in its lifetime, but it can receive and give up control many times. ATTACH logic in KCP creates a task, whereas DISPATCH processing gives it control so that it can execute.

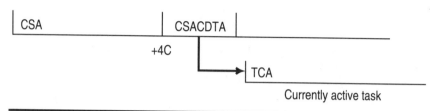

**Figure 3.6** CSA pointer to currently dispatched task.

When Terminal Control issues a DFHKCP TYPE=ATTACH macro, KCP sets up control blocks (see below) for the task and chains it onto a queue for later execution. When KCP's dispatch logic determines that the task is ready to go, it allocates CPU time to the task by passing control to it. When the task needs to wait for an event to complete, such as an EXEC CICS READ command, it gives up control of the CPU to KCP's dispatcher, which dispatches a different task (one which is ready to run) while the first task is being serviced.

In CICS, many tasks may be active, but only one can be in DISPATCH status at any given time. The Common System Area (CSA) has a field CSACDTA (CSA Currently Dispatched Task Address) which points to the current task's TCA at offset X'4C' and is updated every time Task Control dispatches a task (see Fig. 3.6).

Whenever KCP receives an ATTACH request, it validates the task by having the Table Manager Program (DFHTMP) search the PCT for its TRANSID. If it is not found, KCP instead attaches CSAC (the abend transaction), which sends a message to the terminal saying that the TRANSID is invalid. If the transaction is known and was entered from a terminal, KCP does security checking, also attaching CSAC if the user is not authorized for the transaction.

KCP does not stop at validating the TRANSID and user, but continues by checking to see whether there are enough tasks of this type in the system already. Each transaction may optionally be assigned to a class by coding a value (from 1 to 10) in the TCLASS parameter of its PCT entry. In Fig. 3.7, INQY belongs to class 5. The 10-entry Class

```
DFHPCT:
        TRANSID = INQY,
        TCLASS = 5
DFHSIT:
        CMXT = (3, 1, 4, 8, 2, 6, 7, 1, 9, 5)
```

**Figure 3.7** Class maximum matched between CICS tables.

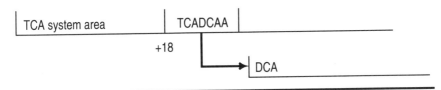

**Figure 3.8** TCA pointer to dispatch control area.

Maximum TASK (CMXT) parameter in the SIT limits the number of class 5 transactions to two at any given time. If there are already two of these transactions in the system, KCP will reject the request. (If TCLASS=NO, KCP will ignore the CMXT check.)

After these checks, KCP finally creates a DCA to hold dispatching information for the task. It is pointed to by the fullword at offset X'18' of the TCA's system area (see Fig. 3.8).

Each task is assigned a priority between 0 and 255. This is a combination of the transaction, terminal, and operator priorities coded in the PCT, TCT, and SNT (Sign-On Table), respectively. The task's DCA will now be linked in a chain of "active" task DCAs in descending priority order. The priority is placed in the field DCATCDP (dispatching priority) at offset X'1A'. Each DCA also has a pointer to the next higher priority DCA at DCAKCFA (forward address) and to the next lower priority DCA at DCAKCBA (backward address). If two tasks have the same priority, the last one in is lower on the chain.

Note in Fig. 3.9a that at offset X'18' in the DCA, the field DCATCDC (dispatch control) contains X'20' if it is ready to run. If not, this byte, also known as the dispatch control indicator (DCI), will explain why. For instance, if the DCI is X'43', the task is waiting for file I/O to complete. Figure 3.9b contains a list of possible DCI values.

Task Control updates the DCI throughout the life of the task to reflect its execution eligibility. When the task is first created, its DCI is set to X'14' to await the next dispatcher scan.

Task Control creates (ATTACHes) a task only once, but gives it control of the CPU (DISPATCHes it) many times. Dispatching is the pro-

| | DCAKCFA | DCAKCBA | DCATCAA | DCATCDC | | DCATCDP |
|---|---|---|---|---|---|---|
| | Pointers to next higher and lower priority DCAs | | Pointer to task's TCA | Dispatch control indicator | | Task's dispatch priority |
| 0 | +C | +10 | +14 | +18 | | +1A |

**Figure 3.9(a)** Dispatch Control Area (DCA).

## 34 Chapter Three

| | |
|---|---|
| 10 | Nondispatchable |
| 11 | KCP-issued GETMAIN failed |
| 12 | Waiting for an ENQed resource |
| 13 | Waiting for terminal I/O |
| 14 | Waiting for AMXT barrier |
| 15 | Waiting for CMXT barrier |
| 18 | Application GETMAIN failed |
| 20 | Eligible for dispatch |
| 21 | Abend requested |
| 22 | Stall purge requested |
| 24 | Terminal read timeout |
| 25 | Deadlock timeout |
| 40 | Waiting for a list of events to complete |
| 41 | Waiting for a page I/O (obsolete) |
| 42 | Task is running in SRB (MVS subtask) mode |
| 43 | Waiting for a single file I/O to complete |
| 44 | In VSE, the TC task is waiting for work |
| 80 | Waiting for a single event |
| 88 | Waiting for an internal (CICS) event |

**Figure 3.9(b)** Dispatch control indicators.

cess of coordinating a multitasking environment by allowing tasks to overlap I/O and CPU processing. Although the dispatcher coordinates many active tasks, aside from subtasking, only one may be executing at any given time and is addressed by CSACDTA at offset X'4C' in the CSA. When a task is attached, KCP creates a DCA to keep track of its priority, disposition, and other information.

### 3.5. Dispatching Active Tasks

The active task chain is a priority-ordered queue of DCAs for dispatchable tasks (see Fig. 3.10). It is chained "forward" in rising priority by CSAACTFA (at CSA + X'B0') and in falling priority by CSAACTBA at CSA + X'B4'.

At the end of ATTACH processing, KCP changes the CSA's CSACDTA field to point to its own TCA in the nucleus, and becomes the dispatcher task. It is now ready to dispatch other tasks.

The KCP task dispatcher is CICS's main processing loop. It decides which tasks may run, what resources they need, and when to give up control to the operating system. When CICS has no useful work to do, it voluntarily gives up control to the host operating system by issuing

## Task Control 35

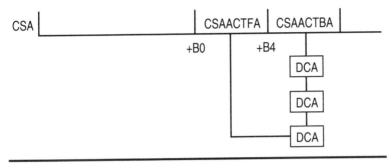

**Figure 3.10** CSA pointers to the active task chain.

an OS or DOS WAIT macro. When the WAIT completes, the operating system hands down control again to the dispatcher.

The dispatcher also can seize control "from underneath" when the currently dispatched task cannot do any more useful work during this scan. If a program changes a task's priority dynamically with the DFHKC TYPE=CHAP macro, the dispatcher still must decide immediately which task on the active chain will execute next. Also, when a task finishes, PCP will issue a DFHKC TYPE=DETACH macro to instruct KCP to terminate the task.

The task dispatcher is itself a CICS task and has its own TCA. This TCA has a TWA and is in the nucleus, and like other tasks is addressed by CSADCTA while dispatcher logic is active. It does not need a DCA because it does not need to be dispatched (it is already running), although the nucleus does contain a dummy DCA (once used for a performance analyzer called PAII).

The way CICS uses the KC WAIT to cause an operating system WAIT is perhaps best illustrated by an example. For instance, if a task needs a VSAM record, File Control (FCP) will create a fullword event control block (ECB) to represent the request and then issue a DFHKC TYPE=WAIT macro on the task's behalf. KCP in turn adds this KC WAIT ECB to its list of OS ECBs when it processes this KC WAIT macro. Thus, an EXEC CICS READ DATASET command leads to a KC WAIT macro issued by the FCP, eventually precipitating an OS (or DOS) WAIT macro issued by the KC dispatcher.

While processing the KC WAIT, KCP adds the ECB to its OS (or DOS) WAIT list (see Fig. 3.11). This list is addressed by KC's TWA field KCECBLA, as shown in Fig. 3.11. The area for the list was reserved during startup by the system initialization module H (DFHSIH1), and is large enough to hold an ECB for each task if the system is at MXT, plus one for each BTAM line. The WAIT list size can be found in KC's TWA field KCECBLL. The physical location of these fields may vary by release from the values given below.

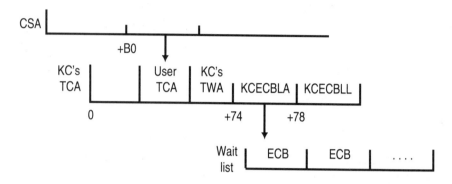

**Figure 3.11** Task Control pointers to the ECB WAIT list.

Dispatcher housekeeping routines are primarily concerned with time. KC begins by requesting Interval Control services three times: first to turn off the runaway task timer and protect itself from being abended as a runaway task; next to update CICS's time-of-day clock in the CSA; and finally to process any time-ordered work. For example, if a task has issued a START request, this third call is where IC checks to see if it is time to attach a task for that TRANSID. The dispatcher also sets one more time value, the STIMER interval, which will be used if no task can be dispatched.

During actual dispatch logic, Task Control examines the DCAs on the active task chain until it finds a task which is ready to execute. The technique used is a Branch on Count (BCT) loop. The maximum number of DCAs which will be inspected is a value coded in the SIT as the Active Maximum Tasks (AMXT) value. The counter is decremented for some (but not all) DCAs the dispatcher encounters during the scan.

When the dispatch loop finds a DCA, it examines its DCI. There is a separate routine in KCP for each DCI setting to determine whether or not the task is dispatchable. If it is, the task is dispatched. This is done by updating the CSACDTA field with the task's TCA address and issuing what is virtually an XCTL to the program associated with the task. The scan is immediately abandoned.

Eventually, the dispatched task will make a CICS request. When it does, the CICS module it invokes will issue a DFHKC TYPE=WAIT, SUSPEND, or DETACH macro. Now that the task has to give up control, a new dispatch scan is entered "from the top."

Whenever an examined task is not dispatchable, KCP has a choice of actions to take. If the task is waiting for an external event (DCI 40, 41, 42, 43, or 80), KCP checks to see whether the event has completed. If it has, KCP marks the task as eligible for dispatch (for the next scan). If not, it ensures that the task's ECB is on the ECB list, and decrements the AMXT counter because tasks awaiting external events contribute to the count. If, however, the DCI is 88, the task is waiting for an internal event, so CICS does not decrement the counter.

Should KCP reach the end of its scan without dispatching a task, it gives up control to the operating system by issuing an operating system WAIT on the entire ECB list, so that if any of these ECBs is POSTed (X'80' in the first byte if OS), CICS normally gets control back and the dispatch scan starts over. Optionally, in OS, the CICS system programmer can keep OS in control longer by coding a completion percent IOCP (up to 50 percent) in the SIT.

What happens, though, if the operating system does not fulfill any of the WAITed-for events? Suppose CICS has nothing for the operating system to do. Then the STIMER value, zeroed by the fourth IC call of dispatcher housekeeping, sets a limit for this waiting period. In other words, the dispatcher gives up control until an event completes or until the STIMER value expires, whichever comes first. This IC limit value is coded by the system programmer as ICV in the SIT. In most systems, there is enough activity to keep the STIMER from ever expiring.

Each active task's DCA is placed on the active task chain (addressed by the CSA + X'B4') in priority order. The dispatcher scans the active chain until it finds a DCA with a dispatchable DCI, and passes control to the associated task. When that task needs a system resource, the dispatcher repeats the scan, giving control to another task. When it cannot find a dispatchable task, KCP gives up control to the operating system, pointing to a list of ECBs.

## 3.6. Suspend and Resume

Although many tasks can be in CICS at any given time, only one at a time can execute. The others are waiting for something. They could be waiting for an operating response, for a VSAM record, for an interval of time to expire, or for some other event to complete. Many of the events, like file I/O, will complete relatively quickly. Other events, like a CONVERSE command which requires operator response, may take much longer.

Task Control separates the long-waiters from the short-waiters by putting their DCAs on two separate chains (see Fig. 3.12). Tasks waiting for long-term events are moved to a chain of suspended tasks. When its long-term event completes, the DCA is moved back to the active chain. Maintaining separate chains speeds up the dispatch algorithm by preventing the dispatcher from searching through long-waiters. The dispatcher searches the active chain whenever it gets control, and the suspend chain is searched only during a system stall.

Tasks are placed on the suspend chain in LIFO order, except for those with a timeout value. Those tasks are placed in progressing timeout order, below the ones that cannot time out. This may not make per-

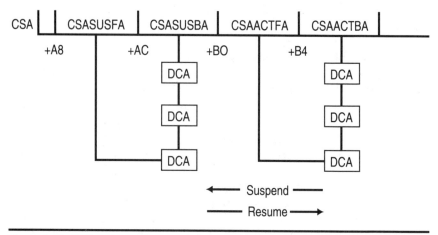

**Figure 3.12** DCA active and suspend chains.

fect sense, but at least the task with the most remote timeout is lower on the chain than tasks with earlier timeouts. The single most imminent timeout task's DCA is addressed by KC's TWA field KCLTPTR.

After placing a DCA on the right chain, KCP updates the MXT and CMXT counters. Terminal Control also must examine the MXT value each time it receives a TRANSID from a terminal to determine whether or not to issue the ATTACH macro to the TCP.

All tasks in CICS are either executing or waiting. If they are waiting for an event which will take a long time to complete, their DCAs are moved to the special suspend chain via the DFHKC TYPE=SUSPEND macro. (TC issues a SUSPEND whenever it receives a CONVERSE command.) When an event completes, the control program which originally requested suspension issues a DFHKC TYPE=RESUME macro to put the DCA back on the active chain. After processing either a SUSPEND or a RESUME, KC always does a dispatch scan.

### 3.7. Enqueue and Dequeue

CICS provides the ENQ/DEQ mechanism to synchronize resources. To CICS, a resource is a symbolically defined object which is only serially reusable and is acquired and released through KCP. The resource can be a storage area, a file, a data record, a control block, an executable code, or any user-defined resource. The DFHKC TYPE=ENQ macro specifies a character string or a 4-byte address. Most enqueueing is implicit; e.g., File Control (not the application) usually issues the ENQs to protect file records.

When KCP receives an ENQ request, it creates a queue element area (QEA) to represent the enqueued resource (see Fig. 3.13). The pointer CSAQETBA (CSA + X'13C') in the CSA holds the address of a special

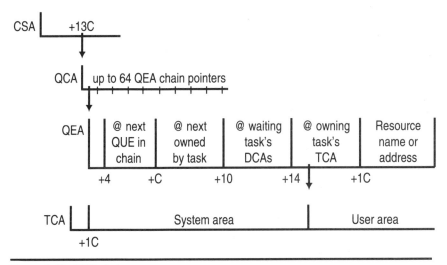

**Figure 3.13** QEA chains.

queue control area (QCA), which in turn can address several (up to 64) QEA chains. KCP uses a hashing algorithm (a rolling exclusive OR) to find the chain it needs. In DOS, KCP searches through all the QEAs sequentially. Each QEA on the chain addresses the TCA of the task which owns that QEA. When a task successfully completes an ENQUEUE, the QEA address is placed in its system TCA at offset X'1C' (field TCAKCQC).

If a task is waiting to ENQ on a QEA, KC suspends its DCA, chains it from the QEA anchor (or the third fullword of an already queued DCA), and changes its DCI to X'12' to show that it is waiting for an enqueued resource. Each QEA also has pointers to the physically next QEA in the QEA chain, as well as to the next QEA in the chain owned by the same task.

The ENQ/DEQ mechanism allows KC to single-thread resource use. Most of this goes on behind the scenes, such as when File Control enqueues to give a task exclusive control of a VSAM record. Each enqueue is represented by a QEA, which is chained from a QCA addressed by a field in the CSA. DCAs waiting for an enqueued resource are in turn chained off the QEA representing that resource. The QEA also points to the task which currently owns the resource.

## 3.8. End-of-Task Processing

A user task terminates by issuing a RETURN request to PCP. PCP determines whether the program is returning control to another program or wants to end the task. If the request is to end the task, PCP issues a DFHKC TYPE=DETACH to terminate the transaction. This makes KCP

**40 Chapter Three**

call the Sync Point Program (SPP) for syncpoint and deferred work element (DWE) processing.

DWEs save information about uncompleted processing which must take place before task termination. For example, a file update request may force creation of a DWE. The DWE remains until the update is performed, a syncpoint is taken, or the task terminates abnormally. DWEs are also used to save information used in dynamic transaction backout (DTB) or in syncpoint rollback. (See Chap. 13.)

After syncpoint processing, KCP calls the Interval Control Program (ICP) to process any task-related Interval Control Elements (ICEs). If the task issued any ENQs, KCP cancels all outstanding QEAs by using a special form of the ENQ/DEQ macro called DFHKC TYPE=DEQALL.

Next, the pointers between the task's TCA and TCTTE are removed, and KCP calls SCP to release the TCA and other storage in subpool 03 or 04. SCP then releases the DCA in subpool 01. KCP then XCTLs to TCP, which performs the final terminal write and updates the TCTTE to show that output is complete.

If the RETURN has a TRANSID parameter, TCP also updates the TCTTE with the specified TRANSID, and subsequent input from the terminal will initiate the designated transaction. This is the technique used to code pseudoconversational transactions.

When a task issues a RETURN to CICS, PC asks KC to DETACH the task. After syncpoint and DWE processing, KCP calls Interval Control to process task-related Interval Control work, and issues dequeues on all enqueued resources. KC concludes by calling SCP to release storage, and requesting Terminal Control to send the final terminal output.

Chapter

# 4

# Program Control

## 4.1. Introduction

The tables and control blocks associated with the Program Control Program (PCP) are discussed here, as well as program linkage levels, CICS program loading, 31-bit addressability, and the benefits and requirements of each type of program call.

The High-Level Language (HLL) Interface and the Executive Interface Structure (EIS) and Executive Interface Block (EIB) are also covered. Major topics include:

- How to code a Program Properties Table (PPT)
- Program loading techniques to maximize storage
- The COBOL extension in the PPT
- Interprogram communication: LINK, XCTL, RETURN, and COBOL CALL
- RSA chaining
- How COBOL becomes pseudo-reentrant
- LOAD, RELEASE, and DELETE and the LLA
- Program Control services flow
- Abend and shutdown processing
- The command-level interface to CICS macros
- HANDLE CONDITION processing
- How the COMMAREA is used
- The assembler language interface

42 **Chapter Four**

The Program Control Program (DFHPCP) is responsible for all program services within CICS. PCP controls program linkage within a task by processing requests to transfer control (XCTL) to other programs or to LINK to them. Application programs reside in a special set of resident program libraries (DFHRPL) and are brought into the region (LOADed) when they are needed. These programs may be brought into the DSA or the nucleus (see Chap. 2). CICS programs may be coded in a variety of languages, and may interface with CICS modules in two different modes. Some applications can even take advantage of XA (extended addressability). PCP controls program execution from the time a task is attached until the time it issues its last RETURN request.

## 4.2. DFHRPL and the PPT

All CICS application programs (and some management modules) are defined to CICS by the system programmer placing them in the Program Properties Table (DFHPPT) off-line, or defining them dynamically with the RDO facility. The RDO facility causes an internal PPT entry, just as if the program was originally coded in the PPT.

## 4.3. Coding the PPT

The system programmer codes a PPT entry for each user load module in the system, and one for the entire PPT as a whole. The first PPT macro is the TYPE=INITIAL entry, which sets the suffix of the PPT load module itself. This macro:

```
DFHPPT TYPE=INITIAL,
    SUFFIX=XY
```

will create the load module DFHPPTXY when the PPT is assembled and link-edited. The DFHSIT should then specify PPT=XY so that CICS will use this particular table.

Each application module needs its own entry in the PPT:

```
DFHPPT TYPE=ENTRY,
    PGMNAME=name,
    PGMLANG={ASSEMBLER|COBOL|PL/I|RPG},
    PGMSTAT={ENABLED|DISABLED},
    RELOAD={NO|YES},
    RES={NO|ALIGN|FIX|PGOUT|YES},
    RSL={0|number|PUBLIC},
    USAGE=MAP
```

All of these parameters are optional except for PGMNAME. Each parameter is represented on the PPT as it appears in storage.

## 4.4. The PPT in Storage

The PPT (see Fig. 4.1) contains all the information PCP needs to control each program. The first 8 bytes of each PPT entry is the program identifier (PPTPI) entry, which contains the name of the CICS program it refers to. This is set by the PROGRAM parameter. Another very important piece of information is the location of each program on DASD. This is not coded, of course, but is set by CICS. On the PPT (in storage), this address is in the PPTDASA (DASD address) field. This area points to the PDS member in a concatenation of load libraries known to CICS as DFHRPL (the resident program library). In DOS, the resident program library is a core image library.

If the program is already in the CICS region, it is addressed by another pointer, the PPTCSA (core storage address; see Fig. 4.2). Just how this program gets into storage is discussed later. For now, let us just say that the PPT always has at least one program pointer (DFHDASA), and sometimes has two (DFHDASA and DFHCSA).

Notice that the programs MYPROG and HISPROG have different sizes. PCP needs to know how large each program is so that it can find space for it in the region. The length of each program is in the PPTSAR field of its PPT entry. In addition to knowing the location and length of each program, PCP needs to know where the first executable code in the program is. When PCP gives control to a program, it gets the entry point (see Fig. 4.3) from the field PPTENTD (entry point displacement).

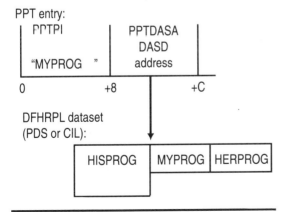

**Figure 4.1** PPT DASD address.

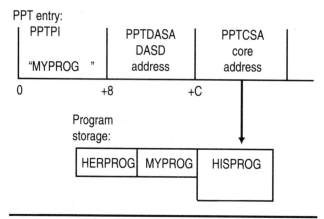

**Figure 4.2** PPT core address.

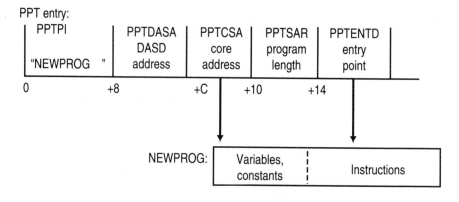

**Figure 4.3** PPT entry point address.

### 4.5. Types of Programs

There are two program indicators in the PPT which describe the type of program (see Fig. 4.4). This includes the language, usage, residency, interface level and status, loading method, definition method, 24/31-bit mode indicators, and new copy information. These flags are located in the 1-byte fields PPTTLR and PPTTLR2.

Because a program may have many of the characteristics described by these fields, CICS applies mask bit settings to the flag bytes. Each

## Program Control 45

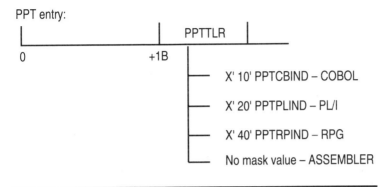

**Figure 4.4** PPT language indicators.

bit in the flag has its own meaning. For instance, if the field contains X'06', then the bit setting is 0000 0110, and we know that the flag contains two indicators (one for each bit set on). Furthermore, we can see that it contains the settings X'04' (binary 0000 0100) and X'02' (0000 0010). In addition, these bit settings have names which describe their meaning. The bit setting X'10' in the first flag (PPTTLR), for instance, shows that the PPT entry describes a COBOL indicator, and is called PPTCBIND.

CICS applications can be coded in COBOL, PL/I, and assembler. (Version 3 of CICS allows C/370 programs.) In addition, CICS under DOS accepts RPG II. This language is discouraged, however, as it is not quasi-reentrant and cannot be multithreaded. Flags in the PPT at PPTTLR tell us which language the program is written in. Note that if none of the language flags is set, the program is written in assembler. The language is set by the PGMLANG parameter for each program.

Usually, programs tend to remain in storage after they are loaded. This means that once they are brought into the DSA, CICS keeps them there. They are deleted only during program compression (see Chap. 2). Occasionally, however, programmers like to have a fresh copy available for each use. This feature is used mainly to load tables or control blocks which are modified by the program loading them.

If RELOAD=YES is coded in a program's PPT entry, PCP will load a fresh copy of the program each time it services a load request. If you want to free the program storage, you must issue a storage control FREEMAIN request. If the FREEMAIN is not issued, the DSA can fill up with copies of this program.

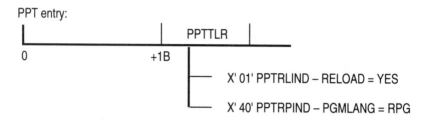

**Figure 4.5** PPT reload indicator.

In DOS, RPG programs are not shared between tasks, and RELOAD=YES must be coded in their PPT entries. CICS will automatically FREEMAIN storage for these programs. The PPTRLIND (reload indicator) setting in PPTTLR tells us whether or not RELOAD=YES was coded for the program. In addition, of course, if PPTRPIND is set, the program is an RPG program (see Fig. 4.5).

In Chap. 2, we said that Storage Control's subpool 08 was reserved for application programs. While it is true that most CICS programs are placed in the Program subpool, it is possible for them to live elsewhere. A very important application program can actually be placed in a part of the CICS nucleus called the resident application program (RAP) area. To force this "residency," the system programmer codes RES=YES, ALIGN, FIX, or PGOUT on the program's PPT entry. This is reflected in PPTTLR by the PPTCRES bit setting.

Another way to keep a program out of subpool 08 is to code USAGE=MAP on the PPT (see Fig. 4.6). This was used at one time for BMS maps, and forced the program into the Shared subpool (subpool 05). As soon as the use count for the program reached zero, the map

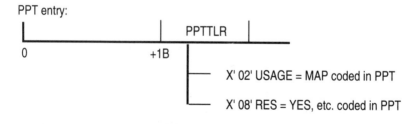

**Figure 4.6** PPT MAP and RES indicators.

was released. The problem was that the map would get overwritten as soon as it was not being used. Since maps should be given the same storage treatment as the programs which use them, this parameter is no longer in general use. If a PPT entry has been coded this way, however, PPTTLR will have the PPTUMAP bit setting turned on.

Programs can communicate with CICS management modules on two levels, macro and command. At one time, the command-level interface did not exist, and all applications used CICS macros to request services. The command-level interface (discussed in detail in Chap. 11) is a simpler and more common method. In addition, macro level will no longer be supported in newer versions, such as 3.1 of CICS, and, of course, is not recommended. PCP needs to keep track of two main types of information as far as level is concerned: Is this a command-level program (PPTEXEC; see Fig. 4.7)? If so, has it been set up for execution (PPTCINIT)? COBOL II, Assembler H, and PL/I programs can take advantage of XA and run "above the line," that is to say, above the 16-Mbyte line. Before XA, all CPU addresses were 24 bits long. The largest number that a 24-bit binary number can contain is about 16,000,000. An XA system allows up to about 2,000,000,000 bytes of addressable storage. However, programs that want to use this space must be able to address it. It takes 31 bits to hold a number this large. A 24-bit program cannot run above the line; a 31-bit program can. If the program can run in the 31-bit mode, PPTTLR2 gets the PPTAM31 bit set.

CICS brings 24-bit programs into storage by itself using a private BSAM loading routine (described in detail later). For 31-bit programs, however, it uses an MVS/XA LOAD macro to get the program into the DSA extension above the 16-Mbyte line. The type of load is shown in PPTTLR by bit settings PPTCPLD and PPTOSLD, respectively.

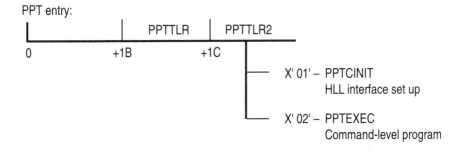

**Figure 4.7** PPT HLL and command-level indicators.

## 4.6. XA and Non-XA Flags

Programs can be defined to CICS on-line by using the CEDA On-line Resource Definition Facility. If this is done, the PPTDYNA (dynamically defined) bit (X'20') will be set in PPTTLR2. When the system programmer requests that a new program copy be brought into the system, he or she uses the CEMT NEWCOPY master terminal command. This happens when a program has been recompiled and link-edited. When PCP receives the NEWCOPY command, it sets the PPTCPYR bit (X'80') in PPTTLR2. Later, when PCP receives a request to use this program, it sees that this bit is on, and gets a fresh copy for DFHRPL.

### 4.6.1. Program status flags

CICS application programs can be in various states at different times, such as disabled, not loaded, being loaded, already loaded, residency location, etc. The field PPTFLGS contains program flags which monitor these states (see Fig. 4.8).

The ALT (Application Load Table) is an optional table which defines the load order for resident programs. These programs must also be defined in the PPT, but the PPT RES parameter will be ignored (CICS uses the ALT parameters instead). This table has the same residency pa-

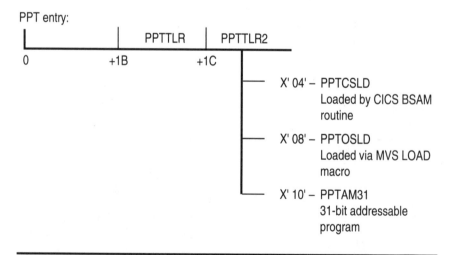

**Figure 4.8** XA and non-XA flags.

rameters as the PPT, and a few more. One very useful parameter in this table is `CLASS={SPECIFIC|GENERIC}`. Specifying `GENERIC` means that CICS will search the PPT (or CSD) for any programs with names beginning with the characters specified in the ALT entry, and load them. For instance, if programs MYPROG01, MYPROG02, MYPROG03, and MYPROGXX are defined in the PPT, the following ALT entry will make them all resident:

```
DFHALT TYPE=ENTRY,
    PROGRAM=MYPROG,
    CLASS=GENERIC
```

Other ALT parameters allow the system programmer to determine where in the RAP area the programs will be loaded, where they will be loaded from, and what type of page alignment (if any) should take place when they are loaded. The `SHR={NO|YES}` parameter determines where the program is to be loaded from. `SHR=NO` tells CICS to get the module from DFHRPL as usual. `SHR=YES` means that the CICS will try to get the module from the LPA (OS) or SVA (DOS). The `ALIGN`, `FIX`, `ADRSPCE`, `PAGEIN`, and `PAGEOUT` values are ignored if `SHR=YES` is coded. This is useful if there are many CICS regions running under the same operating system. `SHR=YES` allows all of them to execute the same module. This module does not have to be loaded into each region. To use this in OS, `LPA=YES` must be coded in the SIT. In addition, all of the modules must be read-only or truly refreshable; that is, they cannot modify themselves. Very few applications meet this requirement.

The `ALT ALIGN={NO|ENTRY|YES}` parameter determines how the program will be aligned on a page boundary. `NO` means that page alignment will not take place at all, and `YES` means that the program will be aligned. This is similar to `RES=ALIGN` in the PPT. In the ALT, we can specify that the entry point of the program should be aligned on a page boundary. This can be useful when the module's working set follows its entry point, and the entry point is not at the start of the module. `ALIGN=ENTRY` will keep the entry point paged in or out consistent with the rest of the module.

## 4.7. Programs in Core

We said earlier that the field PPTCSA contains the core storage address of a program that CICS has brought in from DFHRPL. If there is no core copy of it, that field will be set to hex zeros. When PCP needs to bring the program in, it sets a bit in PPTFLGS called PPTLIPF (load

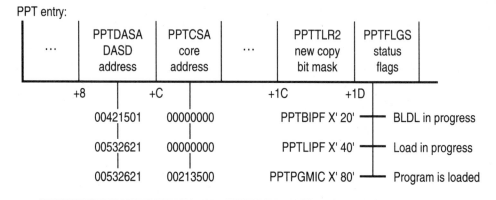

**Figure 4.9** PPT NEWCOPY flags.

in progress flag). This is done to prevent a simultaneous load of the same program. If someone has requested a NEWCOPY of the program, PCP will notice that the PPTNCPRY bit in PPTTLR2 is set.

To get a new copy (see Fig. 4.9), PCP needs to get a fresh copy of the DASD address of the program (PPTDASA); it issues an MVS BLDL macro, which returns the new address. (In DOS, this is handled separately by the DOS Loader subtask.) Before issuing the BLDL, however, PCP sets the PPTBIPF (BLDL in progress) flag in PPTFLGS. After the BLDL completes, the BLDL flag gets turned off, and PCP loads the program, setting PPTFLGS to PPTLIPF as described above. When the load is complete, PPTLIPF gets turned off, and PPTPGMIC (program in core) gets set instead. PPTCSA is then updated with the core address. Note that the BLDL step takes place only if a NEWCOPY has been requested. If it has, PCP goes through the load even if there is a copy of the program in storage, because that is the old copy.

In addition to these, there are some miscellaneous status indicators in PPTFLGS. If a program has been disabled, either by the master terminal operator or by user code, the PPTDSABL (X'04') will be set. This will prevent PCP (and everyone else) from using the program until it has been enabled again. It is possible to share modules across different CICS regions by placing them in the LPA (MVS) or SVA (DOS). These modules must be truly reentrant (remember, CICS programs are only quasi-reentrant). If this program has been loaded from the LPA or SVA, the PPTSHRMD (shared module) bit (X'08') will be on.

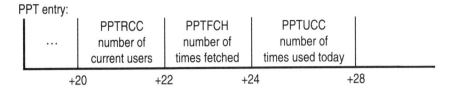

**Figure 4.10** Program use counters.

## 4.8. Program Counters

PCP maintains counter fields to monitor how many tasks are using the same program simultaneously, how often it is used during the run, and how often it has been brought in from DFHRPL. PPTRCC (resident control counter) shows how many tasks are using the same program at any given time. CICS allows only one copy of each program in core. This copy is shared by all programs which need to use it. Because of this, the programs must be quasi-reentrant, that is to say, reentrant between calls to CICS (commands or macros). During program compression (see Chap. 2), SCP checks this field to make sure it is not about to logically delete a program which is being used.

Each time CICS brings a copy of the program from DFHRPL to core storage, it increments a counter in that program's PPT entry called PPTFCH (FETCH count) (see Fig. 4.10). If this number is very high, it means that the program is being subjected to a lot of program compression. The cumulative use counter (DFHUCC), on the other hand, shows how many times the program has been used since CICS started up.

## 4.9. COBOL Fields

Although CICS programs must be at least quasi-reentrant (reentrant between CICS requests), COBOL is not a reentrant language. As we shall see in our discussion of the high-level language interface, Program Control needs to make copies of the Target Global Table (TGT) and working storage for each task executing the program. The TGT is a set of switches and counters used to control the execution of a COBOL program. Working storage contains variables unique to each task's execution of the program. The PPT contains a COBOL extension starting at offset X'28' to keep track of this information. The field PPTCCR contains the size of the TGT. PPTCOTP shows the size of the TGT and working storage combined. PPTCOTGT points to the TGT in

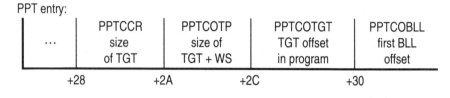

**Figure 4.11** PPT COBOL fields.

the original COBOL program, while PPTCOBLL shows the offset to the first BLL cell (see Fig. 4.11).

## 4.10. The Nucleus Load Table (NLT)

The NLT controls the nucleus load order. It is optional, and allows modifications of the default load order. If it is used, CICS loads all the modules specified, then loads the rest with a default list of management modules in the startup module DFHSIB1. In OS, the system programmer can decide whether the NLT modules from the LPA should be used, and whether NLT modules should be read into protected storage. In DOS, NLT parameters allow CICS to participate in the DOS paging algorithm. In both OS and DOS, the NLT has parameters which allow the system programmer to indicate where the module should be loaded, how it is to be aligned, and whether or not it should be page-fixed.

In OS, SHR={NO|YES} indicates whether or not the link pack area (LPA) module should be used instead of loading a module into the CICS region. This parameter is similar to the ALT SHR parameter. Nucleus LPA modules can be shared among different CICS modules in the same CPU. This results in an overall reduction in operating system paging, because of the reduction in the total working set size. In addition, the LPA is key 0 protected. This means that any CICS module installed there is automatically protected from being overwritten by accident. During startup, CICS checks the SIT to see if LPA=YES has been coded. If it has, it tries to use the LPA versions of SHR=YES modules. If it cannot find a copy of the program in the LPA, it sends a message to the operator, and tries to load the program from DFHRPL. The ALIGN and FIX options are ignored for SHR=YES modules, because the programs are not really loaded. PROTECT=YES is ignored, because LPA modules are already protected. In DOS, CICS' use of SVA modules is determined by the core image library search order. The default search orders forces the use of SVA resident phases.

In OS, the system programmer has the option of specifying that some or all of the NLT modules be protected. To do this, CICS must be initiated as an MVS APF-authorized job step. This means that DFHSIP must be in a library named in the member IEAAPFnn in SYS1.PARMLIB, where nn is supplied during the MVS system IPL. Some CICS modules must be loaded into this storage, and they are named in the default DFHSIB1 load order. Other modules may also be loaded there if they are read-only. To use this option, code PROTECT=YES on the module's NLT entry.

## 4.11. Interprogram Communication

All tasks execute at least one program (the program specified on the transaction's PCT entry). Most tasks, however, use several. These programs pass control to and from one another by issuing LINK, XCTL, and RETURN requests to the PCP. LINK and XCTL pass control to a specified program, and RETURN returns control. These programs can be laid out into logical levels. As the diagram shows, LINK and RETURN change logical levels, while XCTL does not (see Fig. 4.12).

Programs which issue a LINK request get control back when the LINKed-to program issues a RETURN, whereas those which request an XCTL (transfer control) do not. In Fig. 4.13, PROGRAMX LINKs to PROGRAMY, which in turn XCTLs to PROGRAMZ. When PROGRAMZ issues a RETURN, control goes up to the next highest logical level. If PROGRAMX is at the highest logical level (the first program of the task), its RETURN goes to the PCP, which terminates the task.

COBOL II programs may use the CALL verb rather than the LINK command. The CALLed program need not have a CICS environment, such as an EIB. This call is dynamic and processed just like LINK. It is especially useful for program routines CALLed by both batch and CICS systems.

Processing an XCTL request is not too difficult for PCP. In general, it just passes control to the requested program. Handling a LINK, however, is a little trickier. Because the LINKed-to program will eventually

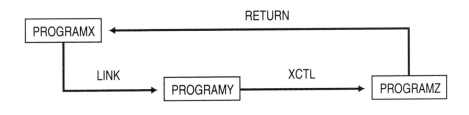

**Figure 4.12** LINK, XCTL, and RETURN.

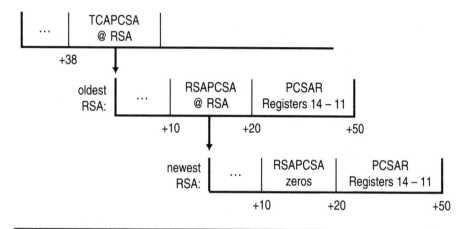

**Figure 4.13** RSA chaining.

RETURN to the LINKer, PCP has to save some information about its processing state.

The most important information is the LINKer's register settings. CICS gets only one set of registers, and these must be restored to the LINKer to allow it to continue processing normally. The RSA (see Figs. 4.13 and 4.14) contains this and other valuable information. The task points to the RSA from its TCAPCSA (TCA Program Control save area). If there is more than one LINKed-to program, the RSAs are chained through the RSAPCSA field.

The RSA itself contains some additional interesting information about the program it is saving registers for. The field RSAPCTA (RSA

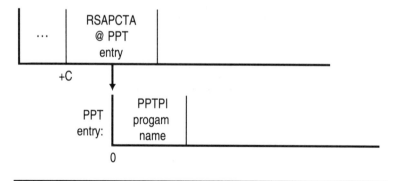

**Figure 4.14** Register save area (RSA).

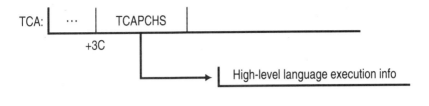

**Figure 4.15** TCA HLL information pointer.

Program Control Table address) points to the program's PPT (not PCT as the name implies) entry. This field is useful for system programmers writing generalized subprograms, where it is often useful to know the name of the program which LINKed to the subprogram.

When the LINKed-to program is written in a high-level language and/or uses the command-level interface, the RSA contains two more useful fields which point to a high-level language save area and a dynamic storage area (see Fig. 4.15). When a high-level program requests a Program Control service, PCP saves some information about the program's execution in an area addressed by the TCA in the field TCAPCHS (TCA Program Control high-level language save). This field is in the Program Control section of the TCA system area (see Chap. 3). During a LINK, PCP saves this information in the RSAPCHS field (see Fig. 4.16).

When a task is executing a COBOL program, that task gets its own copy of the program's TGT and, if it is a command-level program, working storage (see Fig. 4.17). That area is addressed by the TCA system area at offset X'40', and is called the TCAPCCA (TCA Program Control COBOL area). In a PL/I program, this area is the anchor to a chain of PL/I DSAs and is called TCAPCPA. For command-level assembler, it is called TCAPCDSA and points to the program's variable storage area

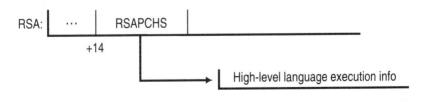

**Figure 4.16** RSA HLL information pointer.

## 56  Chapter Four

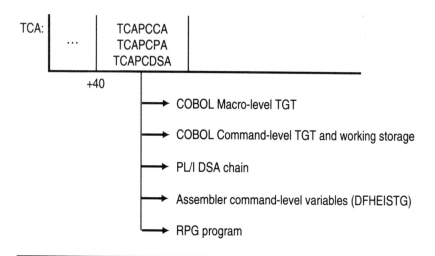

**Figure 4.17**  TCA working storage pointers.

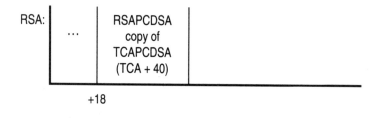

**Figure 4.18**  RSA working storage pointer.

(called DFHEISTG for EXEC Interface storage). For RPG, it points to the entire program, since RPG is completely non-reentrant, and each task gets its own copy of the entire program (see Fig. 4.17).

When Program Control executes a `LINK`, it saves that address in the RSA in the RSAPCDSA (RSA Program Control dynamic storage address; see Fig. 4.18).

### 4.12.  LOAD and RELEASE

Application programs have the option of bringing modules such as tables into storage. These modules are not executed, but may be refer-

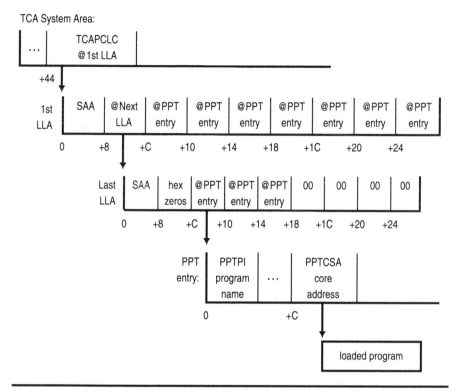

**Figure 4.19** Load list area chaining.

enced. The EXEC CICS LOAD command or DFHPC TYPE=LOAD macro brings programs into CICS and provides addressability to them. When a program LOADs another module, CICS needs to keep track of this information, so that that module can be deleted later. To accomplish this, PCP keeps a list of each task's LOADed programs in a control block called the load list area (LLA).

The LLA (see Fig. 4.19) contains up to seven entries. Each entry points to the PPT of a LOADed program. If there are more than seven, PCP creates another LLA and points to it from the first one. If there are more than fourteen, it creates yet another and points to it from the second LLA, and so on. The LLA pointer in the last LLA is zeros, as are its unused PPT entry pointers. The first LLA is addressed by the task's TCA in the TCAPCLC (TCA Program Control load control) field.

When the task is finished using the loaded module, it can issue the EXEC CICS RELEASE command or a DFHPC TYPE=DELETE macro. PCP

**58   Chapter Four**

finds the program by searching through the LLA chain. If the task does not release its loaded modules, KCP will ask PCP to release all the programs addressed by its LLAs at task termination. If you want to avoid that, code the HOLD option of the EXEC CICS LOAD command, or use the LOADLST=NO parameter of the DFHPC TYPE=LOAD macro. This will prevent PCP from creating an LLA when the LOAD request is processed. If there is no LLA entry, PCP will not delete it. This can be useful for application tables which are built during the day and must not be deleted during the CICS run.

### 4.13.  LINK, XCTL, and LOAD Logic

LINK, XCTL, and LOAD share much of the same logic in PCP, as they often involve bringing a program into storage (see Fig. 4.20). During a LINK, CICS issues a Storage Control GETMAIN for an RSA. In an XCTL, the requesting program is released. Neither of these takes place for a LOAD. PCP calls DFHTM (the Table Manager) to search the PPT for the requested program, increments the use count, and looks to see whether the program is already in storage. If the program is already in storage, PCP does not need to load it again unless the NEWCOPY mask (PPT-NCPYR) is set in PPTTLR2. To actually load the program, PCP branches to code in the SILOADR routine of program DFHSIP, described more fully in Fig. 4.21.

After taking care to see that the program is actually in storage, PCP checks PPTTLR to see if this program uses the HLL interface. If it does, the HLL interface is initialized. If the program will be executed (it is being LINKed or XCTLed to), PCP initializes the HLL entry requirements. If the program is being loaded, PCP places its core storage address (subpool 05 or 08, or nucleus address) in the task's TCA field TCAPCLA (TCA Program Control load address). If the load does not specify the HOLD option, PCP places the program's PPT entry address in the next available LLA entry. If there is no LLA, PCP creates one, and places its address in TCAPCLC. If there is an LLA, but it is full, PCP creates a new one and chains it from the previous LLA.

### 4.14.  CICS Program Load Routine (OS)

The PCP load routine (see Fig. 4.21) is used whenever PCP needs to bring a program into storage to satisfy a LINK, XCTL, or LOAD request. The first thing Program Control does, of course, is to see whether or not the program is already in storage by checking for the PPTPGMIC (program in core) mask setting in the program's PPTFLGS field. If the pro-

Program Control 59

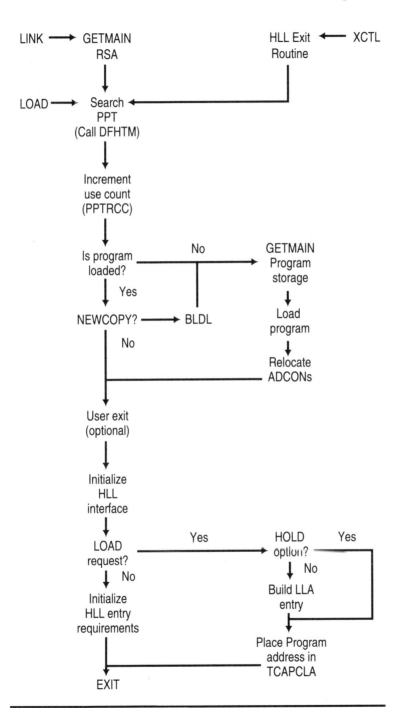

**Figure 4.20** Program Control services flow.

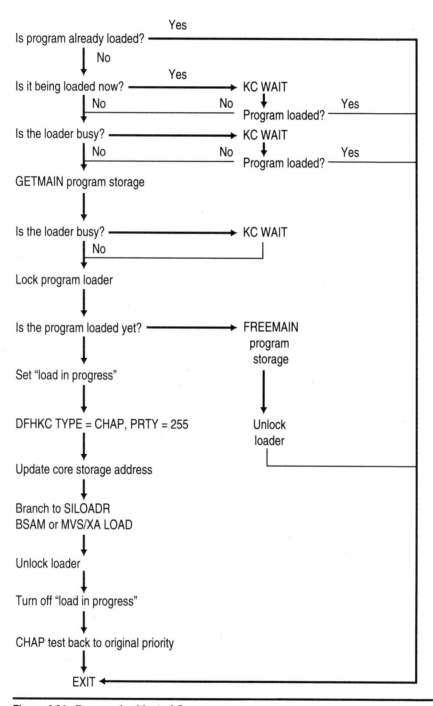

**Figure 4.21** Program load logical flow.

gram is not in core, PCP checks to see if it is currently being loaded by another concurrent PC request. If it is, PPTFLGS will have the PPTLIPF (load in progress flag) bit set, and PCP will issue a Task Control WAIT on behalf of the task. When the WAIT expires, PCP checks to see whether or not the program is loaded. If it is not, PCP returns to its main routine to continue.

The loader routine itself is single-threaded, and "enqueues" on itself by marking an internal storage area called PCENQIND (Program Control ENQ indicator). If this indicator is busy, PCP issues a KC WAIT, and tries later. If, when the WAIT expires, the program is not loaded yet, PCP issues a Storage Control GETMAIN for the program to be loaded, and checks the loader enqueue indicator again. If it is free, PCP locks the loader by setting the enqueue. Just to be on the safe side, PCP checks once more to see whether the program has been loaded yet.

When it is ready to load the program, PCP sets the PPTLIPF flag in the PPT and issues a Task Control CHAP (change priority) macro to give the requesting task the highest possible execution priority. Before going to the actual BSAM or MVS load routine, PCP puts the address of the program storage in the PPTCSA field. PCP branches to the SILOADR routine in DFHSIP, which brings the program in by using BSAM (24-bit programs) or MVS LOAD (31-bit). When the load is complete, PCP unlocks PCENQIND, turns off the PPTLIPF flag, and CHAPs the program back to its original priority.

### 4.15. RETURN Logic

When a program issues a RETURN command or macro, PCP takes the task to the next higher logical program level. PCP releases the program issuing the RETURN, then checks to see whether or not there is an RSA. If there is, PCP says to itself, this program must have been LINKed to. In that case, it restores the program's registers and other information from the RSA, FREEMAINs the RSA, and goes to the program which issued the LINK in the first place. If there is not an RSA, then this task must be at its highest logical level, and the RETURN means that the task should end. PCP deletes any programs which have LLA entries, and issues a DFHKC TYPE=DETACH macro. Task Control takes over from there and performs task termination logic.

### 4.16. Abend Processing

If an application abend occurs, PCP gets control and determines what action to take. If there is a user abend exit active at the current or higher logical level, PCP passes control to it, and that's that. If there is not, PCP calls DFHDCP (the Dump Control Program) to produce a

62 **Chapter Four**

transaction storage dump. Then it releases all of the task's programs (by going through the LLA chain), FREEMAINs all RSAs, and issues an internal XCTL to DFHACP (Abend Control Program). DFHACP performs abend processing. While doing so, it LINKs to a user-written module called DFHPEP (Program Error Program).

## 4.17. Postinitialization Processing

Very often, CICS application systems need to run a few programs to initialize the application's environment. This processing may include establishing a DB2 connection, initialization of files, the CWA, TCTUAs, and other areas. In addition, many vendor-supplied performance, security, and audit programs need to establish their environment before CICS opens for business. This is usually done after system initialization (see Chap. 12) but before CICS starts accepting terminal input.

After initialization, DFHSIP (the System Initialization Program) turns control over to the Terminal Control system task (TC). Eventually, this task will accept terminal input. Before it does, however, TC gives us a chance to execute a few of our own initialization programs. These programs are listed in a DFHPLT (Program List Table; see Fig. 4.22). The suffix of this table is coded by the system programmer in the PLTPI (PLT postinitialization) parameter of the SIT.

When the TC task gets control for the first time, it issues a Program Control DFHPC TYPE=LOAD macro for the table. The PLT must, therefore, be defined in the PPT. After loading this program list, TC LINKs to each program on the list in turn. After all of these programs have executed, TC begins normal processing. PLT programs are also executed during a "takeover" if XRF is used.

Because these programs run under the TC task, special precautions must be taken. If a PLTPI program abends, the TC task abends. CICS will not recover from a system task abend, and the entire region will fail with DFH0601, a system task abend. If this happens during startup, locate the CSASSI2 (CSA system signal indicator 2) byte at offset X'49' of the CSA. If the CSAPLTPI bit (X'10') is not set, TC did not complete PLTPI processing, probably because a user PLTPI program failed. To minimize the possibility of abending the startup process, try to keep processing at a minimum. You may request CICS services, but be sure not to do something which may cause an abend.

There are some other restrictions. The TC task needs to stay at the top of the active task chain. Any CHAP requests may disturb this. In addition, TC's TWA should not be modified. TC has values in this area, and changing them might affect normal TC processing later on.

Remember that all of these programs must run before any other

DFHPLTxy:

TYPE = INITIAL,
SUFFIX = xy,                                   DFHPLTxy
TYPE = ENTRY, PROGRAM = pgmname1,              User startup
TYPE = ENTRY, PROGRAM = pgmname2,                programs
TYPE = FINAL


DFHSITnn:

III

PLTPI = xy                        Use DFHPLTxy for startup

III


DFHPPTnn:

III

TYPE = ENTRY, PROGRAM = DFHPLTxy,         Include DFHPLTxy
TYPE = ENTRY, PROGRAM = pgmname1,         Include user
TYPE = ENTRY, PROGRAM = pgmname2,           startup programs

III

**Figure 4.22**  Postinitialization table entries.

tasks are started. If a START is issued, the started task will not run until the postinitialization phase completes. Therefore, do not wait for any actions to be completed by a task which has been started via Interval Control START or Transient Data ATI (automatic transaction initiation).

If all these restrictions seem intimidating, do not worry. There is a way to avoid most of them safely. In many systems, PLTPI processing is limited to START commands. A PLTPI program can START as many tasks as it wishes. If they are STARTed with an INTERVAL of zero, they will be executed as soon as PLTPI processing completes, and will run under their own TCAs as application tasks. This will ensure that the system (and the system programmer) will not be at the mercy of potentially problematic postinitialization programs.

## 4.18.  Shutdown Processing

When CICS comes down at the end of a normal processing run, applications can schedule programs which perform application termination routines. This may entail writing statistics, finalizing an audit trail,

**64 Chapter Four**

DFHPLTab:

```
        TYPE = INITIAL,
        SUFFIX = ab,                            DFHPLTab
        TYPE = ENTRY, PROGRAM = pgmname3,       First quiesce stage
        TYPE = ENTRY, PROGRAM = pgmname4,         programs
        TYPE = ENTRY, PROGRAM = DFHDELIM        End of first quiesce
        TYPE = ENTRY, PROGRAM = pgmname5,       Second quiesce stage
        TYPE = ENTRY, PROGRAM = pgmname6,         programs
        TYPE = ENTRY, PROGRAM = DLZSTP00,       Quiesce DL/I DOS
        TYPE = FINAL
```

DFHSITnn:

```
        III

        PLTSD = ab              Use DFHPLTab for shutdown
        III
```

DFHPPTnn:

```
        III

        TYPE = ENTRY, PROGRAM = DFHPLTab,       Include DFHPLTab
        TYPE = ENTRY, PROGRAM = pgmname3,       First quiesce stage
        TYPE = ENTRY, PROGRAM = pgmname4,         programs
        TYPE = ENTRY, PROGRAM = pgmname5,       Second quiesce stage
        TYPE = ENTRY, PROGRAM = pgmname6,         programs
        TYPE = ENTRY, PROGRAM = DLZSTP00,       Quiesce DL/I DOS
        III
```

**Figure 4.23**  Shutdown table entries.

terminating the DB2 connection, or closing down performance and security software. In DOS systems using DL/I, the program DLZSTP00 runs to quiesce the DL/I DOS on-line system. To perform these tasks, the system programmer needs to code another PLT, listing all the programs to be executed during a normal shutdown.

The shutdown PLT (see Fig. 4.23) has two parts. During the first part of shutdown processing, terminals are available. Tasks started at terminals, however, are rejected unless they are named in an XLT (Transaction List Table), are system transactions such as CEMT, or are started via ATI. Network or System Control transactions are good candidates for this table. This phase ends when all of the first phase shutdown programs have completed and there are no user tasks waiting to complete.

In the second quiesce stage, TCP and KCP ATTACH logic is disabled. The two quiesce phases are separated in the shutdown PLT by a dummy entry for program DFHDELIM (delimiter).

The PLTSD suffix in the SIT names the PLT to be used during shutdown processing. This name can be overridden by using the PLT operand of the CEMT PERFORM SHUTDOWN operator command. Remember that none of these programs will be executed if CICS is terminated by the shutdown command using the IMMEDIATE operand, or if CICS abends.

## 4.19. The Command-Level Interface

Originally, the only way to request CICS services was to code CICS macros. This meant that application programmers needed to be familiar with CICS architecture. Control blocks had to be addressed, and the formats and content had to be understood by any programmer requesting a CICS service. Applications had to manage their own storage by using the DFHSC macro. To free programmers from these constraints, IBM introduced the command-, or EXEC-, level interface. Today, this is almost universally accepted as the method of choice for application code.

CICS developers first considered using native language calls to management modules, but this idea was rejected for several reasons. A large number of arguments might have been needed. The programmer might have had to specify values he or she did not understand. Execution-time performance problems might have occurred in interpreting function codes and defaulting arguments and options. Compile-time error checking would have been impossible. No conversion or padding of arguments would have been possible; each language would have had to use its own mechanism.

Because of these problems, IBM decided to choose a universal call mechanism: the EXEC command. Each EXEC command is translated to a native language call by a CICS language-specific preprocessor during program preparation. When the generated call is executed during a CICS run, DFHEIP (the EXEC Interface program) intercepts the call and acts as a go-between for application and management modules. EIP analyzes the call arguments, determines what function is needed, and contacts the appropriate CICS control program. When the function completes, EIP returns the response to the application.

The main components of the EXEC Interface are the translators and the interpreter. Each language has its own translator. They all share one interpreter: DFHEIP.

### 4.19.1. DFHEIP initialization

When a command-level program starts executing, the first thing it does is call DFHEIP's initialization code. This code is automatically inserted

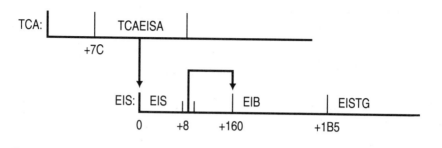

**Figure 4.24** The EIS (Exec Interface Structure).

by the translator at the beginning of a program's executable code. During initialization, EIP establishes the EXEC environment by creating some control blocks, building a parameter list addressing them, and returning control to the application.

The first parameter points to the EIS (EXEC Interface structure). The EIS (see Fig. 4.24) is used to control the command-level environment. Each command-level task has one. It is located in transaction storage as CLASS=USER, and is freed at the end of the task. Its address can be found in the TCAEISA field of the system TCA at offset X'7C'. Like the TCA, the EIS contains three parts: a system area, a user area (called the EIB), and an optional unformatted work area called EISTG.

The system area fields start with the characters EIS and contain information that EIP needs to control the EXEC environment. It holds EIP's RSA, pointers to EXEC request parameters, and system flags. The next area is the EIB (EXEC Interface block). This area is adjacent to the system area, but is also addressed by the EIS at EISEIBAD (EIS + X'8'). This means that IBM might increase the size of the EIS. The EIB contains information that describes the environment to an application.

EIBDATE contains the date in 00YYDDD format. EIBTIME holds the time in 0HHMMSS format. Both of these fields are initialized when a task is created, and can be updated by using the ASKTIME command. The FORMATTIME command can transform these fields to any of various formats. EIBTRNID, EIBTASKN, and EIBTRMID show the current transaction code, task number, and terminal id. Other fields in the EIB show the position of the cursor on the screen, the length of the COMMAREA, and the status of the last request for CICS services. EIBRCODE contains the system response code from the last EXEC command.

## 4.19.2. EXEC Interface flow

When an application issues an EXEC command, it passes control to the stub link-edited with the program. That stub branches to the EIP call point. [At initialization time, the call (or request) entry point of DFHEIP was placed in the stub]. EIP analyzes the request and decides which function stub to branch to. For a File Control request, DFHEFC gets control. DFHEFC transforms the EXEC command to a DFHFC macro, which brings control to DFHFCP. (The last two letters of the stub are the same as the last two letters of the macros it issues.) DFHFCP honors the request, and returns to DFHEFC. DFHEFC then goes back to DFHEIP.

At this point, any one of several things can happen. If all went well, DFHEIP passes control back to the NSI (next sequential instruction) after the EXEC command. If a problem occurred, DFHEIP looks for an active HANDLE routine for the condition. If there is one, it gets control. If not, EIP goes to DFHACP, the Abend Control Program (see Fig. 4.25).

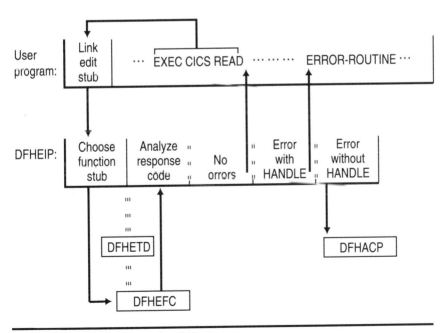

Figure 4.25 EXEC Interface abend handling.

## 4.19.3. HANDLE CONDITION processing

When a program requests a service from CICS, that request may or may not succeed. If it does not, the service module raises an exception condition. To take care of this possibility, an application can have one or more HANDLE CONDITION commands to anticipate exception conditions. For instance, before issuing an EXEC CICS READ command, a programmer would probably code EXEC CICS HANDLE CONDITION NOTFND(NOTFND-ROUTINE). The NOTFND-ROUTINE would get control if File Control could not find a particular record. The EXEC Interface processes the HANDLE at two different times: when the program is prepared, and when it executes.

At translation, each condition is given a number. The translator converts CONDITION names to these numbers. At execution time, the numbers are passed to EIP when a HANDLE CONDITION is issued. If EIP receives an abnormal response to a request, it converts the response into an exception condition number to determine whether a HANDLE label is active for the response.

DFHEIP uses response tables (see Fig. 4.26) in DFHEIP code to perform the conversion. There is one response table per function group. The correct response table is found from an array of offsets indexed by function group codes. The response table entries are 2 bytes long. The argument is usually a bit pattern corresponding to the response. The function is the exception condition number.

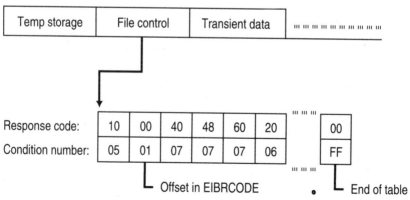

**Figure 4.26** Response tables.

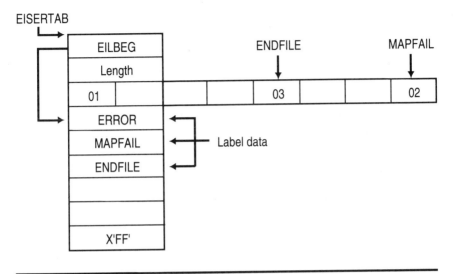

**Figure 4.27** Handle Condition Table.

EIP scans the response table until it finds a bit pattern matching the response in EIBRCODE. In some cases, the response is not the first byte of the response code. If this is the case, byte 1 will be X'00', and the second byte will show the offset in EIBRCODE to be examined. The search is repeated with the appropriate byte from EIBRCODE. The last function byte is X'FF'. If this byte is found, there is no active HANDLE for the condition. This mechanism allows different response codes to be used for the same exception conditions within a function group. This is necessary when several conditions occur simultaneously; EIP can implement a priority ordering scheme to determine which condition it will raise.

When an application issues a HANDLE CONDITION command, EIP remembers the exception conditions named and the label which should receive control if one of those conditions is raised. This information is saved in a Handle Condition Table. This table is allocated when an EXEC program issues its first HANDLE CONDITION, and is addressed by EISERTAB at offset X'98' of the EIS. This table (see Fig. 4.27) contains an index and an array of label information entries.

The index of this table is an array of byte entries corresponding to specific exception conditions. Each condition has a unique number used to address its entry in the index, which was found during the response table search (described above). If no handle label is active, the entry is

# 70 Chapter Four

zero. If one is active, it holds the index to the label information entry for that condition.

Let us take a look at how all this works. Suppose an application has a HANDLE CONDITION for the ERROR, ENDFILE, and MAPFAIL conditions. When the HANDLE commands are translated, these conditions are changed to condition numbers 01, 05, and 07, respectively. When the commands are executed, these condition numbers, and the label information about each one, are saved in the Handle Condition Table addressed by the task's EISERTAB field.

When the program executes a file command and gets the ENDFILE condition, DFHEIP will find the File Control response table by indexing into the function group part of the response table. EIP searches through the table, looking for a response code which matches the one in EIBRCODE (10 in this case). It finds 10, and sees that the associated condition number is 05. EIP then addresses the task's Handle Condition Table, using the EISERTAB field. The fifth entry in the condition number portion of that table contains the number 03. The third entry in the label data part of the table describes the action to take for this condition.

### 4.19.4. HANDLE CONDITION label data

The label data described above tell EIP where to transfer control when a particular error occurs. These data are a little different for each language. For PL/I, each label information entry contains an 8-byte label variable used by the PL/I "go to out of block" code to transfer control to the correct label and to restore addressability to the appropriate PL/I DSA. Since assembler is reentrant, each label information entry has the address of the assembler routine and the DFHEISTG corresponding to the label's environment.

COBOL is not truly reentrant. In COBOL, it is not possible to branch straight back to a paragraph or section. Compiled code could be using register values at the label which are not valid for a branch from outside. EIP must take special steps to get the HANDLE routine, so the translator produces different code for COBOL HANDLE CONDITIONs.

This code starts off with a CALL statement that passes the encoded condition names to EIP. After the CALL, the translator generates a GO TO DEPENDING ON statement, where the list of labels corresponds one-to-one with the list of passed conditions. EIP sets the DEPENDING ON variable to control the branch to the appropriate label. If the variable is zero, control goes to the NSI (next sequential instruction).

When an exception condition occurs, EIP restores the COBOL execution environment by restoring the registers which were valid when the HANDLE that activated the condition was executed. It then sets the DEPENDING ON variable and returns to the GO TO DEPENDING ON after the HANDLE's generated call. The COBOL code then executes a branch to the correct HANDLE routine.

To do all this, EIP needs to save the register corresponding to all active HANDLE commands. Since a given set of registers can apply to more than one condition, it is more efficient to code many conditions in one HANDLE command than to spread them out. The label information entries for COBOL contain a pointer to an RSA and an index to be used as the GO TO DEPENDING ON variable. Since the pointer to the RSA also indicates which HANDLE a label corresponds to, EIP can determine when an RSA can be reused.

### 4.19.5. Command-Level LINK processing

When an EXEC program LINKs to another, the program-dependent EIS data must be saved, so that the new program can use the EIS directly. The saved data include the RSA address, HANDLE information, COMMAREA information, and the program language. Application programs may be in different languages, and the HANDLE mechanism is different for each.

The saved data are stored in a PC LINK table (see Fig. 4.28). This table is arranged as a push-down stack and is addressed by EIS-PCTAB. When control RETURNs to EIP from the LINK, EIP restores the stacked data and frees the table. The halfword EISLINKL at offset X'8C' contains the current link level. Each link entry contains its link level in a halfword at offset X'C'.

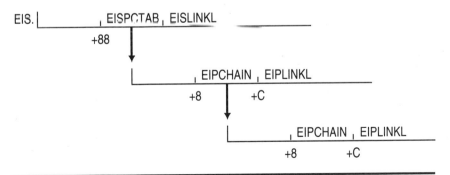

**Figure 4.28** PC LINK table.

**72  Chapter Four**

### 4.19.6. COMMAREA processing

The COMMAREA allows programs to exchange information between LINKs, XCTLs, and RETURN TRANSID. During a LINK, EIP passes the LINKed-to program a parameter list containing the EIB and COMMAREA addresses. XCTL processing is a little different.

The program which issues an XCTL is likely to be terminated, at which point its storage (including its COMMAREA) would be deleted. To circumvent this probability, EIP makes a copy of its COMMAREA and passes the address in EISCOMMX (EIS + X'A8'). When an XCTL is executed, the XCTLer's COMMAREA is freed if it is not a copy of a COMMAREA and it is not being passed to the next program.

RETURN TRANSID with the COMMAREA option allows pseudo-conversational tasks to exchange information. EIP must copy the COMMAREA because the RETURNing program's storage will be freed when the program ends. The address of this COMMAREA is saved in the EIS at offset X'B8'.

### 4.19.7. Command-level File Control processing

Some File Control commands, such as READ UPDATE and REWRITE, interact with one another. To remember this information, EFC (the EXEC File Control function stub) allocates a File Control dataset table when it encounters the first FC request that needs it. This table is addressed by the EIS at EISFCTAB (EIS + X'138').

The internal file table contains dataset names, request ids, and information such as FWA and record id addresses, id types, and key lengths. If the table is full, another is allocated and chained from the previous one. Information from this table is used to check the validity of some request sequences, remember key processing information, and manage storage buffers for READ SET (locate mode processing).

### 4.20.  The Assembler Language Interface

The translator uses one register for dynamic (DFHEISTG) storage, another for code and constants, and another for the EIB. These are all set by the DFHEIENT macro:

```
DFHEIENT CODEREG=(Rc), address executable code and constants
    DATAREG=(Rd), address DFHEISTG (and user storage)
    EIBREG=(Re) address the EIB
```

Before a BAL program can issue an EXEC command, storage for the parameter list generated by the command must be acquired somewhere. The translator provides for this by inserting DFHEISTG and

## Program Control  73

DFHEIEND macros to delimit storage. This dynamic storage can be extended by defining variables in the DFHEISTG DSECT.

In assembler, EXEC commands generate DFHECALL macros to invoke the interface. This macro uses register 15 to hold the entry point of the linked stub, and register 14 to address the return point in the application. Register 0 is used as a work register, and register 1 addresses the parameter list. A typical CICS command is shown below:

```
EXEC CICS READQ TS
    QUEUE(QNAME) ITEM(QITEM)
    INTO(QAREA) LENGTH(QLEN)
```

would be translated into:

```
DFHECALL =X'0A04E8000800008900',(CHA8,QNAME),(____RF,QAREA),
    (FB_2_RF,QLEN),,(FB_2,QITEM)
```

and would generate this at assembly:

```
DS 0H
LA 1,DFHEIPL                         addr parameter list area
LA 14,=X'0A04E8000800008900'         addr parameter list
LA 15,QNAME                          addr the queue name area
LA 0,QAREA                           addr target for queue read
STM 14,0,0(1)                        store parameter list addr,
                                     queue name ,addr, and target
                                     address in DFHEIPL
OI 20(1),X'80'                       show end of parameter list
L 15,=V(DFHEI1)                      addr DFHEIP call EP
BALR 14,15                           go to it and return here
```

Chapter

# 5

# Terminal Control

## 5.1. Introduction

The most standard telecommunication methods are discussed in this chapter. The Terminal Control Program (TCP) and other CICS management modules are explored in depth, in conjunction with key system tables. We will see how a CICS task converses with a terminal, and get a detailed picture of the way VTAM, NCP, and CICS interact to provide terminal and network communication and error handling. The coding of Terminal Control Table (TCT) entries should be of interest not only to 1.7 and 2.1 users who still generate a static TCT, but also to those who want an insight into the internals of Terminal Control. The chapter concludes with a brief look at the Autoinstall feature. Some of the major topics are:

- Overview of terminal access methods
- Major Terminal Control modules and control blocks
- The application request handler (DFHZARQ)
- Terminal Control as a task
- CICS–BTAM interface
- VTAM terminal management
- CICS–VTAM communication
- VTAM message structure
- Coding a TCT
- Generating Terminal Control: SIT and TCT and PCT options
- VTAM–NCP communication and network error handling

## 76 Chapter Five

- Writing a Node Error Program
- Terminal error processing
- Generating Autoinstall

## 5.2. Terminal Control Overview

CICS terminal management programs allow applications to communicate with a wide variety of terminals, printers, and even other software. To do this, the TCPs process requests from user application TC commands and from BMS. A SEND MAP command falls through to a BMS DFHTC macro issued on behalf of the application, while a SEND command goes directly to Terminal Control. User applications never communicate directly with a communications access method; TC chooses the method and forwards the request, whether it is from an application program or from BMS.

### 5.2.1. Terminal access methods

CICS can communicate with a wide variety of terminals. Most users' devices are supported by BTAM, TCAM, or VTAM. BTAM and VTAM are discussed separately in this chapter. TCAM comes in two varieties: TCAM ACB processing and TCAM DCB processing. In TCAM ACB processing, TCAM is under the control of VTAM. In DCB processing, it is somewhat similar to BTAM. In any case, TCAM lines are not dedicated to CICS. In addition, CICS can communicate with sequential devices by using SAM (sequential access method), and with CPU consoles.

### 5.2.2. The Terminal Control Table (TCT)

The major terminal control block is the TCT, which has an entry for each terminal, called a TCTTE. Until CICS 1.7, this was a static table that resided in the nucleus. Now, as we shall see, VTAM terminals can be defined on-line, and even installed automatically. As we can recall from Chap. 3, each task running at a terminal had a pointer from its TCA (in subpool 03 or 04) to its TCTTE. The TCTTE, in turn, pointed to TIOAs in subpool 02, the Teleprocessing subpool. The TIOA is used to communicate a Terminal Control request from the application to CICS. We will see in this chapter how CICS communicates with the terminal itself.

### 5.2.3. Major terminal control modules

CICS has two main terminal control programs: DFHTCP and DFHZCP. ZCP does all the work common to all access methods, and contains all the VTAM code. TCP supports BTAM and the TCAM DCB interface only (in DOS, it also supports consoles). ZCP is required no matter what access methods are being used, as it does the lion's share of the common work. TCP is required only for BTAM, TCAM DCB, SAM, and DOS console support. An MVS installation using VTAM only does not need DFHTCP at all. DFHTCP and DFHZCP are generated separately and are identified separately in the SIT by the `TCP=` and `ZCP=` parameters, so if TCP is not needed, the system programmer can code `TCP=NO` without any problems.

### 5.2.4. The application request handler

ZCP (see Fig. 5.1) has two major CSECTs: DFHZARQ (the application request handler) and DFHZDSP (the dispatcher). Requests for terminal management from applications or BMS always come through ZARQ, while the dispatcher is responsible for turning terminal requests into tasks. Together, these subprograms make up the working set of the application-to-CICS interface. TCP and the VTAM interface portion of ZCP act as an interface between CICS and the terminal network.

The application request handler receives Terminal Control requests communicated through a task's TCA. When ZARQ receives the request, it chains the TCTTE into a work queue to be dealt with later or executes the request directly. If the request implies a WAIT—the CONVERSE command, for instance—TC asks KCP to SUSPEND it by issuing a `DFHKC TYPE=SUSPEND` macro for the task. Later, when the terminal responds, TC will issue a `DFHKC TYPE=RESUME` on behalf of the task.

### 5.2.5. Terminal Control as a task

Sooner or later, the TC task will get control. This happens whenever Task Control gets control back from the operating system. That time is

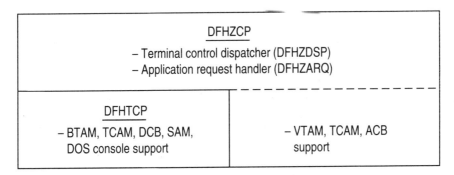

Figure 5.1 Terminal management structure.

**78   Chapter Five**

never greater than the ICV parameter in the SIT. Another parameter that affects this time is the ICVTSD (interval control value for scan time delay). This value is the maximum amount of time that the system programmer would like to have elapse before TC checks the network for input. TC will also get control if an access method tells it directly that it wants some attention. In BTAM, this is done by posting an ECB; in VTAM, by driving an exit. More about that later. If worst comes to worst, TC has a fail-safe value. No more than 1 s will elapse between the time that ZARQ receives a terminal request and the time the TC task is dispatched.

TC is the highest-priority task in the system, and runs under its own TCA. Its job is to perform the requested Terminal Control services. When it receives control, it calls DFHTCP (if there is one). TCP scans the TCT for non-VTAM requests, and returns control to the dispatcher (ZDSP). In a VTAM network, the dispatcher branches to a program which issues DFHKC TYPE=ATTACH macros for any tasks requested by new terminal input. This program is called DFHZATT (attach). After this, ZDSP scans the chain of TCTTEs to see if any work is queued for VTAM logical units. This would include LOGON requests.

When the TC task has finished scanning for input and processing application requests, it returns to KCP and waits for its next dispatch. It is interesting to note, by the way, that in a mixed terminal environment (VTAM and non-VTAM), the non-VTAM network is serviced first.

It is important to remember which actions take place under the user's TCA and which are done by TC as its own task. TC operates under an application task's TCA when the application makes a request, when BMS makes a request, and when Terminal Control carries out an unchained VTAM terminal request. TC operates as a task (under its own TCA) when it is dispatched, when it issues DFHKC or DFHSC macros, and when it executes non-VTAM I/O or chained VTAM I/O.

### 5.3.  BTAM Terminal Management

#### 5.3.1.  The CICS–BTAM interface

There are two major steps to defining a BTAM system. First, local terminals and remote communication lines must be defined to the operating system. The communication lines are defined in a DCB (data control block). BTAM DFTRMLST (Define Terminal List) macros are coded to define the polling and addressing lists for the network. The second step is to define the network to CICS. This is done by defining terminals, lines, and control blocks in the CICS TCT.

CICS-to-BTAM communication is carried out by DFHTCP. Its main functions are to monitor the network for activity, request BTAM terminal polling and addressing, perform EBCDIC (extended binary coded data interchange code) translation, initiate transactions, manage terminal storage, handle terminal errors, and pass user data to terminals. ZARQ receives TC requests and passes them to TCP. TCP issues BTAM macros to send and receive data to and from terminals.

There are three partners in the CICS–BTAM interface. Applications issue Terminal Control commands, or BMS commands which fall through to TC commands. DFHTCP addresses terminals with output and polls the terminal network for input. BTAM initiates channel programs for I/O operations and posts ECBs when the I/O completes.

### 5.3.2. The TCT for BTAM

The TCT contains information that TCP needs to run the BTAM network, and contains descriptions of the network's communication lines and network. More specifically, it contains BTAM polling and addressing lists, and ECBs which track input and output status.

The BTAM TCT (see Fig. 5.2) is structured according to the network's line groups. Even local terminals are defined as line groups. For each group, the TCT contains access method information in TCT TYPE=SDSCI entries, line status and descriptions in TYPE=LINE entries, and descriptions and status of each terminal in their TYPE=TERMINAL entries.

SDSCI (specify dataset control information) entries generate a BTAM DCB for each line group. LINE macros allow BTAM and CICS to track line activity. There is one of these for each remote line and one or more per local group. The LINE entry generates a TCTLE (TCT line entry) which contains the DECB (data event control block) that BTAM needs to track line activity. The TCTLE's line ECB (the first fullword of the TCTLE) is posted by BTAM whenever an I/O event completes on the line. The TCTLE is the main communication area used by CICS and BTAM. Each TERMINAL entry generates a TCTTE (TCT terminal entry), which is the main communication vehicle between terminal management and a user task.

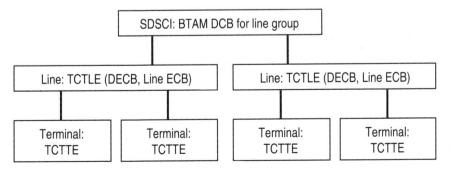

**Figure 5.2** BTAM TCT control blocks.

**80  Chapter Five**

At the end of the TCT is a WAIT list which contains pointers to a CICS timer ECB and to each of the line ECBs. The TC task issues a CICS WAIT on this list when it finishes its processing and has no more work to do, just as KCP issues an operating system WAIT when it has completed its processing.

### 5.3.3. Terminal scanning

Whenever the TC task is dispatched, it scans the TCT to see if there is any I/O to be processed. In Chap. 3, we discussed the ICV, which is the maximum amount of time that the CICS dispatcher will give up control to the operating system. The terminal scan delay works the same way, except that it gets set after a task terminates, or after an output request with a WAIT has been issued.

A timer ECB is set whenever the ICV or ICVTSD expires. A line ECB is posted whenever a terminal event occurs on that line. Whenever the TC task is dispatched, it makes either a full or a partial scan of the ECB. If the timer ECB is posted, it makes a full scan. This means that it scans the entire TCT. If TCP finds any pending output requests (chained earlier), it services them. If line ECBs have been posted (indicating input), TCP receives the data and presents them to the waiting application. If no task is attached, TCP issues a DFHKC TYPE=ATTACH on behalf of the terminal. The full scan continues until each entry has been examined.

If only a line ECB has been posted, TC performs a partial scan to service input requests. Pending output requests found during the scan will also be serviced. A partial scan looks only at terminals associated with lines which have posted ECBs. TC services any input or output requests it finds, and ends when the last posted line has been processed. At the end of either of these scans, TC issues a DFHKC TYPE=WAIT DCI=LIST to Task Control, which begins its task dispatch scan. After KC finishes its scan, gives up control to the operating system, and gets it back again, it looks at these ECBs. If any of them are posted, the TC task gets control and performs a full or partial scan again.

### 5.3.4. BTAM data flow

Let us look at the flow of input from a BTAM terminal to an application within CICS, and the task's output back to the terminal. When CICS receives the message, TCP gets an LIOA (line I/O area) to hold it (see Fig. 5.3). The LIOA size is specified in the INAREAL parameter of the

| Index | STX | CU | DEV | AID | Cursor | Data | ETX |
|---|---|---|---|---|---|---|---|

**Figure 5.3**  Line I/O area (input).

TCT TYPE=LINE macro, and is stored as a halfword in the TCTLEIOA field at offset X'6' of the TCTLE. If the terminal is local, the LIOA will turn into a TIOA. Local terminal messages are read in one block, while remote terminals' data are sent to CICS in 256-byte blocks. If the LIOA is not large enough for the whole message, TCP assembles it into a larger one.

The LIOA is prefixed and suffixed by some BTAM control information (index, STX, CU, DEV, and ETX). These characters identify and describe the location of the device and the start and end of the message text. The AID field and cursor address refer to the attention identifier and position of the cursor on the screen of the sending terminal.

After receiving the input, TCP creates a TIOA (see Fig. 5.4) for it and chains it to the TCTTE (as described in Chap. 3). For local terminals, the LIOA itself is used as a TIOA. The user task is going to be looking at the TIOA and is probably not very interested in the BTAM information, so TCP strips out everything but the data. The AID and cursor position information are placed in the TCTTE at TCTTEAID and TCTTECAD. The data itself is translated from lowercase to uppercase if UCTRAN was specified in the terminal's TCTTE entry. ASCII-to-EBCDIC translation may also take place. The length of the data is in field TIOATDL. TIOAs are chained through the second word of their SAAs, just like any other transaction storage (see Chap. 2). This word is also called TIOASCA in the TIOA. The TIOAWCI and TIOACLCR fields contain BTAM macro information.

After preparing the data, TCP initiates a new task (DFHKC TYPE=ATTACH) or resumes the task (DFHKC TYPE=RESUME) which issued a RECEIVE or CONVERSE and was waiting for the input. If this is a command-level environment, DFHETC (EXEC Terminal Control) copies the TIOA data to working storage, then releases the TIOA. The TCTTEAID and TCTTECAD information is placed in the EIB. If the task is using BMS maps, then BMS interfaces between Terminal Control and the application.

When the application wants to send output to the terminal, it builds a message and issues a Terminal Control command. If the message is actually a map, it issues a BMS command, which in turn falls through to a Terminal Control command. The EXEC Interface (or BMS) acquires a new TIOA and fills it with the output message.

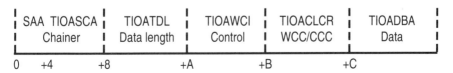

Figure 5.4  Terminal I/O area.

| STX | ESC | CCC | WCC | Data | ETX |

**Figure 5.5** Line I/O area (output).

When Terminal Control processes the request, it moves the TCA request bits to the destination TCTTE and adds BTAM line control characters (STX, ESC, and ETX) for remote terminals. The application request is translated to BTAM control indicators and write characters. The BTAM write control indicator is placed in the TIOAWCI. The write control character (WCC) or copy control character (CCC) is set at TIOACLCR. TC moves the data from the TIOA to an LIOA (see Fig. 5.5) and translates from EBCDIC to ASCII if necessary, then performs a BTAM WRITE addressing the terminal.

When the I/O completes, TCP frees the TIOA and issues a DFHKC TYPE=RESUME (if the request included the WAIT option). If a task RETURNs without waiting for the WRITE to complete, all of the remaining storage will be freed when the TC task inspects the TCTTE for work to be done on that terminal's line. This will not occur until the output completes. If activity is high, it may happen even later.

### 5.3.5 Lines and terminals

Lines and terminals are defined in the TCT, which serves as a communication area between TCP, user tasks, and BTAM. TCP uses the TCT to determine line characteristics, terminal types, special features, error recovery, user areas, and status information. A BTAM environment must be described in an off-line TCT. (Only VTAM may be defined online.) There are five types of DFHTCT macro needed to define a BTAM network to CICS: TYPE=INITIAL, TYPE=SDSCI, TYPE=LINE, TYPE=TERMINAL, and TYPE=FINAL.

Each TCT must start with DFHTCT TYPE=INITIAL. This is where required access methods (VTAM and/or BTAM) are defined. It generates the TCT prefix (see Fig. 5.6), and is addressed by CSATCTBA. This is also where we can define some error handling information. When a transaction error occurs, CICS can display an error message at the terminal.

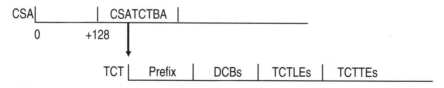

**Figure 5.6** TCT prefix.

The `TYPE=INITIAL ERRATT` parameter determines where it will be displayed. `ERRATT=NO` will put this message at the beginning of the current cursor position. A neater way to display messages is to send them to the last line of the display by specifying `ERRATT=LASTLINE`. Other options of this parameter define additional error message attributes like color and highlighting.

`TYPE=SDSCI` defines the access method information BTAM needs to support the communication line configuration. It identifies a line group, telling BTAM which terminal and line classifications are to be supported, and what type of error recovery is to be used. It generates this information as a DCB, stored in the TCT just after the prefix. Each line's (or line group's) DCB is addressed by the TCTLE + X'8' (TCTLEDCB; see Fig. 5.7).

In the `SDSCI` macro, the system programmer defines the terminal types to be supported by coding the `DEVICE` parameter. These devices can be local or remote 3270 displays or printers (L3270, L3270P, R3270, R3270P) or other devices. The `DSCNAME` will become the symbolic name of the dataset control information. This name is used to associate the `SDSCI` macro with its associated `LINE` macros, so the `DSCNAME`s in each must match. In addition, the `SDSCI DDNAME` parameter must be the same as the `DDNAME` parameter on the DD card which defines a remote line group in the CICS startup JCL.

The `SDSCI ERROPT` parameter determines what type of automatic error recovery and recording will take place. `ERROPT=E` gives basic recovery, such as resending after transmission errors. `ERROPT=C` is a little more complicated. In MVS, it provides LERB (line error recording block) support to collect error statistics. This requires coding a BTAM LERB macro in the TCT, and specifying its label in the `SDSCI LERBADR` parameter. In DOS, specifying the `LERBADR` generates LERB support automatically. In most cases, `ERROPT=E` should suffice.

Each line within a line group needs a `TYPE=LINE` macro, which generates a TCTLE (see Fig. 5.8) used by BTAM and CICS to communicate with the terminals on the line. The TCTLE tells TCP the type of access method to use and the position of the line within a line group. For BTAM, the access method indicator (TCTLEMI) will show either sequential access (X'01'), local access (X'02'), or telecommunication access

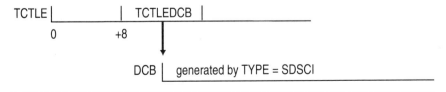

**Figure 5.7** BTAM line entry DCB addressability.

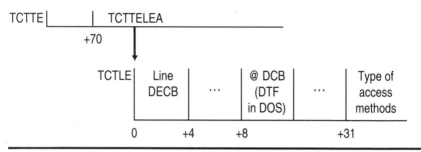

**Figure 5.8** BTAM line entry DECBs.

method (X'04'). The first word of each TCTLE contains a DECB, and is addressed by the TCTTE at TCTTELEA (line entry address). TCTLEs follow DCBs in the TCT.

The LIOA size is defined in the TYPE=LINE macro by using the INAREAL parameter. In general, it should be at least 256, because data is read in 256-byte segments. Local 3270s can be given any value above zero. Remember that for local terminals, the LIOA becomes a TIOA. The INAREAL value should be the length of a typical input message.

Remote communication lines are grouped by terminal type. The line group defines the protocol BTAM uses to interface with all the devices on each line. This means that all lines in the group must represent the same type of terminal. If a network contains only 3270s, then, all the lines could be defined in the same line group (SDSCI). If the system programmer wanted to group them logically, however, he could define multiple SDSCIs. The only restriction is that different terminal types cannot appear within the same line group.

Local terminals are not connected through communication lines. They are still, however, defined in line groups to CICS. The SDSCI contains the DCB that BTAM needs to access the device. The TCT must have at least one SDSCI to define a local line group

One reason to group terminals under multiple lines is to take advantage of the 3270 print request function. This facility allows us to print out a 3270 display on a 3270 printer. To get the print option, code PRINT=PA1 | PA2 | PA3 in the SIT. Whenever this PA key is hit, the display will be printed at a 3270 printer. This printer must be on the same remote control unit or logical line as the terminal. Remote terminals must have FEATURE=COPY in their TYPE=TERMINAL definitions. The printer itself must have a buffer capacity at least as large as the terminal's, and must be in service and not attached to a task. In addition, the printer must have FEATURE=PRINT and COPY in its TYPE=TERMINAL definition.

On a remote line, CICS sends the output to the first available printer on the same logical line. If you want to assign a printer to a particular group of local terminals, you can define a line for that group.

One problem with local printing on a line, however, is that CICS and BTAM can handle only one operation at a time on a local logical line. If something is printing out on the local 3270 printer, the terminals on that line are shut out, and can neither send nor receive data. This is because there is only one TCTLE, and it can handle only one I/O at a time. To get around this problem, code the `TYPE=LINE POOLCNT=n` parameter to generate $n$ TCTLEs. The safest way to do this is to make $n$ the total number of printers, plus one. This means that even if every printer on the line is tied up, there is still one TCTLE left available for terminal I/O.

Because there may be several `LINE` definitions for each `SDSCI`, we need to specify the BTAMRLN (BTAM relative line number) of each line within an `SDSCI` group (see Fig. 5.9). Each group has a DD card in the startup JCL. The DD card for the first group (BTAMRLN=1) has a label matching the `DDNAME` parameter of the `SDSCI` macro. The next concatenated DD card represents the BTAMRLN=2 group, and so on. The BTAMRLN sequence must match the DD card sequence.

Each line definition is followed by a `TYPE=TERMINAL` macro for each terminal on the line. The TCTTE (see Fig. 5.10) defines specific information needed by TC to communicate with applications and other management modules. It defines the terminal id, model, and other information. This macro creates a TCTTE which addresses the TCA of its associated task, the task's TIOA, and the TCTLE.

The first terminal of a local line must be identified to that line by coding the label of the first `TYPE=TERMINAL` macro in the `POOLADR` pa-

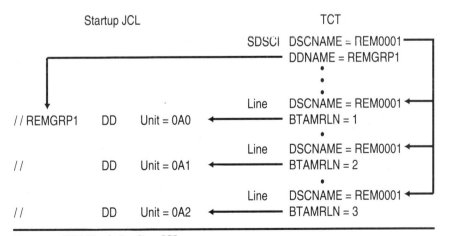

**Figure 5.9** BTAM relative line JCL.

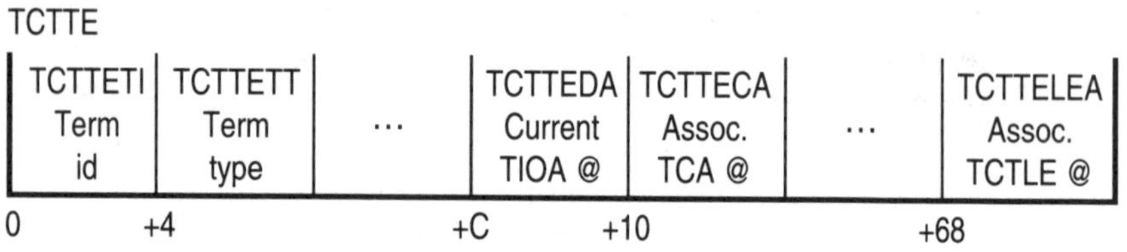

86    Chapter Five

TCTTE

| TCTTETI<br>Term<br>id | TCTTETT<br>Term<br>type | ... | TCTTEDA<br>Current<br>TIOA @ | TCTTECA<br>Assoc.<br>TCA @ | ... | TCTTELEA<br>Assoc.<br>TCTLE @ |
|---|---|---|---|---|---|---|

0         +4                    +C      +10                  +68

Figure 5.10  BTAM TCTTE fields.

rameter of its `TYPE=LINE` macro (see Fig. 5.11). Note the `POOLCNT=2` parameter, coded to facilitate the printer (PRT1).

The last terminal on the line must be identified with the `LASTTRM` parameter. For local lines, code `LASTTRM=POOL`, as shown above. If this had been a remote line, we would have coded `LASTTRM=LINE`.

There is an optional user extension to each TCTTE called a TCTUA (TCT user area). Its size is defined in the `TYPE=TERMINAL TUTUAL` parameter. This area can be used to store information between tasks, and can be useful for terminal-related data. Remember, however, that this area is allocated from the TCT (in the nucleus!) and can take up a lot of storage. For instance, if a network has 2000 terminals, each with a 512-byte TCTUA, we are tying up 1,024,000 non-XA bytes permanently. This can represent about 15 or 20 percent of an entire CICS region.

After all the terminals are defined, we can finish up the TCT by coding a `TYPE=FINAL` macro. This generates some additional control information, including a TCT WAIT list, used for dispatching the TC task to do a TCT scan. This is the list of line ECBs that we discussed earlier.

```
LOCDCB1 DFHTCT TYPE = SDSCI, ...
LOCLIN1 DFHTCT TYPE = LINE, ..., POOLCNT = 2, POOLADR = TRM1



TRM1    DFHTCT  TYPE = TERMINAL, TERMID = TRM1,...
TRM2    DFHTCT  TYPE = TERMINAL, TERMID = TRM2,...
TRM3    DFHTCT  TYPE = TERMINAL, TERMID = TRM3,...
PRT1    DFHTCT  TYPE = TERMINAL, TERMID = PRT1,..., LASTTRM = POOL
```

Figure 5.11  Local line pooling.

### 5.3.6. BTAM polling and addressing

When CICS wants to know if there is any input, it polls the the terminal. The opposite of polling is addressing—the terminal is asked whether it is ready to receive output. To accomplish both of these, CICS maintains polling and addressing lists. Polling and addressing are done only for remote 3270 printers and terminals.

Because remote terminals are attached to control units, BTAM polls the control unit, not the terminal. This is called general polling. The control unit is responsible for asking each of its terminals whether it has any input to send. A polling list keeps track of the address of each control unit and shows BTAM the order in which they are to be polled. Each remote line has its own polling list, which includes the polling characters for each control unit on the line. The control units will be polled according the polling list sequence.

There are three kinds of polling lists. An *open list* asks BTAM to make one pass through the polling list when the TC task is attached. A *wrap list* is the same as an open list, except that BTAM automatically goes back to the top of the list after the last control unit on the line has been polled. An *auto list* moves the responsibility for polling from CICS to the communications controller, saving some host CPU cycles in the process. Auto lists can also be wrap lists, and in CICS, this is the best way to specify polling.

Because addressing involves only one specific terminal, we do not need a multiple list of terminals. Addressing lists contain only one terminal, and are open lists. There is a separate list for each terminal for all write operations.

To define these lists, we need to code a BTAM DFTRMLST (define terminal list) for each remote line in the TCT. They can be placed after all the `TYPE=LINE` and `TYPE=TERMINAL` macros (but before `TYPE=FINAL`), after each `TYPE=LINE` DEFINITION, after the last `TYPE=TERMINAL` for each line, or between the `TYPE=SDSCI` and its corresponding `TYPE-LINE` macros. Use whatever method is easiest to maintain. When the TCT assembles, all the lists will be together after the last `TYPE=TERMINAL` entry no matter where they are coded (see Fig. 5.12).

|        |          | AUTOLST |
|--------|----------|---------|
| symbol | DFTRMLST | AUTOWLST, (polling characters) |
|        |          | OPENLST |

**Figure 5.12** BTAM DFTRMLST macro.

**88   Chapter Five**

```
GENPOL1      DFTRMLST      AUTOWLST
                           (C1C17F7F2D,
                           C2C27F7F2D,
                           3737373737)
```

**Figure 5.13** General polling list.

The first DFTRMLST parameter (AUTOLST, AUTOWLST, or OPEN-LIST) defines the type of list. We need an open list for addressing, so we would code OPENLST. For polling, we would code AUTOWLST.

The hexadecimal polling characters represent each terminal in the list by showing its control unit, device address, and a special ENQ character (X'2D') to show the end of the device's polling characters. In the case of a general poll, the X'7F' is used instead of the device address (see Fig. 5.13).

In this auto wrap list, we have defined two entries: control unit 1 is X'C1', and control unit 2 is X'C2'. For polling purposes, control units 1 to 9 correspond to hex C1 to C9. Control unit 0 is a special case, and is called X'40' instead of X'C0'. (Note that each control unit and device character occurs twice to accommodate the double addressing required by 3270 binary synchronous multipoint communication to avoid intermittent transmission line errors.) The CU characters are followed by X'7F' to show general polling, and each entry is delineated by X'2D'. The 3737373737 string is a set of five EOT (End-of-Text) characters which must follow the last entry of a general polling list.

Each line gets its own polling list. CICS finds this list by using a symbol defined by the TYPE=LINE LISTADR=(symbol,option) parameter. This symbol corresponds to the one coded in the DFTRMLST macro. If the system programmer wants general polling (which is recommended) for this list, he or she would ask for it by coding WRAP in the second subparameter: LISTADR=(GENPOL1,WRAP). In order to get wrap list support for BTAM, WRAPLST=YES must be coded in the DFHSG (system generation) macro when generating the Terminal Control Program.

Remember that for addressing, the terminal is receiving output, so that BTAM can address it directly. For output, then, we need to code an open list (see Fig. 5.14).

```
OUTLST1  DFTRMLST   OPENLST, (E2E2C1C12D)
```

**Figure 5.14** Addressing list.

This macro defines an addressing list for terminal 1 on control unit 2. Terminals 1 to 9 are given hex characters C1 to C9. Again, terminal 0 is a special case, and is called X'40' in the list. For addressing, control units 2 to 9 are coded as hex E2 to E9. Control units 0 and 1 are exceptions, and are identified with X'60' and X'61'. The X'2D' shows the end of the entry. Coding `TRMADDR=OUTLST1` in the `TYPE=TERMINAL` macro for this terminal would identify `OUTLST1` as the addressing list to use when servicing a `CICS SEND` command against it.

### 5.3.7. BTAM terminal error processing

In any given network, any number of things can go wrong during transmission. There may be errors in terminals, modems, lines, communication controllers, BTAM software, and application programs. BTAM and CICS work together to resolve these problems.

If BTAM notices an error, it posts return codes and completion codes to the DECB in the line's TCTLE (see Fig. 5.15). CICS, in turn, runs error recovery procedures which are determined by the value coded by the system programmer in the `ERROPT` parameter of the `TYPE=SDSCI` macro. Generally, BTAM tries to retransmit the data (up to six times) before giving up and telling CICS about the problem.

When TCP finds out about the problem (by noticing a code in the DECB), it gives control to TACP (the Terminal Abnormal Condition Program) to handle the error. TACP performs default actions such as abending the task and putting the line or terminal out of service. These

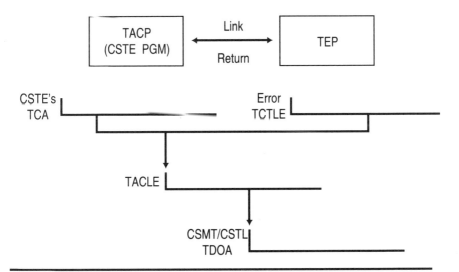

**Figure 5.15** Terminal error control blocks.

90    Chapter Five

actions can be overridden by a user-written Terminal Error Program (TEP).

Both TACP and TEP look at a TACLE (terminal abnormal condition line entry) to get information about the error. It contains error flags, TCTTE addresses, action flags set by TACP, and BTAM return codes.

Let us look at the error process in a little more detail. When an error occurs, BTAM tries to correct it. It it fails, it notifies TCP, which puts the terminal (or line) out of service by changing its TCT entry. It then creates a TACLE, which is chained off the TCTLE associated with the failure. The first 16 bytes contain I/O error information provided by BTAM. The rest of the TACLE is a copy of the DECB as it appeared when the error occurred.

If the task was attached to a terminal, the TCTTE addresses the TCA, which in turn points back to the application. In a pseudo-conversational environment, however, the task will actually RETURN before doing terminal output, and a TCA will not even exist. In either case, CICS attaches the CSTE (CICS terminal error), which executes TACP.

TACP has its own TCA, which points to the TACLE. The TACLE contains an error code indicating the type of problem. Two common codes are X'85' (write request without a TIOA) and X'95' (unit exception occurred on a device on a communication line). TACP inspects the code and determines default actions by setting flags in the TACLE. To log the errors, TACP sends error messages to the Transient Data destinations CSMT or CSTL, using a TDOA (Transient Data output area) addressed by the TACLE.

After logging the error and setting default actions, TACP links a user-written TEP. TEP can access error information in the TACLE and accept or change the default actions set by TACP. It then returns to TACP, which will carry out the default actions, and any specified by TEP.

## 5.4.  VTAM Terminal Management

CICS communicates with VTAM (Virtual Telecommunication Access Method) via the VTAM API (application program interface). VTAM is a separate task from CICS and has its own address space, running at a higher operating system priority. DFHZCP contains code which presents itself as a VTAM application.

### 5.4.1.  A VTAM network

A VTAM network contains many different hardware and software elements. Host processors contain VTAM applications, such as CICS. These are called application LUs (logical units). Communications controllers use the Network Control Program (NCP) to run the communication network. SNA (System Network Architecture) terminal controllers use SNA protocols, or rules, to communicate with applications in the host. Some terminals are connected through non-SNA controllers. Terminal I/O is transmitted over data links to terminals or terminal LUs. VTAM's job is to move data between devices in the network and user applications, using a VTAM application like CICS.

A VTAM environment has three major software components: VTAM, the NCP, and a VTAM application program (CICS, for instance). VTAM handles the data flow between network devices and CICS. It has several responsibilities. It connects, controls, and ends communication between CICS and terminal LUs. It moves data between CICS and terminals. It allows CICS and other VTAM applications, like TSO, to share lines, controllers, and terminals. If there are any locally attached devices (not connected through a controller), VTAM manages them directly. VTAM also can monitor the network and change it dynamically.

CICS identifies itself to VTAM through an access method control block (ACB), as do all other VTAM applications. When CICS opens its ACB, it is "active." To VTAM, a terminal looks like a Physical Unit (PU) and an LU. For instance, the control unit could be a PU, and a terminal would contain an addressable LU attached to it. These LUs can be SNA or non-SNA, local or remote (see Fig. 5.16).

VTAM works with the NCP to control the network. While VTAM is more interested in data flow, the NCP is more involved in the nitty-gritty physical work of managing the network. It controls devices that are remotely attached through a communications controller, such as the IBM 3275. It is in charge of addressing and polling, dialing and answering, and temporary line error processing, including detection, recovering, and logging. In addition, the NCP manages synchronous data

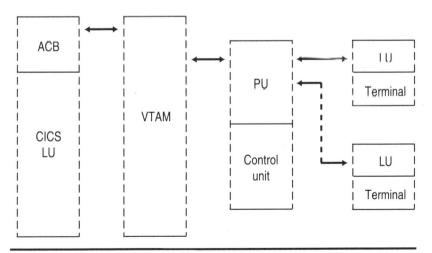

**Figure 5.16** Physical and logical units.

## 92 Chapter Five

link control (SDLC) and binary synchronous (BSC) line control. The NCP is concerned only with remote devices, and acts as an interface between remote SNA or non-SNA devices and VTAM.

### 5.4.2. CICS as a VTAM application

CICS VTAM API code in DFHZCP is the interface between application tasks and the network. This code is responsible for establishing communication with terminal LUs. This means accepting logon requests sent through VTAM. The API code handles all terminal input and passes user communication requests to VTAM. When a terminal LU requests a logoff, ZCP returns the terminal to VTAM. The API code also can ensure a certain amount of message integrity and error recovery. Notice than this code does not communicate with physical devices. That job is shared by VTAM and the NCP.

ZCP communicates with VTAM by issuing VTAM macros which help to create, maintain, and terminate a session, or send and receive data to or from the LU. ZCP and VTAM can exchange either SNA commands or ordinary data. VTAM communicates with ZCP in two different ways. It can post an ECB, or it can drive (execute) an exit routine within CICS itself.

VTAM posts ECBs only for initial transaction input. This means that CICS is not really expecting any input from the terminal. It may be transaction initiation, or even part of a pseudotransaction. In VTAM terms, the terminal was in Continue Any (CA) mode when it was not attached to a task. CICS, however, asked VTAM to Receive Any (RA) input from the system. When the operator hits enter, VTAM receives input from an LU in CA mode while there is an outstanding RA request. Whenever this happens (it happens a lot, of course), VTAM posts an ECB, the TC task gets dispatched, and a task is attached to the terminal.

In any other kind of situation, VTAM drives an exit in CICS. Although this code is in ZCP, it is controlled by VTAM and runs asynchronously to CICS. These exits are specified to VTAM when CICS makes a terminal request.

### 5.4.3. CICS–VTAM control blocks

We know that terminals are defined to CICS in the TCT. The TCT, however, contains many "hidden" VTAM control blocks that control CICS–VTAM communication. These control blocks define CICS itself, terminal requests, error routines, and RA ECBs.

Each VTAM application has one and only one ACB to define and describe itself to VTAM. This presents something of a problem to installations using the VTAM and TCAM ACB interfaces. CICS can have only one of these ACBs open at a time. They can be opened and closed dynamically with a CEMT command, but that is probably not much consolation to shops which want both running simultaneously. The ACB EXLST (exit list) addresses ZCP routines that are driven by VTAM when events occur which are not related to any specific request.

Each VTAM macro points to a request parameter list (RPL) which describes the request. When VTAM completes the request, the RPL contains information about the results of its request execution. The system programmer can define a fixed number of RPLs in the TCT to be used exclusively for RA processing. These are called RA-RPLs. Other requests use RPLs which are not in the TCT. These are created in the RPL subpool for each LU attached to a task. When the task ends, the RPL is released.

CICS uses the node information block (NIB) to identify the session and to show VTAM how communication on the session should be handled. This block exists only during a logon. After the logon has completed, VTAM knows what to do and does not need the NIB anymore, so the NIB is released. The TCT points to a NIB descriptor block that is used as a model to create a NIB when one is needed. There is one NIB descriptor block for each terminal. The NIB addresses an EXLST. This list addresses exit routines which VTAM drives whenever an event occurs that is associated with the LU associated with the NIB.

### 5.4.4. RA processing

CICS requests input from any terminal by maintaining several outstanding RA requests. Each request is represented by an RA-RPL. When an operator enters a transaction code, VTAM accepts it and holds it for CICS in Receive Any input area (RAIA). For each RA-RPL, there is an RA-ECB. VTAM posts when it receives input (such as a transaction code) in response to an RA request. CICS sees that the ECB is posted, and processes the input.

When the TCT is coded, the system programmer can specify the number of RA-RPLs in the RAPOOL parameter of the DFHTCT TYPE=INITIAL macro. These RPLs are reusable, and are pooled among all LUs. The RAIA size is coded as the RAMAX parameter of the DFHTCT TYPE=INITIAL macro. RAIAs are allocated from the TP subpool in the DSA.

Each RA-RPL corresponds to a Receive Any control element (RACE), which contains the RA-ECB (TCTVRAEB) and the address of the RA-RPL at offset 4, which in turn points to the RAIA (see Fig. 5.17).

After CICS receives the input, it moves the RAIA contents to a TIOA (also in subpool 02) and places a pointer to it in the terminal's TCTTE. Once the input is processed, Terminal Control asks Task Control to attach (DFHKC TYPE=ATTACH) the task.

## 94  Chapter Five

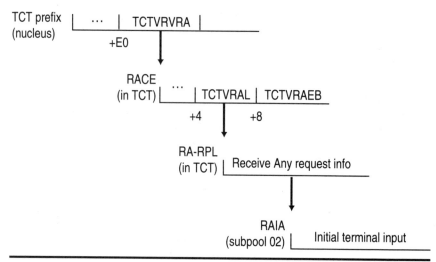

**Figure 5.17**  Receive Any control blocks (1).

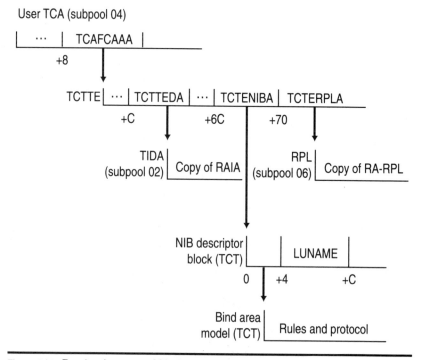

**Figure 5.18**  Receive Any control blocks (2).

During `ATTACH` processing, Task Control calls Terminal Control to bond the TCTTE to the task's TCA (in subpool 04). After the task has been created, Terminal Control copies the RA-RPL to another RPL (in subpool 06), so that the RA-RPL can be used for another RA request (see Fig. 5.18). The address of this new RPL is placed in the TCTTE. The TCTTE also points to the NIB descriptor block described above. This block contains the VTAM LUNAME and points to a bind area model used to describe the protocols for the LU session. VTAM and CICS used this information earlier to create the actual NIB and bind area when the session was established.

### 5.4.5. CICS–VTAM communication

DFHZCP contains several CSECTs which issue VTAM macros. When VTAM wants to communicate with CICS, however, it often does so asynchronously. Instead of issuing a direct request to CICS, it executes some code in the CICS region. This code is provided within the various DFHZCP modules, and is executed when specific events occur in the network. When CICS issues a request, it provides a list of these exits, which are associated with the ACB or NIB and RPL specified in the request (see Fig. 5.19). The NIB itself points to a VTAM EXLST which addresses NIB and ACB exit routines. These routines are also addressed by another EXLST addressed by the ACB. The RPL points to exit routines which are to be driven by VTAM when a request completes.

The completion exit routines addressed by the RPL are associated with a particular request. When the request completes successfully, VTAM will "drive" one of these routines. For example, if an application issues an EXEC CICS RECEIVE, CICS will issue a VTAM receive-specific macro. That macro will be associated with an RPL which addresses a completion exit routine that VTAM calls RESP. The RESP exit is driven when the receive-specific macro completes normally. In CICS, this code is in the DFHZRVX CSECT. (CICS VTAM exits end with the letter X.)

The ACB/NIB exits are driven when an asynchronous event occurs which cannot be associated with a particular request. For instance, if a user starts to log on to CICS, VTAM drives the LOGON exit (DFHZLGX in CICS). In this code, CICS issues a SIMLOGON to VTAM, which logs the user on to CICS. If VTAM detects a catastrophic error, it drives the SYNAD exit (DFHZSYX), which determines the type of error and schedules the Node Abnormal Condition Program (DFHZNAC) to handle it.

### 5.4.6. Terminal Control modules

Terminal Control actually consists of six sets of modules, each of which contains several routines which perform various internal (CICS) and

## Chapter Five

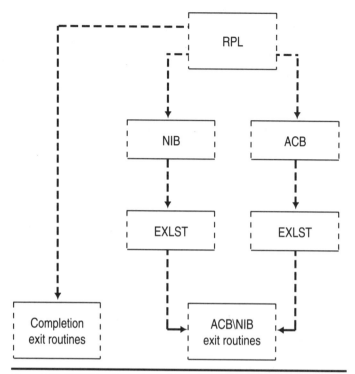

**Figure 5.19** VTAM exit routine addressing.

external (VTAM) functions. A seventh module, DFHZCC, supports ISC and MRO. VTAM refers to the partners of a conversation's LUs. CICS is an applications LU. Terminals are also LUs. As far as VTAM is concerned, then, these CICS modules issue VTAM macros which result in LU–LU communication.

DFHZCP contains routines common to both VTAM and non-VTAM requests. These routines are used very frequently, and comprise part of Terminal Control's working set. The Terminal Control dispatch routine, DFHZDSP, is called each time the Terminal Control task is dispatched. DFHZARQ, the application request handler, analyzes and checks each application Terminal Control request, and services it by calling the appropriate routine or by putting the requesting task's TCTTE on an activity queue. DFHZSUP (the startup program) is called by DFHKCP after it creates a TCA. This routine initializes a newly ATTACHed task's TCA and TCTTE.

DFHZCA is also part of the Terminal Control working set, but contains VTAM-only routines. DFHZACT scans the TCTTE activity chain, and services each request by branching to the appropriate service module. DFHZGET issues DFHSC macros to get storage for Terminal Control blocks, including the NIB, RPL, and bind area. DFHZFRE frees these areas. DFHZQUE processes requests to add and delete TCTTEs from work queues. DFHZRST issues VTAM RESETSR requests to change the terminal receive mode to CA or Continue Specific (CS), and cancels unsatisfied RECEIVE requests.

DFHZCB is another VTAM-only group of working-set routines. The DFHZATI routine handles automatic transaction initiation (ATI). It initiates SNA bid protocols to decide if an LU (a terminal) is available. If it is, it acquires an RPL and issues a DFHKC TYPE=AVAIL macro, telling Task Control that the terminal requested in an ATI request is available. The attach routine, DFHATT, issues a DFHKC TYPE=ATTACH macro when Terminal Control receives a request to start a transaction. This would happen when an operator types in an explicit request, such as a transid or PF key, or when the operator presses enter in the middle of a pseudoconversation. DFHZDET helps Task Control process a DFHKC TYPE=DETACH macro by detaching the TCTTE from the task and cleaning up its status so that another task can use it.

DFHZCX contains non-working-set code common to both VTAM and non-VTAM processing. The DFHZLOC routine processes the DFHTC CTYPE=LOCATE macro, often used by system programmers to locate TCT entries. This routine, in turn, issues a DFHTM macro to the CICS Table Manager Program (DFHTMP). DFHZSTU is used to change the status of a TCTTE or TCTSE (TCT system entry) in response to the DFHTC CTYPE=STATUS. This macro is often used to put a terminal into (or out of) service.

DFHZCX also contains some code to support MRO (multiregion operation) and ISC (intersystem communication). DFHZTSP is used for transaction routing. It converts a request issued against a surrogate TCTTE into a request against the link TCTTE. DFHZISP, DFHZIS1, and DFHZIS2 are ISC system routines used for allocating and deallocating sessions and for coordinating syncpoints across sessions.

DFHZCY, VTAM-only non-working set code, handles asynchronous commands received by VTAM and contains logic error and logon exits. DFHZOPA and DFHZSHU open and close the CICS VTAM ACB. After the ACB is open, the DFHZSLS issues a VTAM SETLOGON START to tell VTAM to accept logon requests, and issues the first RAs for RPLs in the RA pool. This routine also looks at the SIT to see whether on-line terminal definition is being used. If it is, the routine copies SIT parameters to the TCT prefix.

CICS receives terminal logons in the DFHZLGX VTAM exit. This routine scans the NIBs until it finds the one specified by VTAM. If it finds a match, it sets an OPNDST request in the corresponding TCTTE, and places it on the activate queue. If a match is not found, this routine

**98   Chapter Five**

defines a terminal automatically by allocating an auto-define work element which holds a CINIT_RU. The work element is queued for activate scan processing. This process is explained more fully in the "Autoinstall" section of this chapter. If CICS wants to acquire a terminal without having the operator log on, it uses a SIMLOGON generator in DFHZSIM. The SIMLOGON exit, DFHZSIX, is scheduled by VTAM when the SIMLOGON completes successfully.

DFHZCY contains several VTAM asynchronous error routines. DFHZLEX is the logical error address (LERAD) exit, which VTAM drives when it detects a logical error, usually because of an error in coding the TCT. DFHZSYX is the SYNAD exit module, which receives control when a catastrophic error occurs. If VTAM loses contact with a node (terminal), it gives control to the LOSTERM exit (DFHZLTX) with three possible return codes. If the return code shows that the node is lost and recovery is in progress, CICS puts the terminal out of service. If the node is lost but recovery was successful, the TCTTE stops the session and schedules a SIMLOGON. If the node is lost and recovery is unsuccessful or impossible, CICS stops the session and issues a message.

If VTAM detects a network service error (for example, if the link between two nodes is broken), it drives the VTAM NSEXIT, known in DFHZCY as DFHZNSP (Network Service Program). This routine closes the ACB and cleans up in general. When VTAM itself is terminating, it drives the TPEND exit (DFHZTPX), which schedules a CLS-DST (close destination) for each active session, and sets bits in the TCT prefix to set off DFHZSHU when the Terminal Control task gets control.

DFHZCZ handles the logon/logoff aspect of session management. DFHZCLS and DFHZCLX quiesce and terminate sessions. DFHZOPN requests VTAM to bind, or establish, a session. DFHZOPX is the exit VTAM drives when the bind process completes. Error messages on any particular session are managed by DFHZEMW.

### 5.4.7.   CICS–VTAM connection life cycle

Before CICS can communicate with LUs (such as terminals), it needs to connect to VTAM. Before any application can connect to VTAM, of course, VTAM needs to be started. When VTAM comes up, some portions of the network may be activated immediately, while others need to be awakened by the network operator VARY command. This command can also be issued by a VTAM program. When it receives this command, VTAM creates sessions with PUs and LUs, thereby activating them.

When CICS starts up, the initialization program, DFHSIP, issues a request VTAM macro to open the VTAM ACB. The ACB includes a symbolic name which identifies this CICS region to VTAM. This name, the APPLID, is coded in the `DFHTCT TYPE=INITIAL` macro, and must be obtained from the VTAM system programmer who defined CICS to the network. If VTAM is not up when CICS is started, the connection must be made later using the CICS master terminal command `CEMT SET VTAM OPEN`. This command must, of course, be issued at a non-VTAM terminal, such as the system console. After the ACB is open, LUs can be connected, and I/O operations can take place.

Before a CICS application can communicate with an LU, VTAM needs to connect CICS and the LU. Since CICS is also an LU, this connection is called an LU-to-LU session. VTAM maintains this session, and coordinates the I/O (or sending and receiving) between the LU-to-LU partners during the session. The session is initiated by a logon request. These requests can be generated automatically by VTAM or CICS. If a terminal's TCTTE is coded with `CONNECT=AUTO`, CICS will generate an automatic logon request as soon as the ACB is open. An operator can log on to his own terminal by entering the VTAM command `LOGON APPLID(CICS APPLID)`. The master terminal operator can log on to any VTAM terminal in the system with the CICS command `CEMT SET TERMINAL ACQUIRED`. The VTAM network operator can also initiate a logon. Once logon processing completes, a session has been established, and CICS can communicate with its session partner.

During the LU-to-LU session, the terminal may start communicating with CICS by entering a CICS transaction code. CICS applications, in turn, communicate with the terminal by issuing `EXEC CICS SEND` and `EXEC CICS RECEIVE` commands. These requests result in VTAM `SEND` and `RECEIVE` macros issued by CICS Terminal Management modules. Each of these VTAM macros references the RPL associated with the task which made the request.

When communication is to be ended, the LU-to-LU session is terminated by using logoff processing. The terminal operator can log off by entering `CSSF LOGOFF`. `CSSF` is the CICS sign-off transaction, while `LOGOFF` is a request to VTAM to terminate the session. A CICS application can end the session by using the `ISSUE DISCONNECT` command. At the master terminal, an operator can log off any VTAM terminal by entering the CICS command `CEMT SET TERMINAL RE-LEASED`. The VTAM operator can also request a logoff. Once an LU is logged off, communication cannot take place again until another logon is issued and processed.

To disconnect from VTAM, CICS requests that the ACB be closed. Although this request is usually made during CICS shutdown processing, it can also be made by using the CICS master terminal command `CEMT SET VTAM CLOSED`. In this case, CICS would continue operating, but would not be able to communicate with any VTAM devices.

100　Chapter Five

### 5.4.8.　VTAM message structure

When LUs (such as CICS and VTAM terminals) communicate, they need to exchange certain information above and beyond the actual data, or message. More specifically, communication requests must contain the origin address of the sending LU, the message's destination address, and some information about how to handle the request. All of this information is contained in a Path Information Unit (PIU).

The PIU flows from the LU to VTAM or, in the case of a remote LU, from the LU to the NCP and then to VTAM. There are three parts in each PIU: the transmission header (TH), the request/response header (RH), and a request/response unit (RU).

The TH holds the origin and destination addresses. The RH describes both the message and how the request should be handled. The RU contains either data, commands, or, in the case of an error, SNA sense information which describes the problem. The actual user data are contained in the RU.

If the sending LU (a terminal, for instance) is already attached to a terminal when it sends a PIU, it is in CS (Continue Specific) mode, and CICS must issue a VTAM RECEIVE SPECIFIC macro to get the message. (CICS issues the VTAM RECEIVE SPECIFIC when the application issues an EXEC CICS RECEIVE command.) The terminal's message is stored in VTAM buffers until CICS issues the RECEIVE macro.

If the terminal is not attached to a task, VTAM gives the message to CICS in the terminal's RAIA, and posts the RA ECB in the TCT. When the Terminal Control task is dispatched, it notices that this ECB is posted, and processes the message.

When the application receives this message, it will usually format a reply and issue a SEND command, either EXEC CICS SEND or EXEC CICS SEND MAP. In either case, Terminal Management will issue a VTAM macro to transmit the data. In this request, it supplies VTAM with the location of the data, the address of the LU, information about how to handle the request, and whether or not VTAM should return a response from the terminal. When it honors the request, VTAM uses this information to generate a PIU similar to the one described above. The RU contains either the application data or an SNA command.

By looking at the TH, VTAM can determine the destination address of the terminal LU, and it sends the PIU over the network to that terminal. After it receives the PIU, the terminal LU may return a response, but only if the RH shows that one was requested.

### 5.4.9.　The Terminal Control task

Terminal Control, like Task Control, runs both as a request handler and as a task. Very often it accepts a task while running under the requestor's

TCA, and executes it later, when it runs as a task itself. Task Control dispatches the TC task when one of several ECBs has been posted.

The CICS timer ECB is posted when either the partition exit time interval or the terminal scan delay time expires. The partition exit time interval is the longest period of time that Task Control will give up control to the operating system, and is coded by the system programmer of the SIT. See Chap. 3 for more details. The terminal scan delay time is coded as the SIT ICVTSD parameter, and specifies the maximum amount of time that should elapse between a CICS Terminal Control request and its execution. It should be set close to, but not at, zero. If it is set to zero (or defaulted), time-initiated tasks at TWX terminals will not be dispatched. Line ECBs are posted when a BTAM I/O event completes. (These were described earlier in this chapter.) An RA ECB is posted when an RA completes, as described above. The active chain ECB is posted when VTAM drives an exit routine in response to a VTAM request.

When one of these ECBs is posted and Terminal Control is dispatched as a task, it first processes non-VTAM terminal requests. It then examines the RA-ECBs to see if there are any terminals which want to start transactions. After that, it looks to see whether any TCTTEs are waiting to have work completed.

The only way TC can tell whether or not a specific task has requested a service is to inspect its TCTTE. In a modern network, this might mean examining thousands of TCTTEs, of which only a few had a pending request. To cut down this overhead, Terminal Control chains these TCTTEs together when they first make the request. (Remember, the requests are usually processed long after they are made.) Later, when the TC task gets control to actually carry out these requests, it goes through these chains, and so examines only TCTTEs which actually have pending activity. Terminal Control actually maintains five different chains, and addresses them all in the TCT prefix. These chains are divided into two different queues, the activate queue and the system service queue. A TCTTE is added to a particular queue and chain depending on what service it requires.

The activate queue contains TCTTEs which have pending communication requests. There are two chains on this queue: the activate queue chain and the activate process chain. When an application makes a TC request, it is very likely that it will not be serviced immediately. Terminal Control marks the request in the task's TCTTE, and adds the TCTTE to the activate queue chain instead. Whenever a VTAM exit is driven, the associated LU is also added to the activate queue chain. Whenever a TCTTE is added to this chain, the active chain ECB (mentioned above) is posted, and the TC task becomes eligible to be dispatched and thus service the request.

## 102 Chapter Five

Later on, when the TC task is dispatched, it promotes all the activate queue chain TCTTEs to the activate process chain. CICS does not process requests until their TCTTEs are moved to the activate process chain. This is done to prevent conflicts with VTAM. We said earlier that a TCTTE can be added to the activate queue chain when VTAM drives an exit in CICS. Because VTAM usually runs at a higher operating system priority than CICS, it can interrupt CICS. More specifically, it can interrupt a Terminal Control Program which may be accessing the same activate queue chain. To avoid the inevitable conflicts of two programs (CICS and VTAM) simultaneously and asynchronously accessing the same work chain, CICS gives VTAM exclusive use of this chain while it is driving an exit. CICS services requests only from the activate process chain, and never from the activate queue chain.

The system service queue contains TCTTEs for which requests have been processed, but require more work. The response outstanding and response to be logged chains are part of the optional VTAM message protection feature. This feature records messages and SNA sequence numbers on output. If the system fails, CICS uses the Set and Test Sequence Number command (STSN) to coordinate delivery of messages that had not been received at their destination before the failure. Since the 3270 does not recognize STSN, this feature has a somewhat limited usefulness, which, combined with its high teleprocessing overhead, makes it generally undesirable for the vast majority of CICS installations.

The system service queue's NACP chain, on the other hand, is used quite frequently. NACP stands for the Node Abnormal Condition Program, which processes node (VTAM) errors. When a terminal experiences an error, its TCTTE is placed in the NACP chain. Eventually, the TC task will `ATTACH CSNE`, the node error transaction, and the TCTTE will be processed by both NACP and a user-written VTAM error program, the NEP (Node Error Program). We will have a lot to say about both of these programs later in the chapter.

When the last TCTTE in the activate and system service queues has been examined, the TC task issues a CICS WAIT, which returns control to the CICS dispatcher. It will be dispatched again later, when one of the ECBs described above is posted.

### 5.4.10. A conversation life cycle

Let us take a look at what happens when a CICS operator enters data at a 3270 terminal. First, the data are stored in the terminal's control unit (3274) buffer. If the control unit is remote, the NCP moves the data into its own buffers. The NCP runs in a communications controller, usually a model 3705 or 3725. From there, it passes the data to VTAM

Terminal Control **103**

buffers in the host CPU. The NCP step is skipped if the control unit is local to the host.

When VTAM gets the data, it sees that the terminal LU is in session with CICS. VTAM finds an RA-RPL and moves the data from its buffer into an RAIA addressed by the RPL associated with the CICS RA request which caused the input. VTAM then posts the RA-ECB. When CICS originally issued the RA request, the terminal responded in CA mode. VTAM switches the LU's mode to CS.

Later on, when the TC task is dispatched (probably because the RA-ECB is posted), it scans the RA-ECBs and finds the posted ECB associated with the terminal input. Using information in the RA-RPL (which describes the original RA request), TC finds the TCTTE which represents this LU. TC issues a DFHSC (Storage Control) macro to obtain storage for an RPL, then copies the contents of the RA-RPL into the new RPL. TC then issues another DFHSC macro to get storage for a TIOA, and copies the RAIA data to it.

The first 4 bytes of the input data probably contain a transaction code, so Terminal Management issues a DFHKC TYPE=ATTACH for that code. If we are in the middle of a pseudoconversation, however, TC can see by examining the TCTTE that someone issued an EXEC CICS RETURN TRANSID(transid) for this terminal. If this is the case, TC will issue an ATTACH for the specified transid, which was stored in the TCTTE when the RETURN command was processed. If there was no RETURN TRANSID and the input is a PF or PA key, Terminal Control uses a table in its TCT prefix to determine which transaction to attach.

After the input has been processed, the TC task resets the RA-RPL so that it can be used over again, and issues an RA again. Eventually, when the TC task finishes its processing, control returns to the dispatcher, and then to the application task which TC initiated as a result of the terminal input.

When the application wants to send data back to the terminal LU, it issues an EXEC CICS SEND command. Terminal Management services the command by placing the TCTTE on the activate queue chain. When the TC command is dispatched, it moves the TCTTE to the activate process chain and issues the VTAM SEND macro. This macro points to an RPL which contains information about the request. The actual data themselves are moved from the TIOA to VTAM buffers. VTAM then sends the data from its buffers to the NCP's (unless the LU is local), which, in turn, transmit the data to the control unit's buffers, and then to the terminal itself.

When the operator keys in more data and presses the enter key, the data head back to VTAM via the control unit and NCP. When VTAM gets the data, it sees that the LU is in CS mode, so it knows that the terminal is not responding to an RA. If the application has not issued an EXEC CICS RECEIVE yet, however, VTAM does not pass the data

**104 Chapter Five**

to CICS, but holds them in its own buffers. When the application does issue the EXEC CICS RECEIVE, CICS issues a VTAM Receive Specific (RS) macro for that particular terminal LU. VTAM then passes the LU's data from its buffers to the TIOA. The RAIA is not used in this case, because this input is in response to an RS, not an RA.

### 5.4.11. Coding the TCT

Terminals can be defined to CICS either statically in the TCT or dynamically by using RDO. RDO definition was introduced in CICS 1.7, and we will have more to say about it in our discussion of automatic installation later on in the chapter. Many installations are currently using a static TCT or a combination of RDO and the TCT. As a general rule, TCT parameters (except Autoinstall) have equivalent RDO values. IBM provides a utility for converting non-VTAM TCTs to RDO.

The TCT defines terminal devices and other systems to the Terminal Control Program. We will limit our discussion to a non-ISC VTAM system which uses model 3270 terminals. There are three TCT macros that we need to code: DFHTCT TYPE=INITIAL, TYPE=TERMINAL, and TYPE=FINAL. There is one INITIAL macro, a TERMINAL macro for each 3270 device, and one FINAL macro at the end.

The INITIAL macro generates the TCT prefix. This prefix contains many of the control areas we discussed earlier. The activate and system services queues are anchored here. The prefix contains the ACB which describes CICS to VTAM. RACEs and RA-RPLs which facilitate RA processing are also contained in the prefix.

The system programmer describes each terminal by coding a DFHTCT TYPE=TERMINAL macro. This macro generates two main control blocks. The TCTTE describes the VTAM LU to CICS, and represents the terminal to its associated task. The NIB (node initialization block) is used during logon processing to help determine the rules and protocols for the LU-to-LU session.

After all the DFHTCT TYPE=TERMINAL entries are coded, the DFHTCT TYPE=FINAL is coded to generate bind area models, the TCT suffix, and the VTAM exit list, a list of the addresses of VTAM exits (see Fig. 5.20). The exits themselves are within Terminal Management code itself, not the TCT. The suffix contains the TCT WAIT list, which addresses the ECBs associated with the TC task. Remember from our earlier discussion that these are the CICS timer ECB, the RA-ECBs, and the activate chain ECB used to cause a dispatch of the Terminal Control task.

**The TCT INITIAL macro.** The TYPE=INITIAL macro (see Fig. 5.21) will describe the overall CICS network environment, including the number

| TYPE =<br>INITIAL | TYPE =<br>TERMINAL | TYPE =<br>FINAL | | |
|---|---|---|---|---|
| TCT<br>Prefix | For each one:<br>NIBs    TCTTEs | Bind<br>areas | TCT<br>suffix | VTAM exit<br>addresses |

**Figure 5.20** VTAM TCT in storage.

```
DFHTCT TYPE = INITIAL
       ACCMETH =
       APPLID =
       OPNDLIM =
       RAMAX =
       RATIMES =
       RAPOOL =
       RESP =
       ERRATT =
       SUFFIX =
```

**Figure 5.21** TCT TYPE=INITIAL parameters.

and size of many I/O control blocks and areas. The main parameters are described here.

The ACCMETH defines the access method to be used. In a VTAM-only environment, specify VTAM. If both VTAM and non-VTAM must be supported, code VTAM and NONVTAM. The default is NONVTAM.

The APPLID is the name by which CICS is known to VTAM. When CICS issues a VTAM OPEN macro to identify itself and open its ACB, it passes this name.

OPNDLIM is used to control the number of concurrent logons (VTAM OPNDST macros) and logoffs (VTAM CLSDST macros) which can take place between CICS and other LUs. Each of these requests takes up about 1 Kbyte of storage from DOS GETVIS or MVS subpool 229. The higher OPNDLIM is, the more concurrent sessions can take place, and the more storage is used. Lowering this value uses less storage, but slows down logon processing. The default is 10, but OPNDLIM should be set higher for high-volume systems.

The RAMAX and RATIMES parameters govern the size of each RAIA. When CICS acquires an RAIA, it uses the RAMAX value to determine RAIA size. If the area is not large enough, it multiplies RAMAX by the

**106   Chapter Five**

value specified in RATIMES. For instance, if RAMAX is set at 256 and the input is 250 bytes, CICS will use a 256-byte RAIA. If the message is 1500 bytes long and RATIMES is 6, the RAIA will be 1536 (6 * 256) bytes long, and the message will fit. If, however, the input exceeds 1536 bytes, the LU will receive a negative (error) response. In general, RAMAX should equal the average initial input message size the system programmer expects, and should not exceed the largest RUSIZE value on any TYPE=TERMINAL macro. RATIMES should be large enough to result in an RAIA large enough to hold the longest allowable input message. Note that these parameters apply only to SNA devices, and are not used for non-SNA 3270s.

The RAPOOL parameter determines the number of RA requests to be outstanding at any given time. It also sets the number of associated areas to be generated—RAIAs, RA-ECBs, and RA-RPLs. Because terminal task initiation requests result from RA requests, the RAPOOL value limits the number of concurrent task requests which can be accepted from the terminal network. The best way to determine this value is to find the inbound message rate, and multiply it by anywhere between 1.5 and 2. If this is difficult or impossible, start with the number 3. Look at the CICS shutdown statistics for VTAM RPL storage shortages, and increase the RAPOOL value if necessary. It is better to err on the high side with this value; if it is too low, CICS transaction initiation (and apparent response time) will suffer.

The VTAM response level is specified in the RESP parameter. The only protocol allowed (and required) for 3270 devices is RESP=FME (function management end). In SNA terms, FME means definite response, or DR1. There are two possible FME response requests: exception and definite. A request for an exception response means that CICS wants the LU to respond only when the message was not received correctly. This is the standard method in CICS. When CICS requests a definite response, however, it expects the LU to reply when it receives the message whether there was a problem or not. Definite response can be specified in the PCT as a message protection option, and is generally not used. It can also be specified in the SEND command.

When an error occurs in a CICS transaction, CICS will often send a message to the terminal. This happens often when an incorrect transaction code or operator id is entered, or the transaction abends. The ERRAT parameter determines where on the screen the error message will be shown. The default is NO, which means that the message will be displayed at the current cursor position. This looks a little sloppy; it is better to specify ERRAT=LASTLINE, which directs the error message display to the bottom line of the screen. Additional attributes such as color and highlighting can also be specified here. The ERRAT value specified in the TYPE=INITIAL macro sets a default for each TYPE=TERMINAL macro, and can be overridden selectively for individual terminals.

### 5.4.12. The TCT TERMINAL macro

Each CICS terminal in the network is described by a DFHTCT TYPE=TER-MINAL macro. This macro identifies each terminal to CICS; describes the VTAM data flow, protocol, and buffer sizes; and contains other terminal characteristics such as associated printers and startup status.

Each VTAM TCT entry must contain the ACCMETH=VTAM parameter; the TYPE=INITIAL specification does not fall through to TYPE=TERMI-NAL entries. The NETNAME parameter identifies the terminal LU to VTAM, and must match the 1- to 8-character name given in the terminal's VTAM definition. This name is checked by VTAM during logon processing, and is used to build a NIB for the LU. The NETNAME must be obtained from the VTAM system programmer who defined the terminal to the VTAM network.

The TRMTYPE parameter defines whether the terminal is SNA or non-SNA, and whether or not it is a printer. SNA devices are defined differently from non-SNA devices. Non-SNA devices are described as 3270s: TRMTYPE=3270 describes a 3270 display, while TRM-TYPE=3270P represents a 3270 printer. In SNA, however, there are no "terminals," only LUs. Within LUs there are types, such as LUTYPE1, LUTYPE2, and LUTYPE3. A LUTYPE1 is a 3287 or 3289 printer in SNA Character String (SCS), and is coded as TRMTYPE=SCSPRT. An SNA 3270 CRT is a TRMTYPE=LUTYPE2. A non-SCS SNA 3270 printer should be defined as TRMTYPE=LUTYPE3.

The next set of parameters describes how the CICS–VTAM–LU transmission will take place. More specifically, the BRACKET, CHNASSY, RUSIZE, TIOAL, and BUFFER values specify the SNA protocols, buffers, data flow, and data element sizes.

CICS communication with SNA devices uses a set of transmission rules called *bracket protocol*. This protocol is designed to keep track of the transmission state at any given time, and to delimit the user task which processes SNA input. Non-SNA sessions take place entirely within one bracket. If BRACKET=YES is coded, CICS will enforce bracket protocol. This value should be coded for SNA devices. BRACKET=NO is sufficient for non-SNA.

Bracket protocol can be correlated with CICS user tasks. It is implemented by a BEGIN BRACKET (BB) indicator sent with the first message, indicating the start of a CICS task. At task termination, an END BRACKET (EB) indicator is transmitted by CICS to the terminal LU. When the LU has no bracket (is between brackets), it is free to start a new transaction by sending a BEGIN BRACKET along with the terminal data.

This protocol is used to prevent a task from being automatically initiated by CICS after an input message is received, but before a task is attached. In other words, suppose that an operator enters a transid which is sent to CICS. It would be possible, without bracket protocol,

**108 Chapter Five**

for CICS to start an ATI task at that terminal before it processed the operator's input. The ATI task could send a message to the operator's terminal, and it would appear to the operator that his or her input caused that output. To prevent this, CICS checks the LU's bracket state if the terminal supports both ATI and bracket protocol.

When an LU sends a message, it rides in the data part of a PIU (Path Information Unit) called the RU. Very often, the message is larger than the RU defined for that LU, and must be broken into smaller pieces. A single logical message, then, must often by carried by multiple physical messages. The first PIU of the message is called first in chain (FIC), and the last is called last in chain (LIC). Any PIUs in between are called middle in chain (MIC). If the logical message can fit into one physical message, it becomes the only in chain (OIC). The process of keeping track of these bits and pieces of the logical message is called chaining, and applies to both outbound (from CICS) and inbound (to CICS) messages. In CICS, chaining occurs only with SNA 3270s.

There are three parameters that affect chaining: CHNASSY, TIOAL, RUSIZE, and BUFFER. CHNASSY=YES forces CICS to assemble inbound chains and present the entire logical message to the application program in a single TIOA. This parameter is not required for non-SNA 3270s, as chaining does not take place. SNA 3270s require CHNASSY=YES.

The TIOAL value defines the average and maximum chain sizes. The first value must be specified for both SNA and non-SNA values; it is the minimum-size TIOA that CICS will pass to a user task. The second value has meaning only for SNA devices using message chaining, and defines the largest chained message that CICS will accept from the terminal. If an LU passes a larger message, CICS will reject it with an error code.

The RUSIZE is the size of the buffer used for an inbound chain element (FIC, MIC, LIC, or OIC), and is fairly dependent on hardware. The RUSIZE is designed to be used as a maximum to reduce the number of VTAM RECEIVEs that CICS must issue to input small chains. For remote 3274 controllers, use 1024; use 2048 for remote 3276 devices.

BUFFER size is the maximum-size RU that CICS will send to an LU. Whenever a message is longer, it is broken up into chain elements, as described above. The 3270 controller will assemble the chains before presenting them to the display screen. For remote terminals, specify a value of zero for LUTYPEs 2 and 3, and 768 for SCSPRT devices. The zero value means that no outbound chaining will take place. Instead, we will let the NCP perform segmentation. For local devices, specify 786 for SCSPRT, and 1536 for LUTYPEs 2 and 3.

The BUFFER value of 1536 for local LUTYPE2 and LUTYPE3 was chosen merely because this is the maximum, and segmentation is not supported for local devices. The SCSPRT value of 768 will allow some printing overlap regardless of the printer buffer size. This assumes that pacing (an NCP parameter) is set to 1 or 2.

When outbound chaining takes place, CICS issues a VTAM SEND macro for each chain element. If the BUFFER value is zero, CICS will issue only one VTAM SEND macro, which will force VTAM to pass the whole message along to NCP, which will segment the message. The NCP (running in a 37x5) performs segmentation transparent to the LU in order to fit the data and control information into the communication controller's buffers. If the PIU size is larger than the NCP MAXDATA parameter for the controller, the NCP segments the message. Each segment contains one TH plus one or more full NCP buffers. Although segmenting is not the same as chaining, it has a similar result, and can be relied upon to offload "chaining" work from CICS to the NCP. It also gets rid of the distracting "blinking" effect often seen on LUTYPE2 terminals.

CICS uses two TYPE=TERMINAL parameters, CONNECT and RELREQ, to participate in LU-to-LU session management. If CONNECT=AUTO is coded, the LU will be logged on to CICS automatically during CICS startup. CICS issues a VTAM SIMLOGON macro. Another way to cause this is to use the VTAM LOGAPPL parameter of the VTAM LU and TERMINAL statements for the terminal. In this case, VTAM will issue a logon during CICS startup, or during VTAM startup if CICS is already running. The only difference between these methods is whether CICS initiates the logon (CONNECT=AUTO) or VTAM does. If the terminal is used by other VTAM applications in addition to CICS, use the VTAM LOGAPPL parameters. If CICS is the only VTAM application to use the terminal, however, CONNECT=AUTO will work as well.

The opposite of CONNECT is RELREQ, which determines what happens when an operator signs off from CICS. RELREQ has two subparameters which determine whether other applications in the network can interrupt a CICS-to-LU session. The first subparameter tells whether CICS should release the LU, and the second determines whether disconnect requests will be honored.

Each of the two subparameters can have the value YES or NO. Specifying YES in the first value tells CICS to release the terminal if another VTAM application wants it and it is not currently attached to a task. NO instructs CICS not to release the terminal if another VTAM application wants to use it. In the second value, YES tells CICS to honor disconnect requests for the LU by terminating the session. This usually happens because an operator enters CSSF LOGOFF, but it can also be caused by an EXEC CICS ISSUE DISCONNECT command issued from within a CICS application program. Coding NO will prohibit CICS from honoring a disconnect command.

**110 Chapter Five**

The default values are RELREQ=(NO,NO), which means that CICS cannot release the LU to another application and will not allow an operator or an application to log the LU off. Only the VTAM network operator can cause a logoff. To allow another VTAM application to use the terminal and to allow a CICS operator to log off from CICS, code RELREQ=(YES,YES).

There are two ways to generate printer support for a terminal. One way is to configure the control unit (3274 or 3276) print authorization matrix, and specify PTRADAPT in the FEATURE parameter of the LU's TYPE=TERMINAL macro. In this case, the control unit can handle the print operations without any help from CICS. Another way is to request the print function in the SIT, and to code the destination printers in the originating terminals' TCT entries. This method can be used for all VTAM 3270s.

The DFHSIT PRINT parameter allows the system programmer to specify a PA key (usually PA1) which will activate the 3270 print request facility. This will send the 3270 screen display to the printer named in the CRT's PRINTTO parameter. If that printer is not available, the display will be routed to the printer specified in the ALTPRT parameter. (If that printer is also busy, error processing will eventually route the output to the CSPP transient data destination.) Note that PRTADAPT cannot be specified if PRINTTO is also defined for a given terminal.

There is an optional user extension to the TCTTE called the Terminal Control Table user area (TCTUA). As the name implies, any user data can be saved there. These data will survive across tasks (and pseudoconversations). The TCTUAL parameter of the TYPE=TERMINAL macro specifies the length of this area. The problem with this area is that it is allocated from the nucleus, and it exists throughout CICS execution whether the terminal is in use or not. A far better alternative is the COMMAREA, which can be passed between programs (XCTL and LINK) and tasks (RETURN TRANSID). New applications should not use this area. There are some special considerations in using the TCTUA with the Autoinstall feature which are covered later in this chapter.

The TRMSTAT parameter defines how a CICS terminal will be accessed, or what state it will be in when the system is initialized. A terminal can be in one of four states: Transaction, Transceive, Receive, or Out of Service. Once initialized, the terminal's status can be changed with the CEMT SET TERMINAL command.

A terminal in Transaction status will not receive CICS output unless the terminal requests it. In other words, it does not receive unsolicited output. This includes BMS or CICS message switching transaction (CMSG) output. It also means that ATI tasks associated with the terminal will not be started unless the terminal is switched to Transceive status. These terminals are generally used for entering transactions which do not send unsolicited messages to the terminal.

When a terminal is in Transceive state, it can be used for ATI transactions via Transient Data or Interval Control. The difference between Transceive- and Transaction-state terminals is that Transceive-state terminals can receive unsolicited output. This means that terminal input might be interrupted by unexpected transmission of BMS, CMSG, or ATI transaction output. This might be awkward for an operator to handle in the middle of a pseudoconversation.

Terminals in Receive state cannot send output. Receive should be coded for non-SNA 3270 printers. SNA LUTYPE1 (SCSPRT) devices should be defined with TRANSCEIVE to allow operator interrupts to be communicated back to CICS. ATI transactions may be started at Receive terminals. This is, in fact, how most low-volume printing is accomplished in typical CICS application systems. A terminal can be put into Receive state by mistake when an operator signs off with CSSF GOODNIGHT. If this happens, the terminal must be put back into Transceive or Transaction state with the CEMT SET TERMINAL command. To avoid this problem, use CSSF LOGOFF instead.

An Out of Service terminal cannot send or receive until it has been put into service via the CEMT SET TERMINAL command. In addition to the above statuses, there are some additional requirements for ATI: INTLOG and NOINTLOG. INTLOG allows CICS to simulate a logon to establish a session for an LU which is not yet logged on. If an ATI task is supposed to start at terminal X, for instance, and X has not logged on, CICS will initiate the logon so that it can start the ATI task. NOINTLOG prevents this from happening.

VSE Interactive Computing and Control Facility (ICCF) users must make sure that their TCTs meet some special ICCF requirements. The TCTUAL value must be at least 40, as ICCF uses bytes 9 to 40. If there are any applications using these bytes, they must be recoded and recompiled to use some other TCTUA bytes. The TCTUAL value must also be increased to reflect the application change. As an alternative, change the A.DTSGENER TCTOFS parameter of VSE/ICCF to reflect a different TCTUA offset, then regenerate VSE/ICCF. Again, make sure that the TCTUAL values reflect this change.

All nonprinter ICCF terminals must be specified with TRMSTAT=TRANSCEIVE. Generate 3270 printers with RECEIVE. The FEATURE parameter should not include UCTRAN (uppercase translation) if you would like users to have the ability to enter lowercase data. ICCF performs its own translation according to the wishes of the user. Other CICS applications running at these terminals, however, may require the UCTRAN option.

ICCF terminals must be generated with a TIOAL of at least 80. If

**112  Chapter Five**

the ICCF full-screen editor is used, `TIOAL` should be increased so that the full-screen editor input fits into the input area. Try `TIOAL=(256,4096)` for SNA LUs or `TIOAL=128` for non-SNA LUs.

## 5.5. Generating Terminal Control

CICS is shipped in a pregenerated format, and for the most part, these modules serve quite well. However, the Terminal Control modules are pregenerated to satisfy everyone in all environments. Since most installations need only a small part of the entire Terminal Control package, Terminal Control support should be tailored to suit the characteristics of each network. Remember that all of the Terminal Control modules must reside in the nucleus below the 16-Mbyte line. There are lots of modules, and they can each be very large. Performing a tailored TC generation can save lots of valuable non-XA space.

Terminal Control support is generated using a DFHSG macro (see Fig. 5.22). Coding this macro with `ACCMETH=VTAM` generates the six major Terminal Control modules—DFHZCP, ZCA, ZCB, ZCX, ZCY, and ZCZ—described earlier in this chapter. If the network is mixed, do not forget to specify `NONVTAM` also.

To support Transient Data and Interval Control ATI, specify `AUTOTRN=YES`. This is also required for the CICS message switching transaction (CMSG) and BMS paging and message routine. LUs which plan to be associated with ATI transactions should have the `INTLOG` option in their TCT entries.

`CHNASSY=YES` generates support for inbound chain assembly for SNA 3270 devices, as described earlier. This support is needed for SNA 3270 devices. The default, however, is `CHNASSY=NO`.

`PUNSOL=YES` tells the CICS to throw away garbage input from a terminal. Suppose, for instance, that during a period of slow response, an operator presses the reset key. If that input actually received the application, the results would probably be undesirable. If the operator is using an SNA 3270 terminal, the controller will throw out the unsolicited input. Non-SNA 3270 controllers, however, cannot do this, and

```
DFHSG PROGRAM = TCP
ACCMETH =
AUTOTRN =
CHNASSY =
PUNSOL =
VTAMDEV =
```

**Figure 5.22** Terminal Control DFHSG macro.

will forward the input to CICS. If the system programmer codes PUN-SOL=YES, VTAM will purge the buffer containing data for an LU before it responds to a RECEIVE request from CICS. Therefore, data that VTAM read, but CICS did not request, are cleared.

VTAMDEV is where we specify all the different types of terminals and LUs we must support on the network. To support a mixed network of SNA and non-SNA local and remote terminals, code VTAMDEV=(3270,SCSPRT,LUTYPE2,LUTYPE3). The pregenerated version of TCP supports just about everything from TRS80s to CB radios. This is a good opportunity to eliminate some unnecessary code.

### 5.5.1. Terminal Control SIT options

There are several DFHSIT options (see Fig. 5.23) which affect application identification and Terminal Control task dispatching. There are, in addition, several options which affect automatic terminal installation, VTAM applicability, VTAM initialization transactions, and availability of VTAM logon data.

We said earlier that the CICS VTAM ACB name, or APPLID, was coded in the TCT. This name, taken from the VTAM APPL VBUILD parameter for CICS, can also be coded in the APPLID option of the SIT, where it overrides the TCT TYPE=INITIAL definition. CICS system programmers may use this option to exploit its flexibility in testing new systems. Overriding the TCT value in the SIT would avoid having to reassemble the entire TCT. As a matter of fact, since SIT values can themselves be overridden in the startup deck, no assemblies at all need take place.

ICV and ICVTSD do not really have much of an effect on TC task dis-

```
DFHSIT TYPE = CSECT
        APPLID =
        ICV =
        ICVTSD =
        PRINT =
        TCT =
        TCP =
        ZCP =
        VTAM =
        AUTOINST =
        GMTRAN =
        LGNMSG =
```

**Figure 5.23** Terminal Control SIT options.

**114   Chapter Five**

patching any more. As you will recall from our earlier discussion, application requests are services when VTAM drives an exit in TCP, or when KCP dispatches the TC task. The TC task is dispatched when the CICS timer ECB is posted. This happens when the ICV or ICVTSD value expires. TC is also dispatched when a non-VTAM line ECB is posted, and RA-ECB is posted or the activate chain ECB is posted.

These non-ECB timer events are likely to take place long before ICV or ICVTSD expires. Whenever VTAM responds to an RA, it posts an RA-ECB, which triggers TC dispatch. When VTAM drives an exit routine, the activate chain ECB is posted, which also triggers a TC dispatch. In a VTAM environment, Terminal Management is not heavily dependent on CICS timer facilities. In general, ICVTSD should be set to 1 s. ICV can be set to 5 or 10 s. (It could even be a little shorter to avoid a long wait between VSAM data set OPENs which are performed by an MVS subtask.)

The PRINT option specifies a PA key which initiates the automatic print facility. This parameter interacts with the PRINTTO and ALTPRT operands of the DFHTCT TYPE=TERMINAL macro described earlier.

The TCP and ZCP parameters specify which versions of the Terminal Control program are to be used, and should match the SUFFIX operand of the DFHSG PROGRAM=TCP macro. In an MVS VTAM environment, code TCP=NO, as TCP provides only non-VTAM support. In DOS, TCP is required to support the console. If TCP is included, it should have the same suffix as ZCP.

In release 1.7, three new Terminal Control options were added. VTAM=YES should be coded if VTAM will be used. AUTOINST specifies how much storage is to be allocated for automatically installed terminals, and also specifies the name of a user program which will be executed during the autoinstall process. This process is described later in this chapter. GMTRAN allows us to specify a transaction which will be automatically initiated when a terminal logs on to CICS. The default is CSGM, the "Good Morning" transaction which paints the letters CICS on your terminal every day.

### 5.5.2. Terminal Control PCT options

The PCT can be used to define message protection and integrity, outbound message protocol and chaining, and message journaling for transactions which run at VTAM terminals (see Fig. 5.24). The parameters for these options are coded in special PCT TYPE=OPTGRP entries. These entries are in turn referenced by PCT TYPE=ENTRY macros (see Fig. 5.24).

Whatever the system programmer codes in OPTGRP05 will apply to all PCT entries which specify OPTGRP=OPTGRP05.

```
OPTGRP05 DFHPCT TYPE = OPTGRP,
              MSGPREQ =,
              MSGOPT =


         DFHPCT TYPE = ENTRY,
              TRANSID =,
              PROGRAM =,
              OPTGRP = OPTGRP05
```

**Figure 5.24** PCT OPTGRP and ENTRY macros.

There are two flavors of message protection. Required message protection options coded in the MSGPREG parameter mean that the options must be supported by the device attached to the transaction. In other words, if the transaction is running at, say, a BTAM terminal (which does not support any protection options), CICS will not allow the transaction to execute. Optional message protection will allow the transaction to run even if the terminal LU cannot support the protection options. There are two possible problems here. On the one hand, required message protection precludes the execution of some tasks at some terminals. If all terminals in the network support the options (and always will support them), this problem can be avoided. On the other hand, allowing "optional" message protection means that results will be inconsistent across supporting and unsupporting terminals.

The four message protection options allow us to request message integrity (MSGINTEG), message protection (PROTECT), one-write protocol (ONEWTE), and chain control (CCONTROL). Remember that each and any of these can be specified in the MSGPREQ or MSGPOPT parameters of the PCT TYPE=OPTGRP macro.

Message integrity (MSGINTEG) forces CICS to request a definite response from the receiving LU whenever it sends a message. This means that the LU must respond whether it got the message correctly or incorrectly. Normally, the LU responds only if the message was garbled or otherwise damaged during transmission. Until CICS gets a response, it holds on to the TIOA so that it can be made available to the user-written NEP for processing.

Message protection (PROTECT) has the same features as MSGINTEG, and adds logging and resend features. When a message is sent by a protected transaction or a response is sent from its associated LU, CICS records the I/O on the system log. If the system fails, any in-flight messages can be resynchronized and retransmitted during Emergency Restart. The bad news is that this feature is not supported by 3270 de-

## 116　Chapter Five

vices because they do not understand the SNA Set and Test Sequence Number command. There is, therefore, no point in specifying PROTECT for transactions which might run on 3270 devices.

Message integrity might be useful for recoverable tasks (PCT DTB=YES) and for tasks which send output to printers. In the former case, MSGINTEG will incur the additional overhead of the positive definite response. There is a school of thought, however, which believes that this type of integrity should be built into the application, not dependent on hardware or system programming constraints. MSGINTEG makes the most sense for installations which plan to do node error processing for incorrectly transmitted messages, as it forces CICS to retain the TIOA. In the case of CICS printers, bear in mind the fact that the CICS always requests a definite response for output to LUTYPE3 printers, regardless of the message integrity options.

Specifying one-write transmission protocol (ONEWTE) forces tasks to limit themselves to one send by adding an END BRACKET (BRACKET=EB) to their output. If the task tries to do another send, it abends. This parameter is useful for transactions that send only one output message, then execute at LUs that use bracket protocol (BRACKET=YES). It ensures that END BRACKET is sent with the message, rather than as a separate transmission at the end of the task. For single SEND transactions, it reduces output transmissions by 50 percent.

Normally, Terminal Management performs its own outbound chaining if the TCT TYPE=TERMINAL, BUFFER= option is set to greater than zero. When CCONTROL is set, the application issues an EXEC CICS SEND command for each chain element of the message. Remember that one logical message may consist of several physical message units. Usually, CICS will break the message into several chain elements depending on the BUFFER option. CCONTROL may be helpful for transactions which usually send long message chains. If a command-level program sends messages as smaller chain elements, it may save the DSA storage required to hold the entire chain. If CCONTROL is specified in combination with ONEWTE, the ONEWTE single output restriction applies to one chain, not one EXEC CICS SEND command.

If you want to create an audit trail of input or output messages, specify message journaling (MSGJRNL). This option specifies whether input and/or output messages will be written to a user journal. JFILEID specifies the user journal (02 to 99 or SYSTEM) to be used.

### 5.6.　NCP- and VTAM-Related Definitions

There comes the time in every CICS system programmer's career when the time-honored question must be asked: "Do I really want to get involved in NCP VTAM?" To thine own selves be true, gentle colleagues—

the answer is in our selves, not in our stars. Of course we want to know how all that stuff works! What is worse, we would like to be able to explain it to the NCP–VTAM system programmers over lunch some day and hold our heads up high. Please bear with me while we learn everything about NCP and VTAM that we really need to know.

CICS uses VTAM and the NCP to communicate with LUs on the network. First of all, CICS must be defined to VTAM. VTAM will not speak with anyone to whom it has not already been introduced. Introduce CICS to VTAM by coding a VTAM `APPL` statement. The name you specify must also be used in the VTAM `APPLID` statement in the CICS SIT or TCT `TYPE=INITIAL` macro.

Terminals or LUs must be defined to VTAM in VTAM LU statements. The `LOGAPPL` operand identifies CICS as an application which should receive automatic logons. Use `LOGTAB` to identify the VTAM `LOGMODE` tables which should be used when specifying CICS logons. The interpret tables (`USSTAB`) can convert standard installation logons to valid CICS logons.

The VTAM `ITLIM` parameter defines the number of concurrent logons and logoffs that VTAM can support for all combined VTAM applications (including CICS) at any given time. Needless to say, it is futile to specify a CICS `OPNDLIM` value greater than `ITLIM`.

## 5.7. The TCAM ACB Interface

To define CICS as a TCAM ACB interface application, use the following TCAM options: `RAPI=YES` in the `MCP` `INTRO` macro, a PCB macro for CICS specifying `RAPI-YES`, and a `TPROCESS` macro for CICS, also specifying `RAPI=YES` (see Fig. 5.25).

The ACB defines CICS to TCAM. CICS is identified to the TCAM MCP via a DD statement.

Each logical TCAM unit must be described to TCAM by a `TERMINAL` macro with `TERM=LUNT` and with the `GROUP` operand. The `TYPE=TERMINAL` `NETNAME` must match this name.

## 5.8. CICS VTAM Terminal Error Processing

Of all the things that go wrong in a CICS environment, network problems probably come in first for reliable disappointment. What actually can go wrong? The terminal, the modem, the line, the 3274, VTAM, the LU, and, last but not least, user applications have been known to have communications failures. Of all of these, the NCP, VTAM, and the 3274 have communication error software built in. What can we do with errors they can't handle?

**118** Chapter Five

```
CICS:
              OPEN   ACBCICS
                       •
                       •
       ACBCICS   ACB   APPLID = APPLCICS
                       •
                       •
       APPLCICS   DC   X'08', C' APPLCICS'


JCL:
       //APPLCICS DD QNAME = TCCICS
       //CICS                 JOB ...


MCP:
              INTRO   RAPI = YES
                        •
                        •
       PCBCICS   PCB   RAPI = YES,
                       MH = 0
                       RESERVE = nn
                        •
                        •
       TCICS   TPROCESS LU = YES,
                        RAPI = YES,
                        PCB = PCBCICS
```

**Figure 5.25** Defining CICS to the TCAM ACB interface.

### 5.8.1. Non-CICS message error handling

SNA communication controllers can verify messages traveling to and from terminal LUs. Two of the features SNA implements are response protocol and message sequence numbering. When CICS sends a message from a task with `MSGINTEG` specified in its PCT entry, it expects a definite response. This definite response protocol ensures message integrity and, as we mentioned earlier, causes CICS to hold on to the TIOA until it receives a definite response. Remember that CICS also forces a definite response request when it sends output to an `LUTYPE3` printer.

Most messages are sent using exception protocol, where a response will be returned only if there was a problem in receiving the message. Because CICS releases the TIOA when it sends such messages, the output message itself is not available for error processing.

Message sequence numbers can be used to find missing PIUs. As we mentioned earlier, however, 3270 devices do not support this feature.

When messages are transmitted on SDLC lines, all commands and data are followed by Frame Check characters. The NCP uses these to verify remote data link transmissions. If the NCP detects an error, it retries the operation until the transmission succeeds or it reaches a predetermined threshold value. If it cannot send the message successfully, it informs VTAM of the problem. The NCP records errors on SYS1.LOGREC (MVS) or SYSREC (VSE).

If NCP has failed to recover a message for a remote device and has passed it to VTAM, or if there is a local transmission error, VTAM will record the error and try to recover it. Because the NCP has already retried remote messages, however, VTAM does not bother. It retries only local messages. If it fails, it returns an error code and sense information to CICS, and writes a message to the system log, in addition to logging error information to a communications problem determination data set.

There is an IBM product which can help in diagnosing and solving non-CICS message transmission problems. The Network Problem Determination Application (NPDA) collects and interprets communications error records. These records include statistics for NCP error, summary error statistics from SNA 3274 and 3276 devices, and NCP link level tests.

### 5.8.2. CICS message error handling

By the time a VTAM terminal error is handed back to CICS for processing, it is out of the application's reach. CICS has two systemwide terminal error handlers; one, DFHZNAC, is provided by IBM, and the other, DFHZNEP, is written by the system programmer. Working together, these two programs determine the problem by checking the VTAM error code and SNA sense information, and then decide on what action to take.

There are two kinds of errors which can take place in the network: physical errors and logical errors. Physical errors may be returned by line or terminal hardware errors; VTAM, NCP, or CICS software errors; or errors in the CICS, VTAM, or NCP environmental definitions. In general, a physical error is one that causes a failure to deliver a message to CICS from a controller or vice versa. Physical errors return an error code, but no sense information. Logical errors occur when the message was delivered, but the receiving LU returned an exception re-

**120 Chapter Five**

sponse. In this case, both an error code and sense information are returned. Logical errors are also called node errors.

When VTAM notifies Terminal Control that an error has occurred, it passes control to the Node Abnormal Condition Program. This program is variously known as DFHZNAC, NACP, and ZNAC. We will use the name ZNAC in our discussion. As its name implies, ZNAC analyzes abnormal conditions. After determining the problem, it sets some flags in the terminal's TCTTE which set the default actions for the terminal. These actions may involve printing out a description of the error, abending the associated task, aborting a SEND or RECEIVE, or ending the LU-to-LU session.

Before it carries out these actions, however, ZNAC gives control to a user-written Node Error Program (DFHZNEP or, more commonly, NEP). In NEP, the installation can perform additional error processing and can accept or override the ZNAC defaults. Bear in mind, however, that the standard ZNAC routines are fairly comprehensive and cover most situations adequately. One of the most common uses of NEP is to print additional error messages and/or perform user error logging.

When Terminal Management is notified of a terminal error, it puts the terminal out of service by changing its status in the TCTTE. The TCTTE is chained into the NACP chain described earlier. Then it attaches the node error transaction, CSNE, placing the error information in CSNE's TWA. CSNE is associated with ZNAC, which goes through the NACP chain sequentially to process all TCTTEs which have been involved in a transmission error. ZNAC stores information about the errors in its (CSNE's) TWA. Because CSNE is not attached to a terminal, it writes an error message to either the CSMT (master terminal) or CSTL (terminal log) Transient Data destination. (These queues can be either saved or printed on a CICS or JES printer. See Chap. 12 for more information on defining these destinations.)

At this point, ZNAC (the CSNE task) has recorded error messages and has set default action flags in its TWA. Now, it LINKs to a user-written NEP. NEP can try to recover from the problem, and may, at its option, allow the task to continue. It can determine the state of the problem by looking at CSNE's TWA. After NEP RETURNs, ZNAC carries out the default and override actions. There is an important exception to the NEP link. In certain cases, ZNAC may decide that a link to NEP is not necessary or appropriate. In addition, if the ZNAC decision is to terminate the session, NEP cannot override it.

### 5.8.3. Writing a Node Error Program (DFHZNEP)

Before we write a NEP, let us take a look at the standard error procedures provided in ZNAC. They may be adequate for your installation.

For physical errors, ZNAC records a large amount of information which can be helpful in diagnosing errors. As you become more familiar with the errors, a NEP can be used to suppress certain information that is not felt to be absolutely necessary. For logical errors, ZNAC's actions are more varied, and may or may not be suitable to a particular network. For logical errors, system and user sense information is available.

By the time ZNAC makes its link to NEP, many recovery actions have probably already taken place, and there is actually very little that NEP can do to correct the situation. NEP can, however, tailor error output information and decide what to do with undeliverable messages. Tailoring the error information might entail suppressing some printout, or presenting it in a more meaningful format. If the definite response protocol is used, NEP can read the TIOA and do something with the undeliverable message. One solution would be to write the message to a Transient Data queue associated with an alternative terminal. Alternatively, NEP could START a task which would SEND the message later.

There are three possible NEPs in a CICS system. IBM ships two NEPs with the installation tape. The skeleton NEP is simply that: it issues a RETURN to ZNAC, and that's it. If the default ZNAC is adequate, do nothing—this NEP will be included automatically. The sample NEP provides a few basic recovery actions for non-SNA 3270 devices. As an alternative, the system programmer can code his or her own NEP. Let us look at the sample NEP first, then we will see how to code our own.

The sample does not support SNA devices, and is similar in effect to the TEP supplied for non-VTAM 3270s. The sample will either retry the I/O or take the terminal out of service. Only two error conditions are treated in the sample: exception response received and printer not available. If your installation uses only non-SNA 3270 devices, the sample might be usable, if only because of the printer not available routine. For the rest of us, the sample can serve as a basis for our own custom-made NEP.

Like most CICS management programs, NEP has two parts: executable code (DFHZNEP) and a table (DFHZNET). To generate the sample DFHZNEP, use the DFHSNEP macro (see Fig. 5.26).

The Node Error Program Table (NEPT) contains node error blocks (NEBs) which each hold error statistic blocks (ESBs). NEBs can be ded-

```
DFHSNEP  TYPE = INITIAL
DFHSNEP  TYPE = DEF3270
DFHSNEP  TYPE = FINAL
```

**Figure 5.26** The DFHSNEP macro.

**122 Chapter Five**

```
DFHSNET    COUNT = 100
           ESBS = (01, 6, 02, 8),
           NEBS = 20,
           NEBNAME = (T001, T125),
           TIME = (5, MIN)
```

**Figure 5.27** The DFHSNET macro.

icated to certain terminals or can be shared. The ESBs hold accumulated error statistics for the terminals associated with their NEBs. The NEPT also contains threshold counts for certain errors, and a time interval for resetting these counts. To generate this table, code the DFHSNET macro (see Fig. 5.27).

In this sample NEPT, up to 100 errors (COUNT=100) can accumulate in 5 min or less [TIME=(5,MIN)] before the error processors will start to get a return code. There are two ESBs in this table. ESB 01 has a length of 6 bytes (enough for a time stamp, perhaps), while ESB 02 has a length of 8 bytes. There are 20 NEBs. This first two are dedicated to terminals T001 and T125.

There are several things that can and should be done in a user-written NEP. A good NEP can provide some measure of message data integrity by rerouting or redirecting definite response messages. In addition, NEP can be used to try to keep terminals in service, to record errors, to put out user-friendly error messages, and to collect installation-specific debugging information.

If we wanted to add some SNA error processors to the sample, we could do it by adding a TYPE=ERRPROC macro (see Fig. 5.28). Remember that if we were writing our "own" NEP rather than altering the sample, we would use DFHZNEP instead of DFHSNEP.

```
DFHSNEP    TYPE = INITIAL,
DFHSNEP    TYPE = DEF3270,      sample non-SNA 3270s
DFHSNEP    TYPE = ERRPROC,      sample SNA
           CODE = (81, BA, DC),
           GROUP = 3
USING      *, 15
           user–
           written
           error
           processors
DFHSNEP    TYPE = FINAL
```

**Figure 5.28** Defining a node error processor.

Terminal Control **123**

This processor will act on sense codes 81, BA, and DC. `GROUP=3` is coded to avoid conflicts with groups 1 and 2 already generated for the sample NEP. The actual code within the error processors could alter some ZNAC default action flags to override ZNAC's selected actions. Let us take a look at where we might find some relevant error information.

ZNAC (the CSNE task) passes error information to NEP via its TWA. (NEP also runs under the CSNE task, and thus shares its TWA.) The TWA contains error codes, the address of the problem TCTTE, default ZNAC action flags, and SNA sense codes. The TCA is addressed by register 12.

How did all this information get there in the first place? First, VTAM sent a return code to Terminal Control, which passed the code to ZNAC through the CSNE TWA. Then, ZNAC generated an error code, and stored it in the TWAEC field of its TWA. After looking at the error, ZNAC set default action flags in its TWAOPTL field, and stored the SNA sense codes in TWASENSR. (To get a copy of this DSECT in your NEP, copy DFHVTWA.) Next, ZNAC wrote an error message to CSMT or CSTL, and then linked to NEP. Now, NEP can look at the TWA, decide what it wants to do, and override ZNAC's default flags. Finally, NEP returns to ZNAC, which performs the actions according to the bit settings in TWAOPTL. Remember that (as we described earlier) NEP cannot always override ZNAC.

Appendix B of the CICS Customization Guide gives a list of VTAM-associated errors. There are four column headings: Error Message, Error Code, Condition, and Action Flags. Let us look at one now (see Fig. 5.29).

The error messages, starting with the characters "DFH" and followed by four numbers, represent the messages that DFHZNAC writes to CSMT or CSTL. The error code column shows the hex code

| Error Message | Error Code (symbolic label) | Condition | Action Flags |
|---|---|---|---|
| DFH3400 | X'45' (TCZCHMX) | Chain exceeds maximum chain size. If chain assembly has been specified in the TCTTE, the chain being assembled does not fit into the TIOA for a maximum chain. The remaining space in the TIOA is smaller than the maximum RUSIZE. | X'20600400 |

**Figure 5.29** CICS–VTAM error messages.

124 **Chapter Five**

passed to NEP in the TWAEC field. This column also contains the hex code's symbolic name used in the DFHVTWA DSECT copy book. The condition column describes some possible reasons for this error. The default action flags show the settings of TWAOPFL. By the way, what is the problem here, and how can we fix it? (Check the DFHTCT TYPE=INITIAL macro.) Directly after this list is a similar one which contains the heading System Sense Received instead of Error Code in the first column.

The TWAOPTL field contains 4 bytes, labeled TWAOPT1 through TWAOPT4 (see Fig. 5.30). Each of these bytes (option fields) contains mask bit settings which pertain to a particular type of action. (For an explanation of how mask bits work, see Chap. 4.) TWAOPT1 controls which fields will be printed for debugging purposes. TWAOPT2 fields indicate what action will take place for the task connected to the terminal. TWAOPT3 is node-, or terminal- related. The last byte, TWAOPT4, contains information related specifically to the error message.

The SNA sense code area, TWASENSR, is also 4 bytes long. Two bytes are dedicated to system sense information, and 2 to user sense information. Each 2-byte area has a major and a minor area. The first byte (major) identifies the error category, while the second identifies a specific error within the category. The system sense code major and minor areas are called TWASR1 and TWASR2, respectively, while the user sense areas are named TWAUR1 and TWAUR2. In CICS, the user fields are not useful, as they are reserved for private conversation protocols. The first byte of TWASENSR (TWASR1), then, tells us what the problem is in general. The possibilities are 80 (path error), 40 (request header error), 20 (state error), 10 (request error), and 08 (request rejected).

To find out exactly what the system sense code is telling us, use Appendix B of the Customization Guide as described above. TWASENSR is not used for physical errors, as they do not generate SNA sense codes.

### 5.9. Automatic Terminal Installation

Starting with release 1.7 of CICS, LUs can be installed in CICS without having to be defined in the TCT. The way CICS manages this is to check the VTAM LOGMODE parameters in the VTAM definitions, so this will require some cooperation and involvement of the VTAM systems programming group. They can help in defining the MODEL statements and BIND images needed in CICS to accommodate the autoinstall feature. Autoinstall supports all LUs plus locally attached non-SNA 3270 devices.

## TWAOPT1 - Debugging information

X'80' - Print action flags
X'40' - Print RPL
X'20' - Print TCTTE
X'08' - Print TIOA
X'10' - Print bind area

## TWAOPT2 - Task-related

X'80' - Abort SEND
X'40' - Abort RECEIVE
X'20' - Abend task
X'02' - SIMLOGON required
X'08' - Good morning message required

## TWAOPT3 - Node-related

X'80' - INTLOG allowed
X'40' - No INTLOG allowed
X'10' - Close session (can be reset by NEP)
X'08' - Close session (cannot be reset by NEP)
X'04' - Send negative response
X'02' - Leave node out of service
X'01' - Cancel session

## TWAOPT4 - Message-related

**Figure 5.30** TWA action flags.

### 5.9.1. Autoinstall overview

Before a terminal can be installed automatically, it must be defined to VTAM. Alternatively, the VTAM system programmer can use VTAM/NCP dynamic reconfiguration to change the network by adding new LUs without having to quiesce VTAM, NCP, or CICS. This should be of particular interest to those who want real 7-day, 24-hour availability.

The CICS system programmer defines some all-purpose generalized terminal definitions using `TYPETERM` and a unique `TERMINAL` defini-

**126** Chapter Five

tion specifying AUTOINSTMODEL=YES or ONLY, and giving the definition a name using the AUTOINSTNAME option. This RDO group of terminal definitions is then installed. (See the Resource Definition Guide—Online for more details on this procedure.)

When a VTAM terminal (unknown to CICS) tries to log on, DFHZLGX (the LOGON exit) calls the Autoinstall program (DFHZATD) to choose a model definition and give the terminal a CICS terminal id. DFHZATD checks the CINIT table built by VTAM from its LOGMODE tables, and calls DFHZCQ to install the terminal. When DFHZCQ finishes, DFHZATD schedules an OPNDST to establish a connection for the new TCTTE created by DFHZCQ. When the user logs off, DFHZNAC schedules the terminal for disconnection by issuing a CLSDST. This request gets passed to DFHZATD via the activate scan chain. DFHZATD calls DFHZCQ, which performs the deletion.

### 5.9.2. Generating autoinstall

The most important Autoinstall parameter is the DFHSIT AUTINST=(number,program name) parameter. The number is the maximum number of concurrent logons that may be queued for Autoinstall logon processing. It is not the maximum number of Autoinstall terminals. (This could be tracked, if desired, in the user autoinstall program.)

With VTAM release 3.1, CICS will ask VTAM to suspend CICS LOGON and SCIP (session control initialization point) exits when this number is reached. This prevents further LOGON requests. These LOGONs are then queued in VTAM (MVS subpool 229 storage) until CICS asks VTAM to resume scheduling them. This will occur when CICS has processed enough of the queued requests to fall below the AUTINST limit. With a pre-3.1 VTAM, CICS rejects logon requests after the number has been exceeded.

### 5.9.3. Autoinstall and terminal naming conventions

During Autoinstall, CICS gets the terminal's NETNAME from VTAM, and uses this eight-character name to create a four-character CICS TERMID. Unfortunately, the way it does this is to use the last four non-blank characters of NETNAME, a procedure that is probably in conflict with many installations' naming standards. It is not IBM's fault (no single naming technique would satisfy everyone), but it does mean that we probably cannot use the sample Autoinstall program and will have to code our own. This might involve maintaining a VSAM file which could correlate TERMIDs with NETNAMEs. CICS, by the way, will not allow two identical TERMIDs to be autoinstalled at the same time.

Terminal Control **127**

### 5.9.4. Autoinstall TCTUA considerations

Many application systems use the TCTUA to store terminal-related data. Often, this area is initialized by a PLTPI program and retrieved by a PLTSD. Well, guess what? The TCTTE might not exist at startup any more! It might not even be around when the system comes down. (Question: With 24-hour availability, when does the system come up and down?) In addition, TCTUA data will not be saved between LOGONs. They will not be saved during emergency restarts.

TCTUA users will have to devise a way to save this information, such as saving it on a VSAM file. User information in the TCTUA is not available to the user autoinstall program during logoff processing.

The best place to put this code is probably in DFHZNEP (DFHZNEP, as you will recall, is the user-written Node Error Program). DFHZNAC gets called every time an autoinstall terminal is involved in `LOGON` or `LOGOFF` processing. Since DFHZNAC calls DFHZNEP, this seems to be the logical place to save and/or process TCTUA data.

Chapter

# 6

# Terminal Hardware and Mapping Programs

## 6.1. Introduction

In this chapter, we will take a look at how CICS supports the 3270 device, by far the most common terminal in today's CICS networks. Basic Mapping Support (BMS) is a facility which allows easy and portable coding of terminal screens. To implement BMS on 3270s, CICS has programs which work in concert with the Terminal Control programs described in the previous chapter. CICS uses these programs to send data streams to its terminals.

The reader will learn:

- Reasons for using the BMS interface
- What services exist within BMS
- BMS maps and commands contrasted with native Terminal Control
- Various options for controlling 3270 features
- What a 3270 data stream looks like and what BMS does with it

## 6.2. Basic Mapping Support (BMS)

When a program executes a Terminal Control (TC) SEND, it must insert control characters in the "raw" data to signify new lines, character attributes, cursor position, etc. In order to free CICS programmers from the burden of writing 3270 data streams, IBM introduced BMS. Originally, this was an optional feature, so the BMS pointers and control information are in the Optional Features List (OFL), not in the CSA.

**130   Chapter Six**

The mapping facilities provided by BMS provide application programmers with device independence and format independence. In other words, the application need not know about the device, or how the device expects to be presented with terminal data. BMS itself looks at the TCT to find out about the device, and finds out about the presentation requirements by reading a BMS map prepared by the programmer. This map is a CICS load module defined in the PPT (see Chap. 4). Different versions of a single map can be defined for different devices.

### 6.3.  Map Definition

To send and receive maps, programmers use SEND MAP and RECEIVE MAP, specifying the name of the map in the MAP option. To send a map, BMS takes the terminal characteristics from the TCT, the preassembled map, and merges it with the data named in the SEND MAP command. It passes this output (in a TIOA) to the TCP, which then sends it to the device. When the operator receives the map, he or she fills in fields on the map and presses the enter key. Terminal Control receives the input and hands it over to BMS. BMS interprets the data stream according to the device characteristics and presentation requirements described in the TCT and the map, then passes it to the application.

The map itself describes the presentation requirements for the I/O data. These data are divided into fields. Each field has a position on the screen, a length, and one or more attributes, such as highlighting or color. Optionally, the fields may have a default value, such as blanks or zeros. The DFHMSD, DFHMDI, and DFHMDF macros are used offline to generate maps. These macros are assembled twice. The first assembly produces a physical map (CSECT), which is stored in the CICS program library (DFHRPL) and is defined in the PPT. The second assembly produces a symbolic description map (DSECT or COPY book), which is included in the program which uses the map. The COPY book, of course, corresponds to the CSECT.

An easier way to make maps is to use the IBM Screen Definition Facility (SDF). SDF is an on-line program which runs under CICS. Using SDF, programmers can define maps interactively with no knowledge of the BMS macros. SDF output, however, consists of BMS. Think of SDF as an on-line application development interface between a programmer and the BMS facility.

What the COPY book or DSECT produces in the assembly is a set of COBOL, PL/I, or assembler statements defining a data structure. The elements of this structure represent fields in the source map. Each field in the map has at least one element in the structure. One element is for the data. Usually (but not always) there are other elements which describe the length and attributes of the data. The data element can be

## Terminal Hardware and Mapping Programs   131

defined with a default character string or numerics when the map is assembled. The same is true of attributes and lengths. On output, the application can override the attributes and data by changing the elements. During input, the program can examine these elements to see what data the operator entered and what length they are.

### 6.3.1. Partition maps

Some displays (the 3290) support more than one logical screen. These logical screens are called partitions, and are displayed on viewports, the physical area of the display screen. Each logical screen uses part of the terminal's buffer, called the presentation space. The partition which contains the cursor is called the active partition, and can be changed by the operator by pressing the JUMP button. A CICS program can also change the active partition. The layout of these displays is described by the system programmer as a partition set by using the DFHPSD and DFHPDI macros. These definitions are stored in the CICS libraries just like maps. Applications refer to partition sets by using the SEND PARTNSET command. Alternatively, the system programmer can identify the partition set by coding the PARTSET option of a transaction's PCT entry.

To associate a map with a particular partition, use the PARTN operand of DFHMDS and DFHMDI. An application can then use the OUTPARTN and ACTPARTN options of the SEND command to specify the destination partition and to make that partition active. When receiving a map, the program can make sure that the operator is using the right partition by coding the INPARTN option of the RECEIVE MAP command. To receive input from any partition, and determine on input which partition that is, use RECEIVE PARTN.

### 6.4. BMS 3270 Feature Support

3270 devices have several control features which can be manipulated by the programmer. These features include cursor positioning, the audible alarm, and a magnetic slot reader (MSR). The SEND MAP command can include options to operate these features, or the programmer can use a special BMS command, SEND CONTROL. The cursor can be positioned at a specific screen offset ("hard offset") or under the first character of a particular map field ("soft position"). The advantage of the latter method is that the cursor position will change if the field position moves. (It might if the map is changed and reassembled.)

In addition to maps, BMS provides aids in sending simple text strings, which may contain embedded blanks, new line characters, and character attribute controls. BMS takes these data and formats them into lines which will fit on the destination terminal. The first byte of

## 132 Chapter Six

each line is a blank attribute byte. BMS provides a word wrap facility by ensuring that words will not break between lines. If the output will not fit on one page, BMS will split the text into screens, or "pages," using optional headers and footers defined within the program. The command for this service is SEND TEXT. The JUSTIFY, JUSTFIRST, and JUSTLAST options of this command control the position of the text lines.

The SEND ACCUM option causes BMS to accumulate data until the screen overflows, allowing an application to handle arbitrary amounts of data and still make the best use of the available screen or page size. This size is defined by the PGESIZE and ALTPGE operands coded in the DFHTCT TYPE=TERMINAL macro for the 3270 terminal or printer. BMS will send the screen or page when it is full. When the program wants to send the last page (which is probably only partially full), SEND PAGE will force the output.

### 6.5. 3270 Device Support

Working together, BMS and Terminal Control allow CICS applications to implement the functions of 3270 terminals. These programs map information onto 3270 fields. Other controls are provided for individual character attributes, cursor positioning, data erasure, screen size, buffer size, and output control operations.

### 6.5.1. 3270 display fields

3270 display screens and printer data streams can be divided into fields. The first byte of each field contains a Start Field (SF) order, which is followed by a set of attributes for the field, such as whether the field is highlighted. This attribute set is a set of mask bits all contained within 1 byte. Although it occupies space in the device buffer, it is displayed (or printed) as a blank. Some terminals can use the extended data stream to use functions like color or programmed symbols. For these devices, the beginning of each field has a Start Field Extended (SFE), followed by a set of type and value pairs which name the attribute type for the field and set the value for the field. For instance, one type–value pair may indicate the attribute type "COLOR" and the attribute value "BLUE."

Using native Terminal Control to construct and understand these fields can be unwieldy. For output operations, the program needs to insert an SF or SFE order at the start of each field. In addition, this order must often be preceded by a Set Buffer Address order, followed by the screen address of the field. The SBA order positions the field in the display (or printer) buffer. On input, the program locates a field in the

Terminal Hardware and Mapping Programs **133**

3270 data stream by looking for the SBA order and start address which delimits it.

The alternative is to use BMS, where field lengths and positions are defined in BMS maps. On output, field attributes and data contents are specified in the map definition (default values) or stored by the application program in the symbolic map produced during map assembly. On input, BMS moves the 3270 field contents to the program element within the map structure which corresponds to the field. This includes length and attribute information. If a field is not changed (is unmodified), the elements are set to nulls, or LOW VALUES in COBOL.

It is possible to send free-form unformatted data to terminals. Unformatted data are not divided into fields and are supported by Terminal Control. The application program is responsible for sending the data without including SF or SFE indicators. When receiving data, the program will find data only (no SBA orders). BMS does not support unformatted data on output. On input, BMS will not format the data, but will pass them to the application program, raising the MAPFAIL condition.

Terminal Control can set the screen's cursor position by placing an Insert Cursor (IC) order in the data stream. After a RECEIVE, DFHETC (EXEC Terminal Control) places the cursor position in EIBCPOSN, a halfword (2-byte) binary field in the EIB. BMS allows the cursor to be set at a particular location within the map. It can be at an offset from the first screen position or under the first character of a field. To accomplish these, programs use the CURSOR option of SEND MAP, SEND TEXT, or SEND CONTROL. The initial position of the cursor can be defined during map definition, as can the fields which the cursor should skip.

### 6.5.2. Controlling 3270 features

To erase the entire screen (or print buffer), a program can use BMS and TC options on the SEND, SEND MAP, SEND TEXT, SEND CONTROL, and CONVERSE commands. If only the unprotected fields are to be purged, the ERASEAUP option can be specified on SEND MAP, SEND TEXT, or SEND CONTROL. The operator can erase the whole screen, of course, by using the clear key. A by-product of this operation is that CICS resets the terminal to the default screen size. The default size and alternative screen sizes are set in the TCT TYPE=TERMINAL macro, and selected in the transaction's PCT entry. When CICS detects the clear key, it adds the ERASE options to the next SEND command bound for that terminal.

In addition to sending data to the terminal, an application program can use TC and BMS to control other 3270 terminal facilities. Using

**134 Chapter Six**

Terminal Control, the program can send a Write Control Character (WCC) by specifying and setting the CTLCHAR option of a SEND or CONVERSE command. Omitting CTLCHAR effectively defaults to a WCC which specifies keyboard restore and reset MDT (Modified Data Tag). Options of the BMS commands SEND MAP, SEND TEXT, and SEND CONTROL can have the same effect. The option key words are the same for BMS and Terminal Control. To set off the audible alarm, use ALARM. Keyboard restore is set by FREEKB. To reset the MDTs, use FRSET. These options can also be generated during map definition by using the CTRL operand.

### 6.5.3. Special 3270 input options

A terminal can generate input by means other than keyed data. Special keys such as PA, PF, CLEAR, CLEAR PARTITION, and CURSR SEL can be used, in addition to special light pen and magnetic slot reader 3279 options. The device generates an attention identifier (AID), a 1-byte code in the data stream which indicates the type of special input. When CICS receives the input, it strips the AID from the data stream and stores it in the EIBAID field of the receiving application's EIB.

The CURSR SEL key and the selector light pen allow an operator to select a field or group of fields from the screen and transmit them to the host. To create a field which can be detected, it must contain a special "detectable" attribute and have, as its first character, a designator of "?", "&", space, or null. When the designator is "?", the field is called a selection field. The designator toggles back and forth between "?" and ">" when the operator selects it. If the operator selects the field, for instance, "?" changes to ">". If the operator selects the field again, the ">" changes back to "?". If the operator hits ENTER after the "?" changes to ">", however, the field will be transmitted as a modified field.

When the designator character is "&", a space, or a null, the field is called an attention field. If it is selected, a transmission to the host will be started immediately. For designators of a space or a null, the input message contains the buffer address of selected and/or modified fields. If the designator is "&", only the address and contents of modified fields and selected ">" and "&" fields will be sent. The AID sent with the input data stream will indicate the ENTER key if the "&" attention key is used.

These functions can be implemented by either native Terminal Control or BMS. For native TC, the application must insert the detectable attributes and designator characters in the output stream. When data are received, the data stream is passed to the application, but the AID is removed and stored in EIBAID. BMS is more flexible. The definition of the output map specifies the detectable attribute for light pen or CURSR SEL fields. These fields can either be initialized with their designator characters or these characters can be placed there during execution by the application program. In either case, the designator belongs in the first byte of the field. For an input-only map, BMS will generate fields of only one character each for selectable fields. Input/output maps contain normal data structures. When BMS receives detectable input, it sets the first character of a light pen–selected field to HIGH VALUES (hex FF).

The trigger AID can be used to facilitate fast, uninterrupted keystroking by a terminal operator. When the cursor leaves a trigger field, that field's contents (and the trigger AID) are sent immediately to the host. The operator can continue keying in data while the CICS application in the host acknowledges the trigger negatively or positively. If the response is positive, the queued keystrokes (input after the trigger was sent) will be processed. A negative response will reject the stored input. This feature can be used to initiate field validation without interrupting the operator's input.

To use trigger fields, the field must be defined with a trigger validation attribute, either in the map definition or during execution. When CICS receives the AID, it raises the HANDLE AID condition. Alternatively, EIBAID can be queried after the execution of a RECEIVE or CONVERSE command. The trigger is accepted or rejected via a SEND command.

### 6.5.4. 3270 printer control

CICS supports printing on 3270 printers defined in the TCT. To go to the top of a new page, the application must include a Form Feed order (hex 0C) in the data stream. The X'0C' must be the first print position on a line. The BMS FORMFEED option of SEND MAP, SEND TEXT, and SEND CONTROL will generate an FF in the first byte of the terminal buffer. SCS (SNA character string) printers that are supported can use printer tabulation to shorten the data stream. Instead of sending blanks to pad out to a print position, the application can "tab" out. Before sending the output, the tab stops must be set by inserting Set Horizontal Format (SHF) and Set Vertical Format (SVF) orders in the data stream.

### 6.5.5. Extended 3270 functions

To understand partitions, magnetic slot readers, programmed symbols, and how to determine terminal characteristics, we will need to take a brief look at structured fields. Extended 3270 functions are supported by data streams which contain structured fields. These fields

**136 Chapter Six**

contain a length, an operation code, and data subfields. The length of the data subfields depends on the structured field type. A `SEND` or `CONVERSE` may generate several structured fields. These fields are built by the application, and the `SEND` or `CONVERSE` command must contain the `STRFIELD` option. CICS does not generate write control characters (WCCs) for this option. The WCC must be embedded in the structured field data. Structured fields are described in more detail later in this chapter.

A partitioned 3270 terminal contains several logical screens, each of which has a 1-byte partition id, a viewport, and a presentation space. The partition containing the cursor is the active partition, which can be changed by the operator (using the partition jump key) or by an application. The clear key erases the entire display screen, destroying all partitions and resetting the device to its base state. The clear partition key clears only the active partition. Both Terminal Control and BMS support partitions.

Partitions are controlled by structured fields. To create a partition, previous partitions should be destroyed by using a Reset Usable Area structured field. To destroy a single partition, use a Destroy Partition structured field. At this point data can be sent to the partition via an Outbound 3270 structured field. The partition is activated by an Activate Partition structured field. After the partition is created, the terminal is placed in partitioned state.

Now, when the operator enters data into a partition, pressing the enter key causes the data to be returned in an Inbound 3270 structured field. For normal (not partitioned) 3270 input, CICS puts the cursor position in the application's EIBCPOSN and copies the AID to EIBAID. When Terminal Control gets a structured field from a partition, however, it does something a little different. Terminal Control sets EIBCPOSN to zero, and EIBAID to hex 88. It is the application's responsibility to determine the cursor position and AID by examining the Inbound 3270 structured field. There is a special partition called partition zero which sends its data back in a normal 3270 input data stream. Before accessing partitions with native Terminal Control, code `PARTSET=OWN` on the application's PCT entry.

As usual, dealing with partitions is made quite a bit simpler with BMS. The system programmer defines the terminal's partition layout in a partition set with the DFHPSD and DFHPDI macros. The macros are assembled, and the load module is stored in the CICS program library (DFHRPL). When the application uses the `SEND PARTNSET` command, it references the associated partition definitions. Alternatively, an implicit reference can be made by using the `PARTSET` parameter of the PCT entry for the application. Be sure not to use the `ACTPARTN` option for single-partition devices. To make sure that the terminal operator is entering data in the right partition, the programmer can use one of two methods. One method is to specify the partition in the INPARTN option of RECEIVE MAP. The other is to receive any partition, and to use RECEIVE PARTN to determine which partition was received. For both methods, BMS will force EIBCPOSN and EIBAID to contain the cursor position and AID values.

The magnet slot reader (MSR) has no bells and whistles per se, but it does have colored lights (red, amber, and green) and a buzzer. The buzzer produces both short and long buzzes, allowing a CICS program to (theoretically at least) send Morse code. How about dah-dah-dah dit-dit-dit dah-dah-dah accompanied by a flashing red light to signal a transaction abend? Using native Terminal Control, the MSR is controlled by an MSR Control structured field. BMS provides an MSR option for SEND MAP, SEND TEXT, and SEND CONTROL.

It is possible to provide some 3270 terminals with character sets defined by the application. These characters are called programmed symbols (PS). This feature is typically used to produce italic lettering or Greek letters. For each device, up to six character sets can be defined, each one containing as many as 191 characters. To produce these symbols, they must be loaded down to the terminal within a Load PS structured field command referenced by the SEND STRFIELD command. It is probably a good idea to prohibit application programs from doing this arbitrarily. Instead, write a transaction which is STARTed by a PLTPI program which can load down the character sets for the installation. This transaction should use EXEC CICS SEND FROM (symbol set data area) LENGTH (length of data area) WAIT STRFIELD. For more information on the contents of the FROM field, use the IBM display guide manual for the device, such as the 3270 Information Display System: 3274 Control Unit Description and Programmer's Guide, GA23-0061.

The Query structured field allows CICS or an application to determine the characteristics of a terminal which supports the 3270 extended data stream. The device replies to the Query with a Query Reply structured field containing the terminal characteristics. The Query structured field should be sent with the Terminal Control CONVERSE command.

Starting with release 1.7 of CICS, CICS can determine the device characteristics for BMS by specifying Query at terminal definition time. Specify FEATURE=QUERYCOLD or QUERYALL in the DFHTCT TYPE=TERMINAL macro. If you are using RDO, add QUERY(COLD or ALL) to the CEDA DEFINE TYPETERM command. CICS will issue a Query structured field to the device either after the device's first logon or after every logon, depending on whether COLD (QUERYCOLD) or ALL (QUERYALL) is specified.

138   Chapter Six

## 6.6.   CICS 3270 Data Streams

When a terminal access method receives data from a terminal, it passes a buffer to CICS which holds data, codes, and origin information. The contents of these buffers are known as the data stream. Conversely, when a CICS application requests output, CICS puts the message in a buffer and passes it to the access method, together with control information such as the message destination. The access method merely transmits the data stream. CICS, and sometimes an installation's system code, must be capable of both interpreting and constructing these data streams. Although BMS makes the CICS interface to 3270 data streams transparent, users of native Terminal Control must understand them fully.

### 6.6.1.   Input

Input from a 3270 is first detected by a communications controller, such as a 3274, as a result of a polling operation. When the 3270 is polled, it performs a Read Modified operation. The Read Modified operation pulls all the data in the buffer except null characters. If the screen is formatted, however, only data in fields which have their modified data tags (MDTs) set will be transmitted (see Fig. 6.1).

A field's MDT is set when an operator keys over the field, touches it with a light pen, etc. In addition, an application can deliberately set the MDT on before output, so that the subsequent Read Modified operation will pick up the field regardless of whether it was modified by the operator.

A terminal is ready to send data whenever one of many different operator actions takes place. Pressing ENTER, CLEAR, CLEAR PARTITION, CNCL, a PF key, or a PA key will put a terminal in send state. Using the selector light pen or the CURSR SEL key on an attention selector light pen field also initiates input. The use of various peripherals such as the operator identification card read, magnetic slot read, or magnetic hand scanner will also cause Read Modified execution. In addition, input can be initiated by moving the cursor out of a primed trigger field, that is, a trigger field which has been modified by the terminal operator.

The 3270 transmits an AID (attention identifier) to indicate how the transmission was initiated. The AID surfaces later, in EIBAID. Unless the AID is a PA, CLEAR, or CLEAR PARTITION KEY, the cursor po-

| AID | Cursor address | Field data | SF order | Attribute character | Field data | SF order | Attribute character | ... |
|-----|--------|-------|-------|-----------|-------|-------|-----------|-----|
|     |        |       |       |           |       |       |           | ... |

Figure 6.1   Read Modified data stream.

sition will also be sent in the data stream, to be converted by CICS to a 2-byte binary value in EIBCPOSN. If input is triggered by the enter key, a PF key, an operator identification card, a magnetic slot reader, or a magnetic hand scanner, the addresses and contents of all modified (MDT set on) fields are also transmitted. In contrast, using the CLEAR, CLEAR PARTITION, CNCL, or PA key will send only the AID, even if there are fields with their MDTs set on. Moving the cursor out of a trigger field sends the AID plus the trigger field only. What the selector light pen or CURSR SEL key sends depends on the designator character. A designator of space or null will send the AID, cursor position, and addresses of modified fields. The "&" designator causes transmission of the AID, cursor position, addresses of modified fields, and, in addition, the data in those fields.

When CICS receives the 3270 data, it passes it to the application. If the data is in response to a Terminal Control command, the application gets the entire data stream, minus the AID and cursor position, which are reflected in EIBAID and EIBCPOSN.

The input data stream sent by a terminal can take one of three forms: field mode, extended field mode, and character mode. The form is selected by the application with a Set Inbound Reply Mode structured field (see Fig. 6.2). BMS requires that all inbound data be in the field mode. If the terminal does not support structured fields, it will transmit in field mode only.

If the input is from a partitioned terminal, the input data stream depends on whether the partition identifier (PID) is zero or not. If the active partition is zero (background), the data stream will look the same as that from an unpartitioned terminal. If it is not, however, the data stream will be an Inbound 3270 structured field.

The pseudo-AID of hex 88 identifies the data stream as an Inbound structured field. Terminal Control will strip this AID from the data stream and store it in EIBAID. The rest of the data stream will be presented unchanged to the application, which is why the 2-byte length field which follows does not include the AID. The next byte further identifies this data stream as a 3270 Inbound structured field. The PID

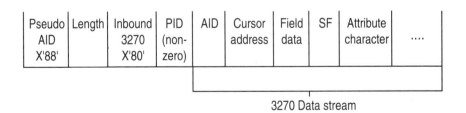

**Figure 6.2** Inbound 3270 structured field.

**140 Chapter Six**

will show that this is a nonzero partition. The remainder of the 3270 structured field data stream contains a normal 3270 data stream as would be sent from a normal unpartitioned 3270 device.

### 6.6.2. Output

CICS uses the Write command to send data to a 3270 display unit in response to a SEND or CONVERSE command. The basic command, Write, has four variations: Write, Erase/Write, Erase/Write Alternate, and Write structured field. The ordinary Write command is used if the transaction uses the default SCRNSZE in its PCT entry. Using the ERASE option of SEND or CONVERSE causes CICS to use Erase/Write instead, so that the screen will be wiped clean before it receives the input. If the transaction's PCT entry specifies the terminal's alternative SCRNSZE, Terminal Control will send Write (if ERASE is not specified) or Erase/Write Alternate (if ERASE is specified). If the command carries the STRFIELD option, CICS will use the Write structured field 3270 command.

In addition to the Write command, a 3270 Outbound data stream (see Fig. 6.3) contains other codes which describe ancillary operations, 3270 orders, and the data themselves. Using Terminal Control, the application is responsible for the entire content of the data stream except for the 3270 Output command and the WCC. To erase an entire screen, an application often issues the TC ISSUE ERASEUP command, which generates a 3270 Erase All Unprotected command. The ERASEUP option of a BMS SEND command generates a similar command called 3270 Erase Unprotected to Address order (EUA).

Except for structured field commands, the first byte after the command is always a WCC. The WCC specifies additional operations, such as whether the alarm should be activated. The CTLCHAR option of SEND and CONVERSE can be used to convey a WCC.

SBA (Start Buffer Address) and SF (Start Field) are orders which control how the data will be written to the control unit's buffer. SF shows that the next byte is an attribute character which describes the data following it. SBA tells the control unit which buffer a Write operation will start or continue from. Not shown is the Insert Cursor (IC) command, which repositions the cursor. Each SF command corresponds to a field on the screen and, presumably, in a BMS map.

When the control unit reads the data stream, it puts the data in the terminal's I/O buffers in consecutive character positions unless it sees

| Write command | WCC | SBA | Buffer address | SF | Attribute character | Data | SBA | Buffer address | SF | .... |
|---|---|---|---|---|---|---|---|---|---|---|

**Figure 6.3** 3270 Output data stream.

an SBA, RA (Repeat to Address), or EUA command. If it sees an SBA, it will be followed by the 2-byte address of the buffer where the data starts. An RA is followed by the 2-byte address of the character to be repeated. The RA simply copies the character into the terminal buffer until the specified address is reached. An EUA is also followed by a 2-byte address, and it places nulls in all the unprotected characters between the current buffer address and the stop address.

There are three types of buffer addresses: 12-bit, 14-bit, and 16-bit. The 12-bit addresses are supported by all 3270s, and allow buffer addresses up to 4095. These bits are transmitted and received as two printable characters, so CICS programs using native Terminal Control must be able to perform the conversion. To convert the address, remove the 2 high-order bits from each character. Shift the low-order 6 bits of the first character so that they are contiguous with the bottom 6 bits of the second character. For instance, the character address A1 is C1 F1 in EBCDIC. The C1 F1 bit pattern is 11000001 11110001. When we drop the high-order 2 bits from each character, it becomes 0000 0111 0001, which is 71 in hex, or 113 in decimal.

Terminals which support extended features use a 14-bit address, which is just a 2-byte binary address with the 2 top bits set to zero. Since characters never start with two zeros, the 14-bit address can be positively distinguished from a 12-bit address. These terminals will transmit a 14-bit address only if the buffer is larger than 4095 characters. When the Create Partition structured field is used to create a partition, the buffer address may be 12, 14, or 16 bits long. Because the 16-bit address is a 2-byte binary address, it can be mistaken for a 12-bit address.

Field attributes are set by 3270 orders in the data stream (see Fig. 6.4). SF, SFE (Start Field Extended), and MF (Modify Field) set the field attributes. SA (Set Attribute) sets character attributes. While all 3270s support the SF attributes, only certain models support SFE, MA, and SA. The SF order is followed by a 1-byte attribute code which is stored in the display buffer with its data. The attribute byte appears to be a space on the screen, and cannot be overtyped. This attribute can specify whether its field is displayable, protected, numeric, highlighted, light pen selectable, etc. While this is normally handled by BMS, an application can insert the SF order and attribute bytes itself in native Terminal Control mode. When the operator hits the clear key, the whole 3270 buffer, including the attributes, is set to null.

| ... | SFE order | Attribute count | Attribute type | Attribute value | Attribute type | Attribute value | .... |
|-----|-----------|-----------------|----------------|-----------------|----------------|-----------------|------|

**Figure 6.4**  3270 SFE Output data stream segment.

142   Chapter Six

Terminals which support the SFE order have more available attributes than SF can provide. SFE is followed by an attribute count byte showing how many attributes have been specified. That byte is followed, in turn, by the attribute specifications. Each attribute specification has an attribute type indicator followed by an attribute value. In addition to SF attributes, SFE supports explicit color attributes (extended color), extended highlighting (blinking, underscore, and reverse video), programmed symbols (PS), and some forms of data validation.

MF allows a program to change a single attribute of an already established field. This order should follow an SBA order which finds the first locations of the field. The SA command defines attributes on a character, rather than field, basis. The SA is followed by a 2-byte attribute specification which applies to all subsequent data until the next SA order or the next 3270 Output command.

Earlier, we said that structured fields support functions like programmed symbols, queries, alternative character sets, partitions, and magnetic slot readers. A structured field has a length field (2 bytes), a structured field type code (1 byte), and a variable-length field which holds the structured field data. To send one of these fields without using BMS, build it in an output area, and use the STRFIELD option of SEND or CONVERSE.

To process a SEND, CICS transmits all characters in output data streams. That includes blanks. To improve performance, it is sometimes desirable to compress the data stream by replacing the blanks with instructions to repeat a single character many times. The most logical place to code such a routine would be in the BTAM or VTAM Terminal Control output exits, XTCOUT and XZCOUT1, respectively. In this routine, bear in mind that data preceding the first 3270 order cannot be compressed by using RA during a write, because the data address depends on the cursor position, which is as yet unknown.

### 6.6.3. Printing considerations

Although output to a printer is handled very much like display screens, there are a few differences which are worth pointing out. The WCC is different in that it contains printer format bits describing a line width of 40, 64, or 80 bytes, or the maximum allowed by the device. In addition, the WCC contains a start print bit which indicates that the buffer is to be printed. Non-SCS printers also understand additional orders, like New Line (NL) and Form Feed (FF).

SCS printers receive SNA character string output. SCS control codes are similar to 3270 orders, but perform a wide range of controls and functions. SCS printers can also transmit data as well as receive data. If an operator presses PA1 or PA2 after a Read Modified command has

### Terminal Hardware and Mapping Programs   143

been received, the SCS printer will send out the character string 'APAK 01' or 'APAK 02', along with an AID. If there is no read outstanding, the terminal will send a signal command, raising the SIGNAL condition in the CICS program. This usually happens when someone hits a PA key while the task is issuing a series of SEND commands.

One way to take advantage of this is to code a transaction which sets the horizontal and vertical tabs for the printer, and give it a transaction code of APAK. When CICS receives the 'APAK...' character string transmitted by the SCS printer, APAK will automatically set its formatting controls. The terminal status of the printer must be set to TRANSCEIVE instead of RECEIVE.

Chapter

# 7

# File Control

## 7.1. Introduction

CICS programs can access VSAM and BDAM files by making requests
to the CICS File Control Program (DFHFCP). Among the specific services provided are random and sequential retrieval, update, addition,
and deletion. In addition to the TCA, applications use several file work
areas to communicate with FCP. FCP, in turn, uses access method
macros and OS areas to pass along the requests.

The material presented in this chapter lays the groundwork for the
understanding of further concepts such as nonstandard file processing,
enqueueing of resources, and exclusivity of access. Here we cover basic
file processing concepts and their ramifications in detailed discussions
of the following topics:

- The two primary file management programs within CICS
- Defining VSAM files to CICS through the File Control Table (FCT)
- How BDAM file entries are coded
- Services provided by FCP
- How applications communicate with FCP (FIOA, FWA, FBWA, and
  VSWA)
- The importance of buffers and strings
- Basic concepts of local shared resources (LSR)
- Off-loading File Control requests to VSAM subtasking
- The meaning of data set states

**146 Chapter Seven**

## 7.2. File Management Programs

CICS has two primary file control programs: DFHFCP and FDHFCS. DFHFCP carries out requests against application data sets (VSAM and BDAM). DFHFCS is used to change the state of a file. In other words, it can OPEN, CLOSE, ENABLE, and DISABLE a data set. To carry out these functions, FCP and FCS communicate with other CICS programs, with VSAM and BDAM, and with the application programs themselves.

When an application program issues a File Control command, the EXEC Interface File Control Program (DFHEFC) issues a DFHFC macro instruction, which sets some fields in the task's TCA. File Control then examines the TCA and takes action. First, it requests storage from Storage Control to manage I/O buffers and other areas. To actually execute the request, it may issue a VSAM or BDAM instruction. As we will see later, much of this takes place asynchronously through the use of a special subtask.

While the request is being handled by the access method, File Control places the task in a WAIT state. If journaling or logging is to take place, File Control calls the Journal Control Program (DFHJCP). After the request has been fulfilled, FCP places the address of the associated control block in the task's TCAFCAA (TCA File Control associated address) field, and returns control.

Sometimes a request may involve a state change. If an application tries to read a data set which is closed, for instance, CICS will open it. To do this, DFHFCP uses the DFHPC TYPE=LINK macro to pass control to DFHFCS. The request is conveyed in the task's TCAFCARG (TCA File Control argument) field. This field addresses parameters which supply information to DFHFCS. After the data set's state is changed, DFHFCS issues a DFHPC TYPE=RETURN to get back to DFH-FCP. DFHFCP executes the original request, and returns control to the application program.

## 7.3. The File Control Table (FCT)

When the CICS File Management module receives a File Control request from an application program, it searches the FCT for the correct entry. This table describes the file, the location of its control blocks, and the type of actions CICS will perform against it. The system programmer must code an FCT entry for each application file, whether it is VSAM or BDAM. Like most CICS tables, the FCT contains a TYPE=INITIAL entry, which must be coded before the TYPE=DATASET entries required for each file. The INITIAL entry is used to set the table suffix: SUFFIX=nn. This suffix number is then coded in the SIT FCT= parameter to determine which copy of the FCT CICS is to use for the run.

Each file is described by a `TYPE=DATASET` entry in the FCT. The `DATASET=` parameter is coded with the CICS name of the data set, that is to say, the name used by the application programmer in making a request. This name can be from one to eight characters, and is also the file's `DDNAME` in the CICS startup JCL. File Control determines the type of file by examining the `ACCMETH` parameter, which is filled in with either BDAM or VSAM. In pre-1.7 versions of CICS, ISAM can also be coded here.

In CICS, the system programmer can limit the types of access an application program may request against a given file by coding the `SERVREQ` parameter of the FCT `TYPE=DATASET` macro. These services include `ADD`, `BROWSE`, `DELETE` (VSAM only), `UPDATE`, and `READ`. For BDAM files, `KEY` means that records can be retrieved from or added to a keyed data set.

The `RECFORM` parameter defines the format of the file's records. This parameter is coded with three combinations of subparameters:

```
RECFORM=(UNDEDFINED, VARIABLE, or FIXED,
    BLOCKED or UNBLOCKED,
    DCB format)
```

For VSAM, the CICS default is `VARIABLE` and `BLOCKED`, and it is required for VSAM ESDS (entry-sequenced data set) files which require abend backout protection. For VSAM KSDS (key-sequenced data set) files and unprotected ESDS files, the system programmer can code `FIXED` if the file was defined with fixed records. This means that the average size is the same as the maximum size, and that all records in the data set are of that size.

The FCT also contains definitions which affect backout and recovery, buffer use, dynamic allocation, and special BDAM processing. We will discuss the use of these values from time to time as they come up in our discussions.

## 7.4. BDAM Considerations

There are some special considerations for coding BDAM file entries. A special `RECFORM` subparameter for BDAM files is DCB format. Using this field is the only way to put format information in the DCB created when the FCT is assembled. To indicate whether a BDAM file is `FIXED` or `VARIABLE`, code `BLOCKED` or `UNBLOCKED` in the `RECFORM` parameter. For example: `RECFORM=(FIXED,BLOCKED,FBS)`.

BDAM key lengths can be specified in either the `BLKKEYL` or `KEYLEN` operand. If the data set has a physical key, code the key length (a value from 1 to 255) in the `BLKKEYL` parameter. If, on the other hand, the data set contains blocked keys, use the `KEYLEN` parameter. As we shall

148    Chapter Seven

see, CICS can use the physical key and block reference to place the record under exclusive control. The starting position of the key is coded in the RKP parameter. For variable-length records, this value must include the 4-byte llbb field found at the start of each record. RKP must be coded for data sets which are browsed, or which have keys within each logical record. The RELTYPE parameter specifies that either relative (BLK), zoned decimal (DEC), or hexadecimal (HEX) addressing will be used for the block reference portion of the record identification field. The SRCHM parameter can be used to force a multiple-track search for keyed records. Code the number of tracks (or blocks) to be searched.

The maximum length of a logical record is coded in the LRECL operand, while the BLKSIZE parameter is coded with the length of the block. If the file contains variable or undefined blocks, specify the maximum block length. If the SERVREQ parameter specifies ADD or BROWSE, and the data set contains fixed-length data set with keys, this value should be the sum of LRECL and BLKKEYL for unblocked records, or BLKKEYL added to the product of LRECL and the blocking factor for blocked records. This operand allows two subparameters. To generate a BLKSIZE value in the DCB, use the second subparameter, such as BLKSIZE=(300,250). The second value (250 in this case) is the true block size, and will be placed in the DCB generated when the FCT assembles. This value must always include the BLKKEYL value. The first value (for the FCT itself) must never be less that the actual block size of the data set.

## 7.5.  File Request Areas

Each task uses the common control portion of its user TCA for File Control requests (see Fig. 7.1). Let us take a look at a few of them.

When an application issues a File Control command, DFHEFC (EXEC File Program) sets a 1-byte indicator at TCAFCTR to show the specific type of request. Macro programs update this field directly. These requests could be for:

- Random selection
- Random update
- Random insertion
- Random deletion (VSAM only)
- Sequential retrieval
- LOCATE mode read-only retrieval (VSAM only)
- Mass insertion (VSAM only)

File Control   149

| System TCA area | User TCA area | TCAFCTR and TCAFCAA | TCAFCID and TCAFCARG | TCAFCNRD and TCAFCURL | ... | TCAFCBRI | TCAFCTR2 flags, TCAFCRI |
|---|---|---|---|---|---|---|---|
| 0 | +80 | +84 | +8C | | +98 | +9C | |

**Figure 7.1** TCA File Control area.

TCAFCAA occupies the last 3 bytes of the area from offset hex 80 to 84. It contains the address of the file area which will be used to pass record information between the program and FCP. This area can be either a file input/output area (FIOA), a file work area (FWA), or a VSAM work area (VSWA). The name of the FCT entry is in the FCAFCDI field (see Fig. 7.2).

The FWA (see Fig. 7.3) is acquired from subpool 04 when an application makes a request to read or update a VSAM or blocked BDAM record, to insert a record, or to browse a file. The FWA does not hold a true I/O area. FCP moves records between the FWA (seen by the application) and an FIOA or FBWA (seen by the access method).

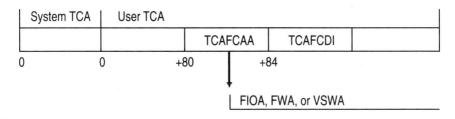

**Figure 7.2** TCA file area addressing.

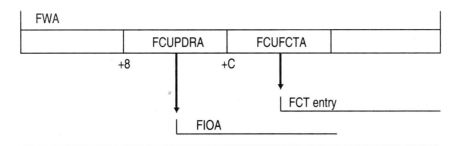

**Figure 7.3** FWA addressing.

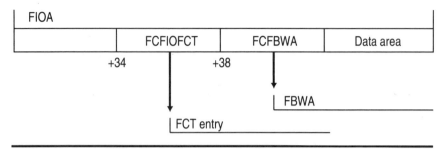

**Figure 7.4** FIOA addressability.

The FIOA (see Fig. 7.4) is used for I/O to BDAM files, and is acquired from Transaction storage (subpool 04). TCAFCAA addresses this area only if the request is for read-only access to an unblocked BDAM file. Otherwise, the FIOA is addressed through the FCUPDRA field of the FWA. The actual data is at hex offset 40 into the FIOA (field FIOADBA), which is a true I/O area used to read and write records to the file. The FCT entry is addressed at data area FCUFCTA.

The file browse work area (FBWA) is used to maintain positioning during a BDAM file browse operation, and is acquired when DFHEFC or the application program issues a DFHFC TYPE=SETL macro. The FBWA is released at the end of the browse. This area is never addressed directly by TCAFCAA. Instead, it is addressed by the FIOA's FCFBWA field at hex offset 38.

CICS applications do not access VSAM records in the actual I/O buffer. Instead, they use either the VSWA or their own working storage area. The VSWA contains a VSAM RPL (Request Parameter List) in the locations VSWARPL (offset 8) through VSWARPLL (offset 4C). For XA systems, the VSWA can reside above the 16-Mbyte line. If the application is not written in VS COBOL II, of course, it cannot access areas above the line, and CICS will copy the record from the buffer into an area which the non-XA COBOL program can access.

## 7.6. Buffers and Strings

Application VSAM files need special groups of areas, controlled by File Control, to allow task access. These areas are called buffers and strings, and are defined in the FCT. These areas can be shared among different files, or can be dedicated. For the purposes of our discussion right now, we will be referring to dedicated buffers and strings. These dedicated resources are often called nonshared resources (NSR). Local shared resources (LSR) will be discussed in the next section.

Each request against a VSAM data set uses a string. The STRNO= parameter determines the number of strings maintained for each data set. Each of these strings uses about 4 Kbytes of storage. If an application issues a READ, WRITE, or DELETE request, CICS obtains a string. This string is released when the command completes successfully. A READ UPDATE string is held until the task requests a REWRITE, DELETE, UNLOCK, or SYNCPOINT, or ends. A STARTBR string is released by an ENDBR, a SYNCPOINT, or the end of a task.

If an application makes a request against a file, and all of that file's strings are in use, FCP places the task into a WAIT state. This is called a string WAIT, and it will last until there is a free string to the file. This WAIT is a DFHKC TYPE=WAIT,DCI=CICS macro. For read-only requests, FCP issues the WAIT against ECADDR=FCTDSMSW. Whenever the file's STRNO limit is reached, CICS marks this ECB nonposted. When a string is released, the ECB is posted.

When an application makes a non-read-only request, FCP checks the number of strings in use. If 80 percent or more are being used, FCP issues DFHKC TYPE=WAIT,DCI=CICS,ECADDR=FCTDSPSW for the task. This is done to allow read-only access at any time. In MVS CICS releases prior to CICS 1.7, the system programmer could vary this percentage by using the STRNOG parameter, which reserved strings for get-only processing. Because read-only requests complete much faster, the 80 percent algorithm generally provides much faster throughput. The FCTDSPSW ECB is posted when the number of strings in use drops below 80 percent again.

To debug a string WAIT, find out which tasks are holding the strings for the problem file, and determine why they cannot run. To do this, examine the task storage on the active and suspended DCA chains, looking specifically for VSWAs. Each VSWA represents a string.

When a VSAM file is opened, CICS reserves buffers for the data and index components of the file. In XA systems, this storage is the extended private area above the 16-Mbyte line. The number of data buffers is determined by the FCT BUFND= operand. This number must be higher than the number of strings for the file. The number of index buffers is determined by the BUFNI= operand, and must also be higher than the number of strings. For direct access processing, BUFND should be equal to the number of strings, plus one to service control interval (CI) splits. BUFNI in this case should be equal to the number of strings plus the number of index levels minus one. The number of index levels can be obtained from an AMS LISTCAT for the data set. To help keep high-level indexes in core, give them different sizes from the data component.

### 7.7. Local Shared Resources (LSR)

LSR allows files to share up to eight different pools of buffers and strings. This is usually very helpful when many data sets are open, and each transaction accesses many data sets. To use this feature, the sys-

**152   Chapter Seven**

tem programmer codes parameters in the participating files' FCT entries. In releases prior to CICS 1.7, code the SHARE key word in the SERVREQ= parameter to allow a file to participate in the LSR pool. Starting with release 1.7, however, there are seven pools. The LSR-POOL= parameter tells CICS which one to use.

Each of the LSR pools is defined in the FCT with the DFHFCT TYPE=SHRCTL macro. These entries define the size and type of each pool referred to by the LSRPOOL= parameter of the TYPE=ENTRY macros of files using the pools. All of the files which use the same LSR-POOL= value will share the same buffers and strings. CICS builds each pool the first time a file belonging to the pool is opened. If a SHRCTL macro has not been coded, CICS will calculate the necessary values by examining each FCT entry belonging to the pool. This can be time-consuming. If the files are not allocated, CICS uses only the information it has available, which may later be inappropriate (when the files are allocated) and will probably degrade performance. The best strategy is to code the macro for each pool, using explicit values. Each pool is identified by the LSRPOOL= parameter in its TYPE=SHRCTL macro.

In the BUFFERS= parameter, the system programmer specifies pairs of buffer sizes and counts. A specification of BUFFERS=(1024(10),512(5)) will allocate 10 buffers of 1024 bytes and 5 of 512. The buffer size must be the same as a legal CI size (512, 1024, 2048, 4096, 8192, etc.). The number of buffers must be at least 3 and no higher than 32,768. The KEYLEN parameter contains the maximum key length of any data set using the pool. STRNO defines the total number of strings which will be shared by users of the pool. It must be between 1 and 255. If the BUFFER and STRNO parameters are omitted, CICS will calculate the needed resources by examining the FCT entries of the data sets which use the pool. If this method is used, the system programmer can use the RSCLMT= parameter to specify the percentage of the total BUFFER and/or STRNO value to use. The default is 50 percent of the total.

Sometimes a task which issues a request against a file using an LSR pool will wait. This can be caused by a string WAIT or a buffer WAIT. If all the strings for the pool are being used, FCP adds the FCT entry to a chain anchored in the FCT at FCTSRBWC. CICS issues a WAIT for the task using the FCTDSBWE ECB. This ECB will be posted when the string is released.

Let us take a look at some of the differences between LSR and NSR. Often, VSAM performance is enhanced if the software can search the VSAM buffers before actually bringing data in from DASD. This is called "lookaside" processing, and is generally beneficial. There are some differences in the way it works with NSR and LSR. With NSR, the only lookaside processing which can take place is for the VSAM index set, and then only if the index set is not associated with an active (in use) string. LSR allows lookaside processing for the index set, the sequence, and the data themselves. With NSR, we specify both index and data buffers. LSR definitions include explicit size and amount definitions—CICS decides whether it will use them for an index or for data.

Browse operations using LSR can be tricky. LSR will not do any read-ahead at all; only one data buffer will be used. A file which has high performance requirements for sequential processing should not be in the LSR pool. NSR will allow read-ahead processing. If the CI is very large, however, read-ahead processing may not be helpful.

LSR represents a tradeoff between real storage and CPU cycles. In other words, it cuts down on CPU storage requirements, but increases processing overhead. If real storage requirements are higher than what is actually available, CICS tasks will wait. If the system is short on real storage, but has lots of CPU cycles to burn, LSR can help. Since cycles usually cost more than storage, however, LSR may not be as cost-effective as many believe. In any case, LSR performance should be monitored very carefully.

## 7.8. VSAM Subtasking

In CICS, VSAM reads and writes are performed by the VSAM/BSAM subtask program, DFHVSP. This is an MVS subtask which operates asynchronously to CICS. The purpose of this mechanism is to offload the VSAM work from the CICS region, thereby taking advantage of multiprocessors, attached processors, and dyadic processors by allowing CICS and VSAM work to overlap.

When CICS starts up, the initialization module DFHSIJ1 attaches the MVS subtask DFHVSP, and then waits for it. If DFHVSP abends, so will the DFHVSP CICS task. When File Control receives an application request, it issues the DFHSQEM macro, which adds a subtask queue element (SQE) to DFHVSP's work chain. The application goes into a CICS WAIT (`DCI=CICS`) on VSWACECB. FCP activates DFHVSP by posting its MVS ECB VSCASECB.

When DFHVSP starts processing, it moves all the SQEs from the request queue to a process queue. This is done to prevent conflicts with CICS. If DFHVSP used the original queue, it might have to process the queue while CICS was changing it. VSP examines each request on the process queue, executes the appropriate request, and moves the request to a wait queue. When the process queue is empty (all requests have been issued), VSP examines the wait queue. If any of the requests have completed, VSP posts VSWACECB. This will give control to CICS, which will in turn post the application, which will then be dispatched. When VSP has no more work to do, it waits for any pending requests to complete, or for another post from FCP.

**154   Chapter Seven**

VSAM and BSAM subtasking is designed for large, tightly coupled environments with lots of real storage. Its advantage is that it allows processing overlap. On the negative side, it incurs WAIT/POST overhead. It does affect the use of AMXT. Because the CICS dispatcher does not wait for the VSAM I/O to complete, the number of OS WAIT list entries is decreased. As the applications wait on an internal CICS ECB (DCI=CICS), and the AMXT counter skips these tasks, AMXT has less of an overall effect on performance. This is acceptable, however, because AMXT is designed to reduce the working set for systems with real storage constraints.

### 7.9.   Alternate Indexes

CICS applications can process a VSAM data set either directly via the file's base or by using an alternative index path defined over the base. This requires separate FCT entries for the base and for each path. In this case, the DSNAME parameter of each FCT entry should contain the name of the VSAM data set to be accessed. The BASE   parameter should contain a name to tie the entries together for performance reasons, but it has no effect on how CICS determines bases and paths. CICS gets this information from the VSAM catalogs themselves when the files are opened.

Another way to access a VSAM data set is to process it via a path which has been defined to VSAM as an alias for the base data set. In addition, the system programmer can associate more than one FCT entry with the same base data set by using the same DSNAME   in each one. In all of these cases, FCP will realize that the FCT entries are connected to a single base data set.

The FCT DSNSHR   parameter can be used to provide read integrity between AIX paths and the base data sets. DSNSHR=ALL   will force VSAM data set name sharing in the VSAM ACB when the file is opened. DSNSHR=UPDATE   will set data set name sharing in the ACB when the file is opened only if SERVREQ   specifies DELETE, ADD, or UPDATE. All of the paths and bases which participate in DSN sharing have the same VSAM SHAREOPTIONS.

### 7.10.   Data Set States

CICS data sets can be in two different states at any given time. A file can be ENABLED or DISABLED, and can be OPENED or CLOSED. The initial state of a data set is controlled by the FILSTAT   parameter of the DFHFCT TYPE=ENTRY macro:

```
FILSTAT=(ENABLED/DISABLED,OPENED/CLOSED).
```

Coding ENABLED ensures that normal processing will be allowed against the data set. If DISABLED is coded, command-level requests will raise the DISABLED condition in the program. If a macro-level program makes a request against the file, the task will abend. The default is ENABLED.

If the system programmer codes OPENED in the file's FCT entry, the data set will be opened by the transaction CSFU, which is initiated automatically after CICS system initialization. CLOSED (the default) will keep the data set closed until it is opened by the master terminal operation, by a DFHOC macro, by the EXEC CICS SET command, or by an application request to access the file.

Let us look at the combinations: If (ENABLED, CLOSED) is coded, the file will be opened the first time it is accessed. This is the default FCT setting. If we change the setting to (ENABLED, OPENED), the file will be opened automatically after initialization. This could slow down our CICS startup time appreciably. If the file is set at (DISABLED, OPENED), the file will be opened, but any requests against it will raise the DISABLED condition. It is important to remember that the NOTOPEN condition is not raised any more by CICS. CICS merely opens the file. HANDLE CONDITION DISABLED is an alternative. The file can be ENABLED by the master terminal operator. Coding (DISABLE, CLOSED) will ensure that the file is CLOSED until an application implicitly opens it. Because it is DISABLED, however, the application will be transferred to its HANDLE CONDITION DISABLED code.

Chapter

# 8

# Database Management

## 8.1. Introduction

This chapter covers the advanced area of database management systems as used with CICS. It discusses two popular types of database, hierarchical and relational, using as examples IBM's two major product offerings, IMS and DB2.

Standard CICS interfaces to IMS (DL/I) and DB2 databases are given. The emphasis is on DB2, which is the newer technology.

Topics include:

- Why use a DBMS, and which type to use
- The DB2 subsystem
- The CICS–DB2 attachment architecture
- DB2 security and recoverability within CICS
- The purpose of threads and the RCT
- How two-phase commit protocol synchronizes CICS and DB2
- The DB2 plan as a CICS transaction
- How an application's SQL request is processed
- The CICS DL/I interface
- DL/I integrity (program isolation, logging, and journaling)
- How shared database allows batch access through CICS
- CICS DL/I initialization process

## 8.2. Using CICS with a Database

There are many advantages to using a database management system (DBMS) to hold corporate data. A DBMS provides its own comprehensive backup and recovery systems. Instead of asking all programmers (and programming departments) to understand a VSAM record layout, a good DBMS is capable of presenting a unified view of the data to all applications. Security can be managed on the DBMS level instead of the CICS level. If managed correctly, a database can prevent potentially dangerous data redundancy. In short, the database is a concept which can ideally provide data independence, that is to say, separation of code and information.

Right now, there are two major types of databases which are compatible with CICS—relational and hierarchical. For our discussion in this chapter, we will focus on IBM's DB2 (relational) and IMS (hierarchical). Both products support database calls within CICS applications. A single CICS application may, in fact, call both databases with complete integrity. DB2 is the newer technology, while IMS is a workhorse which has served faithfully for many years. DB2, because of its flexibility, data independence, and ease of use, is gradually easing IMS out, but IMS will continue to be supported for many years. The latest version, IMS/ESA version 3, which includes the new CICS–IMS interface DBCTL (see Chap. 15), proves that IMS is still a strategic performer which continues to get support and enhancements from IBM.

There are, in addition to these two products, many other databases supported (directly or indirectly) by CICS. These include ORACLE, IDMS(R), ADABAS, SQL/DS, and SUPRA, to name but a few. Figure 8.1 presents a DB2 overview.

DB2 is IBM's relational database management system for MVS. The user interface to DB2 is the Structured Query Language (SQL). Data are accessed on-line through CICS and TSO. Together, DB2 and CICS make up a comprehensive database/data communication (DB/DC) sys-

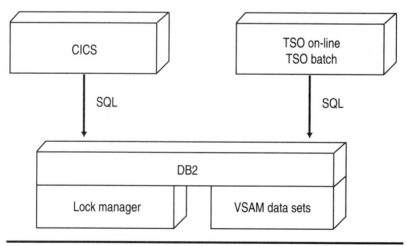

Figure 8.1  DB2 overview.

tem. TSO provides interactive query and batch access. The actual data which DB2 controls, interprets, and returns to the application are stored on DASD in VSAM data sets.

All work in DB2 is done within "units of work" called transactions. When an application needs data, it passes the request to DB2 using SQL. In the case of a failure, transaction recovery is coordinated by a set of protocols which guarantee that data will be synchronized at a point of consistency. To ensure access to "clean" data, database changes are coordinated by using a lock manager.

DB2 is an MVS subsystem. When MVS is initialized, DB2 EARLY code is invoked (Fig. 8.2). DB2 EARLY code is in the link list, functions as a resident part of the operating system, and exists whether or not DB2 has been started. This code establishes DB2 as an MVS subsystem, and makes it eligible to receive commands via the MVS subsystem interface (SSI). DB2 commands are identified by a unique first character chosen by the installation. The default character is a hyphen (-).

When DB2 EARLY code senses the START DB2 command, it starts three tasks, each with its own address space: one for DB2 system services, one for database management, and one to provide database integrity (IRLM). To be on the safe side, DB2 always "restarts" in case

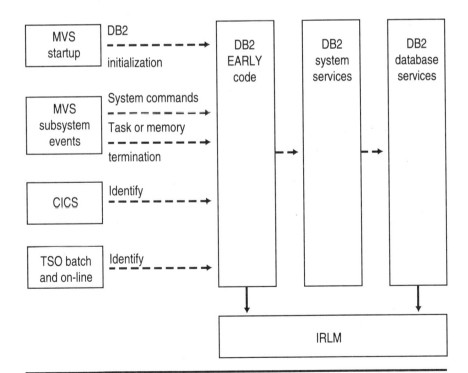

**Figure 8.2** DB2 subsystem.

## 160 Chapter Eight

anything went wrong during the last execution. There is virtually no operator control over DB2 restart processing; it is all controlled by DB2 itself. During restart, the subsystem finishes any work that was outstanding during the previous run and ensures that all data are at a point of consistency.

After DB2 is up, EARLY code intercepts commands and passes them to the system services address space. If it receives a command during restart, the command is saved until the DB2 subsystem is ready for it.

TSO and CICS communicate with DB2 through attachments. Attachment code resides in the application's address space. When the attachment receives a request from the application, it locates DB2 via the SSI and sends an MVS IDENTIFY request to EARLY code. This establishes a connection between the application and DB2. After the connection has been established, the attachment communicates directly with the subsystem services address space, which passes the request to the database services address space. EARLY code waits for task and memory termination events in the application. If the application ends before finishing its work, DB2 cleans up the connection and takes steps to ensure consistency of the database.

## 8.3. The DB2–CICS Relationship

CICS is attached to DB2 by sets of threads. In this multithread connection, each CICS transaction calling DB2 uses a different thread to DB2. Each thread, in turn, uses an MVS control block called a TCB (task control block), which represents a cross-memory service (XMS) call to DB2. This allows the attachment to take advantage of the MP or dyadic capability of modern computer architecture. Although a task which calls DB2 goes into a CICS WAIT (DCI=CICS), CICS itself does not wait. The code for the attachment itself is shipped with DB2, but its installation requires that we modify two tables with which we are already familiar—the PCT and the PPT. We must, in addition, add a new table, the Resource Control Table (RCT). This table defines the threads and how they will be used by the various CICS transactions which make DB2 calls.

The attachment offers operational facilities to facilitate starting and stopping and recovery/restart. The connection itself can be started and stopped by using a special CICS transaction which controls the connection. This same transaction can also be used to monitor the connection. We said earlier that one of the advantages of using a DBMS is its integrated recovery/restart facility. A CICS transaction can update both DB2 and non-DB2 resources. CICS will synchronize these updates by using a protocol called two-phase commit protocol (TPCP). This means that all updates will be committed or backed out together.

To monitor the DB2–CICS environment, the system programmer must use a combination of CICS and DB2 tools. In CICS, we can use CICSPARS, the CICS trace, and shutdown statistics. Within DB2, DB2PM (DB2 Performance Monitor) can be used to read and interpret the SMF 100 and 101 records. The object of tuning the environment will be to allow the most efficient use of threads. To do this, the system programmer will need to tune the number of threads used and the way they are assigned to different transactions. As we shall see, there is a special feature we can use called the reusable thread. These reusable, or protected, threads have been responsible for driving transaction rates up to about 60/s in some installations.

Security can be handled on several different levels. CICS provides transaction-level security either internally or externally. Internal security implies that the system is using the sign-on table (DFHSNT) and either the IBM-supplied sign-on program (DFHSNP) or one provided by a vendor, such as OMNIGUARD. To use the external manager, the system programmer codes `EXTSEC=YES` on the SIT, and installs either RACF or a vendor-supplied security manager such as ACF/2 or Top Secret. In either case, the security is provided by CICS.

DB2 provides additional security. When a CICS region connects to DB2 (usually as a part of CICS startup processing), DB2 will call RACF to verify that CICS is authorized to connect. Later, when transactions issue DB2 calls, DB2 uses a different type of authorization checking. When a CICS program has a DB2 request, the attachment asks DB2 to execute a corresponding DB2 "plan." Each transaction in CICS has a corresponding plan in DB2. The plan is the DB2 part of the transaction, and is stored in DB2. When the attachment passes the application's request to DB2, it also passes an authorization id (usually the sign-on id) to DB2, which checks to see whether the user is authorized to execute the plan.

To prepare a CICS application, a programmer follows the usual procedure, except for a couple of extra added steps. First, the programmer must go through a special DB2 precompiler (before the CICS precompiler) The precompiler produces a database request module (DBRM). This DBRM must then be "bound" (added) to DB2. The "bind" output is an application plan. In other words, the application will have two parts: a load module and a plan. The load module has all the non-DB2 code, and the plan contains the DB2 request execution code.

In practice, the precompiler output of several programs is usually bound into one plan. (A plan may be bound from several DBRMs.) The reason for this is that the CICS–DB2 relationship is on a transaction level, not a program level. As we all know, of course, a transaction may consist of several programs. Each of the DBRMs involved in a transaction must be bound into that transaction's plan. Each program which

**162  Chapter Eight**

issues a DB2 call will have a corresponding DBRM. Binding these programs together, however, can create a very large plan. Although this will increase the chance that a thread will be reused, it may increase storage requirements within the DB2 address space.

Let us look at these features in a little bit more detail, and see what we can do to make the attachment work efficiently.

### 8.3.1.  DB2–CICS attachment architecture

TSO, IMS, and CICS access DB2 through the MVS subsystem interface (SSI) protocols. Before any of them can access DB2, however, they must connect to DB2 and create threads to DB2. In the CICS attachment, a thread is a two-way path between a CICS task and DB2. The path can be to an application plan or to the command processor. CICS uses a single address space subsystem (SASS) connection, which allows many concurrent CICS tasks to call DB2 at the same time. Each thread uses cross-memory services to communicate. This attachment is similar in many ways to the IMS DC attachment.

When a program calls the DB2 database, it uses EXEC SQL statements, which look very much like EXEC CICS calls. SQL stands for Structured Query Language, which is the data language used to access DB2 data. (This language is also used by many other relational database products.) Each SQL call starts with EXEC SQL and ends with END-EXEC. In PL/I, it ends with a semicolon. Each CICS program which calls DB2 has a special module link-edited into it called DSNCLI (DSN CICS language interface). The precompiler replaces the EXEC SQL statement with a parameterized call to DFHCLI.

At execution time, the application branches to DFHCLI, which branches to the attachment. Does this all sound familiar? It should, because it is very similar to the way the EXEC CICS interface works. A CICS–DB2 command-level program has two link-editied stubs. DFHECI handles EXEC CICS commands by routing them to the EXEC Interface Program (DFHEIP). DSNCLI routes EXEC SQL commands to the CICS–DB2 attachment.

A CICS programmer may use any combination of CICS and DB2 facilities. Within DB2, the program can access databases and define DB2 objects. One limitation, however, is that a program which contains EXEC SQL statements must have a command-level environment. In addition, EXEC SQL statements cannot be function shipped. When a program accesses DB2 and non-DB2 resources such as VSAM, Transient Data, and DL/I, all updates will be fully synchronized. The attachment uses the CICS Task-Related User Exits facility to actually send the request to DB2.

In addition to program requests, the attachment can handle commands that the system programmer or operator might issue to change or monitor the system. These commands can start or stop the DB2–CICS connection, modify the connection, or display the connection's current status. These attachment facility commands can be authorized by CICS internal or external security. DB2 authorization does not get involved. After the connection has been established, CICS users can also issue commands concerning DB2 itself. In this case, DB2 will do authorization checking, and will see that the user has been granted the privilege to issue the command. (In DB2, the GRANT command is used to give specific privileges to users.)

CICS and TSO have program code called "attachments" to provide connection protocols to DB2. The attachment issues an MVS IDENTIFY command to request a connection to DB2. CICS can have many transactions running at the same time, each making SQL requests to DB2. When a transaction starts, the attachment asks DB2 to create a thread (see Fig. 8.3). A thread ties together a transaction's requests and resources. Once inside DB2, the thread is attached to a DB2 plan, which executes the SQL request. A DB2 plan corresponds to a CICS transaction or a TSO user. A transaction is the execution of one or more related programs in the host application region. CICS has a multithread connection, while TSO is single-threaded.

When CICS connects to DB2, it must create threads to be used by transactions which issue EXEC SQL statements. When an application

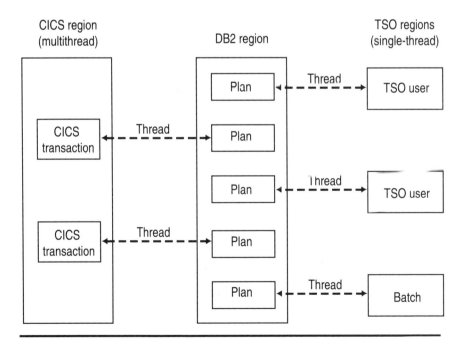

**Figure 8.3** Threads and the RCT.

## 164 Chapter Eight

makes a DB2 request, the attachment will assign it to a thread. There are, in CICS, three kinds of threads—command, dedicated, and pool. In general, these threads are defined by the system programmer on the RCT.

Each RCT starts with a `DSNRCT TYPE=INITIAL` entry. In this entry, the system programmer specifies the total number of CICS–DB2 threads (`THRDMAX=nn`). When coding this value, consult with the DB2 system administrator, who codes the total systemwide DB2 thread limits in the DB2 installation parameters. Like other CICS tables, the RCT can have a suffix. Unlike the others, however, that suffix can have only one character. It is coded in the `SUFFIX=` parameter. The connection is started with the `DSNC STRT x` transaction. The x is the RCT suffix. If the x is omitted, the attachment assumes O. It is possible to start up the attachment in a PLTPI program; in this case you specify the table in the DFHSIP EXEC statement.

Command threads are used for both attachment and DB2 commands. When the RCT is generated, it will automatically produce two of these threads. The command threads cannot be coded. Whenever someone enters the DSNC transactions to issue a command to DB2, the attachment will try to use one of these threads. If there are none available, the request will overflow to a general-purpose pool thread.

Dedicated threads are specific to a transaction (or group of transactions), and are coded in `DSNRCT TYPE=ENTRY` macros. Each of these specifies one plan (`PLAN=`) and one or more transaction ids [`TXID=(tran,tran,…)`]. When the attachment receives a DB2 request, it searches the RCT for a dedicated thread with a transaction code match. If it finds one, it sends the request over that thread to DB2, along with the plan name. DB2, in turn, executes the plan, and so on. These threads are defined in sets. A dedicated RCT thread entry specifies a number of threads: `THRDA=n`. We might, for instance, have an entry which specifies five threads for transaction `INQY`, which is associated with the DB2 plan `INQYPLAN`. This means that there can be five concurrent DB2 requests from tasks with the name `INQY`.

Each thread contains two parts: a TCB on the CICS side, and an allocated plan on the DB2 address space. When an application makes a request, the attachment usually has to create a TCB and ask DB2 to allocate a plan. Wouldn't it be nice if these threads would hang around for a while? Suppose there is a pseudoconversation going on? Maybe we have a transaction with a very high volume rate. What we can do is ask the attachment to defer the termination of some of the threads. If we coded `THRDS=2` for the `INQY` example above, for instance, the attachment would try to keep two of the threads active (for up to 60 s) for the next `INQY` task.

In our `INQY` example, we coded `THRDA=5` to allow for five concurrent `INQY` task DB2 requests. What happens when the sixth request comes in? The `TWAIT` parameter in the thread entry determines what action the attachment will take if all threads are in use. If `TWAIT=YES` is coded, the task will simply wait for an available dedicated thread. If, for some perverse reason, the system programmer wanted the task to abend, he or she would code `TWAIT=NO` on the transaction's RCT entry. There is a compromise, however. We can ask that the request overflow to a pool thread by coding `TWAIT=POOL`.

The system programmer can define a pool of threads (`DSNRCT TYPE=POOL`) with any number of threads (`THRDA=n`). These threads can be used by commands which overflow the command threads, transactions which have overflowed their dedicated entries (as above), and transactions for which the system programmer has forgotten to define dedicated entries. In the last case, the attachment uses a default plan. This technique is not efficient, or even workable in most situations. The pool threads do not support reuse. The `TWAIT` parameters are `YES` (wait for a thread) or `NO` (abend the transactions). DB2 enforces a minumum of three threads in the pool entry.

### 8.3.2. CICS–DB2 transaction flow

When a transaction issues its first DB2 call (EXEC SQL), it branches to DSNCLI (the CICS language interface). The branch to DSNCLI is inserted by the DB2 precompiler. The DSNCLI stub is link-edited into each EXEC SQL program. DSNCLI formats the SQL request, and calls the CICS attachment via the Task-Related User Exit (TRUE) facility. The TRUE is activated when CICS first connects to DB2. The attachment facility searches the thread for a dedicated entry which names the transaction. Remember that the attach uses EIBTRNID, so don't alter it.

Having found the correct RCT entry, the attachment proceeds to schedule a thread to handle the request. If the plan named in the entry has an available thread, the attachment will, of course, use it. If there is no thread, the attachment creates one. This means creating a TCB, allocating a plan, and checking authorization (this is where reusable threads help performance).

By the time a task makes a DB2 request, it has already passed through CICS security. There is, however, security within DB2, and the transaction must get authorization to execute its plan. To facilitate this, the attachment can pass an authorization id to DB2. This id can be one of several items: a three-character operator id, a terminal id, a transaction id, or a simple character string. The type of id to use is coded in the entry's `AUTH=` RCT parameter. Probably the most useful is the eight-character external sign-on id, usually the same as the TSO id. If the thread is a reusable thread, authorization checking is bypassed if the transaction code and user id are the same, or if the user has used the thread recently.

Internally, the thread TCB is posted (MVS POST), and the task goes into a CICS WAIT (DCI=CICS). The request is passed to DB2 via cross-memory services, and DB2 executes the request. When the request completes, DB2 passes the data (and return codes) to the attachment. The task's CICS WAIT completes, and it is dispatched, while the thread goes into an MVS WAIT. The attachment returns control to the program's DSNCLI code via the Task-Related User Exits Program. DSNCLI returns to the next instruction after the EXEC SQL request. The task at this point has received the data and return codes and continues executing. Figure 8.4 illustrates the flow of services.

DB2 uses cross-memory services, which allow multiple address spaces to process synchronously without using SVCs. This is more efficient, as it provides direct communication among the various DB2 components and TSO or CICS.

Application processing is split between the data communication subsystem (CICS or TSO) and DB2. Most of the processing actually takes place in CICS or TSO. Only specific data requests are handled in DB2.

The next time the application makes an SQL request, the same process is repeated, except for the thread search. Since the thread is in an MVS WAIT, the attachment merely posts the WAIT complete. When, however, the task ends or issues an explicit syncpoint, the attachment asks DB2 to commit all changes, and the thread may be terminated. In the case of a reusable thread, the thread termination will be delayed for 30 to 60 s.

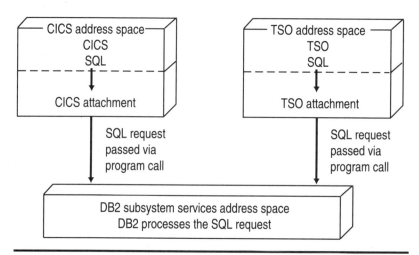

**Figure 8.4** Attachment processing.

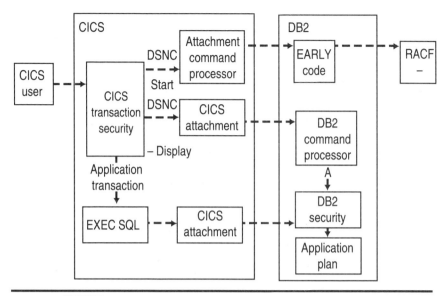

**Figure 8.5** CICS/DB2 security.

Security in the CICS–DB2 environment, as shown in Fig. 8.5, regulates CICS users' access to DB2 and CICS resources, and involves mechanisms which act on several levels. To operate the attachment facility, users need authorization to:

- Connect to DB2
- Enter attachment facility and DB2 commands
- Execute application plans using CICS transactions

This security is provided in the SSI, CICS, and DB2 by RACF, CICS, and DB2 security, respectively. When CICS connects to DB2, DB2 calls RACF, and passes it CICS's address space id and connection request. The address space id is the user id of the CICS job card. CICS always requests a single address space subsystem (SASS) connection, and RACF verifies that the user id is authorized to connect. DB2 is defined to RACF as a protected resource in the DSNR class, which CICS may access using the SASS protocol.

Attachment facility commands entered through the DSNC transaction do not involve DB2 directly, and are secured within CICS on the transaction level. DB2 commands entered through DSNC, however, are routed to DB2. These commands are differentiated by a subsystem recognition character, usually a hyphen. After a DSNC DB2 command

**168 Chapter Eight**

is passed to DB2, DB2 security checks that the user is authorized to enter that particular command.

Every CICS user must have authorization to sign on and to execute particular transactions. That security is provided through IBM- or vendor-supplied security packages which run within each CICS region which accesses DB2 resources. In addition, each transaction must have authority to execute its corresponding application plan in DB2. This security is provided by CICS and DB2 when the CICS attachment sends DB2 an SQL request on behalf of a transaction. For a variety of considerations, including performance, application security should be provided primarily within CICS on the transaction level.

## 8.4. Two-Phase Commit Protocol (TPCP)

DB2 requests are made within the framework of a transaction. A transaction is a set of actions which must commit or abort as a unit. This means that within a transaction, the data will be consistent. Transactions normally end by asking DB2 to commit or abort work. CICS, as the transaction manager, coordinates commit and abort processing. DB2 and CICS each have their own logs to keep track of database changes and transactions, respectively. Because TSO does not use the log write-ahead protocol (see below), DB2 coordinates TSO batch and on-line itself.

Problems could occur if two transactions tried to access the same data at the same time. To prevent this, DB2 "locks" some of the data, preventing two transactions from accessing temporarily uncommitted information. This is all handled by the Internal Resource Lock Manager (IRLM). To make sure that the data will remain consistent if a transaction fails, DB2 logs the data before it is changed. If the transaction aborts, the changes can be reversed. If DB2 or CICS ends before the transaction does, DB2 can redo committed changes and undo aborted changes at restart. This is called the log write-ahead protocol.

To protect against data inconsistency, DB2 ensures the physical integrity of data regardless of software or hardware failures within the MVS environment by allowing CICS to coordinate all commit/abort processing. CICS determines the disposition (commit or abort) of a transaction and informs DB2 of its decision. DB2, however, may or may not be able to cooperate. The TPCP determines the final transaction disposition.

In commit phase 1, CICS notifies DB2 that it is prepared to COMMIT database changes. DB2 responds by indicating whether or not it is prepared to commit database changes. If DB2 is ready, it must be prepared both to commit the changes and to back them out if CICS experiences a failure. This is done by forcing log information to DASD before telling

CICS that it is ready to commit. Until CICS confirms the commit request in commit phase 2, the database change is uncommitted, or, in DB2 terms, it is INDOUBT. The period of time between DB2's response and commit phase 2 is called the INDOUBT period.

If DB2 is not ready to commit the database change, it will tell CICS. DB2 will back out database changes, and CICS will back out any CICS-related changes. This is called dynamic transaction backout (DTB) in CICS.

If DB2 fails before responding in commit phase 1, it will abort the change at the next DB2 restart. After restart, CICS will ask it whether it wants to commit or abort database changes, and DB2 will respond that it wishes to abort.

If DB2 fails during the INDOUBT period, it will, of course, be restarted. During restart, DB2 will ask CICS for the disposition of the transaction associated with the INDOUBT transaction (this is also called an INDOUBT thread). The database change will COMMIT or ABORT according to CICS's decision as the resource manager. If, however, CICS is not available during DB2 restart, any INDOUBT data will be locked to protect the integrity of the database. When CICS is restarted, it will issue an IDENTIFY to DB2 and inform it of the disposition of all INDOUBT threads. This requires that CICS be restarted with its memory intact; that is, it must be restarted with a START=AUTO or START=EMER DFHSIT specification or PARM override. If CICS comes up cold at this point, it will not resolve the INDOUBT threads. At this point, the INDOUBT threads must be resolved manually by the operator.

Commit phase 2 begins when CICS receives a reply from DB2. CICS logs the outcome to DASD. If DB2 replied that it was prepared to commit, CICS logs the reply and notifies DB2 that commit phase 2 is starting. This is the point of no return, and is called the "must complete notification." If CICS starts commit phase 2 by signaling COMMIT, DB2 must make committed changes accessible, and must forget all prior forms of the data. If, for some reason, CICS started commit phase 2 by signaling ABORT, DB2 would reverse the database changes by using information from its log. DB2 saves the response (either COMMIT or ABORT) on its own log. After either COMMIT or ABORT, data locks are freed, and the TPCP process is over.

## 8.5. IMS and CICS

CICS programs can use DL/I to access DL/I databases for update and/or inquiry. The CICS shared database facility allows batch regions to use the same DL/I databases as CICS on-line transactions. If an application needs to access a DL/I database, it can use the CICS DL/I interface.

## 170  Chapter Eight

The interface can handle the database activity of several tasks on a multithread basis. The program isolation (PI) facility of DL/I ensures integrity for concurrent use and update of several databases. Its enqueue/dequeue mechanism allows many different CICS tasks to access the same segment types for update in a database. At the same time, it prevents concurrent access to the same occurrence of a given segment.

The interface uses CICS logging and journaling to record changes, and the standard DTB mechanism to back them out in case of an error. The DTB routines will, in addition, call IMS backout routines to make sure that backout/commit processing is synchronized between DL/I and non-DL/I resources. Although the command-level interface is not required in general, it is required for function shipping DL/I requests.

### 8.5.1. Batch DL/I and CICS

A batch DL/I application can run in two different modes: It can be completely independent of anything else in the system, or it can access common databases managed by CICS. The first method is a batch environment; the latter, a shared database environment.

In a batch environment, the application needs to have exclusive use of all the resources it will need. It is operating in a standalone mode, and is completely independent of any other job running. No resources can be shared. CICS cannot use any resources that the batch job accesses. To get around this problem, the batch job can be run in the shared database environment. In this case, CICS manages the databases, and acts as a database resource manager. Any access to the data will be controlled by CICS. Note that a batch program does not need to be changed to run in a shared environment, just the JCL.

When running shared, the DL/I code and the databases are associated with a CICS, which uses MVS services to communicate between the CICS shared and on-line regions. The shared database region contains a DL/I batch program which needs to access databases managed by and attached to the on-line CICS region. There can be many shared regions, and each of them can execute different programs concurrently. They are all controlled, however, by the CICS on-line region. The on-line region contains the CICS nucleus, DSA, etc., and all the on-line programs. As usual, it controls the terminals, files, and other CICS resources.

The on-line region is initialized like any other CICS region, through job cards or an MVS START command. All CICS resources are connected to this region. When it wants to switch control information and DL/I data to a shared database region, it issues a type 2 SVC.

When two or more CICS tasks or shared database programs update the same database, CICS uses DL/I program isolation to ensure database integrity. CICS and DL/I back out database changes made by failing programs by using the CICS dynamic log. All DL/I logging is done on the same log tape, using standard CICS log facilities.

The shared database region runs a batch application program which processes DL/I data. Like any other job, this application is scheduled by MVS job management. The job's JCL specifies the CICS batch region controller. The program uses DL/I calls for database references. One limitation here is that an application program executing in a shared database region can access only DL/I databases that are attached to the CICS on-line region. Changes made by the program are recorded on the CICS log. The shared database region program can use VSAM and other data sets connected to the batch region. These data sets will, however, be dedicated to the shared regions, and changes to them will not be recorded on the log.

To help concurrency, the batch job should issue periodic DL/I CHKP calls. Because the job may be making a lot of updates, these calls will free the updated segments, making them available for on-line CICS transactions or other shared database programs.

### 8.5.2. CICS–DL/I initialization

Initialization is a joint project of DB2 and CICS, and performs three functions. First, the interface must be initialized. Next, since we are using CICS, and not IMS DC, CICS must simulate the IMS initialization functions. Finally, CICS must call the IMS DB batch initialization routines.

Before CICS can use IMS PSBs and DBDs, they must be expanded to an internal control block format. This is done by the IMS application control block generation (ACBGEN) utility. The blocks themselves are stored in the ACBLIB data sets. After they are expanded, they are called PSBs and DMBs (data manipulation control blocks). The PSB directory (PDIR) is then loaded. It is used to control the PSBs, and contains an entry for each one. Each entry shows the size, status, storage location, and disk address (in `IMSVS.ACBLIB`) for each PSB. The DMB directory (DDIR) list is assembled and link-edited before the interface uses it. It shows the same information for DMBs as the PDIR shows for PSBs. The DDIR has an entry for each physical database, including index DBDs. It should not contain entries for logical DBDs, because no DMBs are created for them. This will raise the "not found" condition during CICS startup.

The number of concurrent threads to IMS is governed by the `DLTHRED` parameter of the CICS SIT (System Initialization Table, remember?). This is the maximum number of CICS tasks that can schedule a PSB concurrently. The value should include the shared database batch programs dependent on the region. This number is dependent, in turn, on the `SESNUMB` parameter in the `DFHTCT TYPE=IRCBCH` macro. The maximum `DLTHRED` value is 31.

## 172 Chapter Eight

When an on-line task issues a call, the interface attempts to schedule one of the threads. If the `DLTHRED` limit has been reached, the task goes into a CICS WAIT until another task releases a thread. This can be done by an implicit or explicit `TERM` call. When a shared database program wants to issue a call, it uses a mirror task in the on-line region. If that mirror task issues a call and no threads are available, the program abends.

### 8.5.3. Enqueueing

The IMS program isolation facility can ensure database integrity when many tasks or programs process the same database in a CICS environment. To do this, it enqueues the database's elements, pointers, free space elements, etc., between CICS syncpoints. To perform the enqueue, control blocks are built in the CICS DSA. This storage is allocated during CICS startup, and cannot change while the system is running. Each of the control blocks is 16 bytes long. The default for the entire pool is 2 Kbytes, which should be all right for most on-line environments. If a shared database is being used, this number should probably be increased.

A much better approach, however, is to use `CHKP` calls in the batch programs. This will avoid a very large number of enqueue control blocks. It will also increase concurrency. The enqueue pool size is set in the `DFHSIT ENQPL` parameter.

### 8.5.4. Performance tips

Usually, a shared database program will degrade the performance of the entire CICS region. This is because of buffer pool saturation. The batch program will often cause on-line transaction data to be flushed earlier than they would be otherwise. The LRU (least recently used) algorithm gives preference to the batch program, as it can generate requests more quickly. Response time will go up, and more I/O will be needed to re-retrieve the flushed data. To help alleviate this, increase the size of the database buffers in a shared database environment.

If the system has a long-running shared database job, Emergency Restart time can increase dramatically. Transactions cannot be entered until everything is backed out. If the program has made a lot of changes, but has not issued any `CHKP` calls, backout may take some time. Issue `CHKP`s as often as is practical.

Because of the overhead of interregion communication with the online environment, a program running in a shared database environment will take much longer to run than it would in a standalone batch environment.

Chapter

# 9

# Intercommunication Facilities

## 9.1. Introduction

This chapter provides an overview of the CICS intercommunication facilities, both interregion (IRC) and intersystem (ISC) communication. It provides a description of the various services available under each facility, as well as examples of where each would be appropriate. Multiregion Option (MRO) and Cross-Memory Services (XMS) are discussed as the methods of interregion communication. For intersystem communication, IBM's LUTYPE6 protocol for advanced program-to-program communication (APPC) is highlighted. You will learn about:

- Types of intercommunication (ISC and IRC)
- Function Request Shipping
- Transaction Routing
- Asynchronous Processing
- Dynamic Transaction Processing (DTP) conversations
- Advantages of LU6.2 protocol

## 9.2. Overview

Intercommunication facilities allow CICS systems to communicate with each other, and with other non-CICS systems which support the SAA application program-to-program communication (APPC) protocol, which is implemented in the CICS Resource Manager interface (RMI) and in SNA LUTYPE6. These facilities fall into two categories: using remote resources, and communicating with remote tasks.

174    Chapter Nine

There are six types of remote resources which may be accessed by a CICS task: files, Transient Data destinations, Temporary Storage, terminals, DL/I databases, and transactions. (The Interval Control START of remote transactions is discussed in Sec. 9.4.3. "Asynchronous Processing." DB2 resources are accessed through special attachment code implemented in the RMI, also known as the task-related user exit. There are two ways to access these resources—Function Request Shipping and Transaction Routing.

A CICS task can communicate with remote tasks either synchronously or asynchronously. Asynchronous communication uses the IC START, PUT, and RETRIEVE facilities to start remote tasks, send data, and allow the remote task to receive the data.This communication is indirect. In other words, each task has its own LUWs, and tasks communicate only by exchanging data occasionally.

The Distributed Transaction Processing (DTP) facility allows two or more tasks to communicate directly. Although these tasks are running on two different systems or regions, they may share the same LUWs and communicate with SEND and RECEIVE commands. The basic difference between these two types of facilities is that Function Request Shipping and Transaction Routing use IBM-supplied tasks specific to supplied service routines. They are utility transactions, and are not customized to a specific application's requirements. Remote task communication, on the other hand, is user-written code.

## 9.3.  Connections

All the facilities (Function Request Shipping, Transaction Routing, Asynchronous Processing, and Distributed Transaction Processing) are implemented over two types of connections. A CICS system can communicate with another CICS in the same host CPU by using multiregion communication (MRO), also known as interregion communication (IRC). This connection uses cross-memory services (XMS), which is independent of any communication network facilities. Intersystem communication allows CICS to communicate with SNA LUTYPE6 partners (CICS or other systems), and takes place over the VTAM communication network links, making the connection independent of the host processor locations.

## 9.4.  Why Use Intercommunication Facilities (ICF)?

One of the main justifications for these facilities is that they allow a single system image to be presented to a user. Although a transaction may appear to be taking place on a terminal connected to a given processor, the work may actually be shared by several regions, or even systems, in different locations. Connecting to a remote CICS region provides access to data and resources that are not on the local region. This presents the opportunity to share data between data centers, departments, divisions, and, in some cases, even different companies, as is the case in the financial, insurance, and other industries.

Many single-region systems experience virtual storage constraints, and to some extent ICF can provide some relief. A large CICS region can be split into smaller ones. Some of the applications can be moved into the additional regions, and users will still be provided with transparent access. Another strategy is to split the region into a terminal-owning region, called a TOR, and another region which owns the applications and files or databases, called an AOR. Systems which because of software constraints have as yet been unable to take advantage of the extended storage available through 31-bit addressing have used this approach to obtain VSCR (Virtual Storage Constraint Relief). With the widespread use of multiprocessors, this technique may be able to exploit multiprocessing techniques to some degree.

Storage isolation, another important concern, can be addressed by these techniques for pre-ESA systems. Very often, the hardiness of a region is jeopardized by applications which "misbehave." These applications not only abend themselves but, because of the nature of CICS processing, can also abend the CICS region, and therefore all other applications. Separation of regions also allows different tuning and availability options which are specific to the region which owns them. This can have political ramifications, such as: "My application is more important than the others, and requires its own region."

### 9.4.1. Function Request Shipping

Function Request Shipping (or, more simply, Function Shipping) allows a command-level request to be transparently shipped to a remote region. Because of this, the application can "think" that the local CICS owns the resource. As a result, applications can be written without regard for the physical location of the resource. The actual location is recorded in the appropriate CICS environmental table, for example, the FCT. The actual request is shipped from the local region to the remote owning region over an intersystem link. This may be an ISC or MRO link.

ISC uses VTAM as a teleprocessing access method, and `LUTYPE6` as a communication protocol. The MRO method uses either cross-memory services or, in older systems, DFHIRP to "switch" the data via MVS SVC instructions. In either case, the `LUTYPE6` protocol is used. A protocol is, after all, just a protocol, or way of doing things, not a piece of

**176 Chapter Nine**

software. Human beings, for instance, can use the same protocol on the telephone that they use in face-to-face communication.

Most CICS resources are supported. Remote VSAM and BDAM files can be accessed through a shipped File Control command. Transient Data and Temporary Storage commands can be shipped. DL/I requests can also be shipped, but not to an IMS/VS region. It is possible, however, to make a request to another CICS system which owns a DL/I DB, and programmers can avail themselves of the batch CICS/IMS interface if necessary. DB2 SQL requests cannot be shipped, but can use DTP to communicate with a CICS running on the same machine as the target DB2 system.

Transactions can be accessed via a shipped Interval Control START command. This is actually a form of asynchronous processing. Although remote terminals can be accessed, this facility falls into the category of Transaction Routing. To facilitate this shipping feature, a "transformer" program formats the requests and associated data in shippable format (actually an LUTYPE6 data stream). In the remote region, a "mirror" transaction receives the request, transforms it to an executable command, and executes it. It then transforms the result to a shippable format and sends it back to the local region. The "transformer" program converts the response back to command-level format, and returns it to the task which originally issued the command.

There are actually seven different mirror transactions, named CSM1, CSM2, CSM3, CSM5, CSMI, CLS1, and CLS2. Although they map to a single mirror program (DFHMIR), they each correspond to particular architected process names. CSM1 is the system message model, and is used internally. CSM2, the scheduler model, is used to execute START commands. The queue model, CSM3, handles Temporary Storage and Transient Data commands. CSM5 is the DL/I model, while CSMI is used to ship File Control commands. If LUTYPE6.2 protocol is used, the transactions CLS1 and CLS2 are used. Whichever mirror transaction is used, its purpose is to re-create the original request on the remote system. After execution, the mirror returns the results to the originating region.

The program which transforms the request during the shipment process is DFHXFP. It encodes and decodes the command. In the requesting system, XFP turns the EXEC command into a transmittable form (XFORM1). In the remote system, XFP turns it back into a command form (XFORM2). After the request is issued, the results are changed to a transmittable form (XFORM3). Upon receipt of the data and return codes by the local region, the last transform to EXEC format takes place (XFORM4). There is an additional program called DFHXFX (the short path transformer) which does not use the full architected LUTYPE6.2 format.

Although exclusive control and recovery/restart facilities are available, they are not entirely foolproof. Protected resources are given exclusive control on the remote system. When the local task issues a syncpoint, the remote mirror also takes one. If the mirror's syncpoint fails, CICS will send a notification to the master terminal. Failures can occur at various points. The local transaction or remote mirror may abend. The intersystem link may fail. One or both systems may fail. If one fails, the surviving system treats this as a session failure, and the standard action in this case would be to abend all involved transactions.

Backout, whether dynamic or during restart, should resynchronize recoverable resources. However an "in doubt" period may exist between the time that a syncpoint request is sent and the time that a positive response is returned. Installations may need to develop procedures which can evaluate and handle the "in doubt" situations.

### 9.4.2. Transaction Routing

Transaction Routing supports both command- and macro-level programs, and allows a terminal owned by one system to execute transactions on another system. This facility is transparent, and the user need never know which system is actually running the transaction. The PCT indicates which system owns the applications, and requires entries in both systems.

If the transaction is initiated through ATI (automatic transaction initiation), it may acquire a terminal in the other system. The transaction can run in one system, while terminal activity is routed to the other. In the early days of transaction routing, only the MRO link could be used, but routing is now supported over ISC using the LUTYPE6.2 protocol.

When a user enters the transaction code for a remote application, the program that executes in the TOR is a relay program called DFHCRP. The terminal-owning transaction executing CRP is usually called the *relay transaction*. CRP routes the transaction request to the AOR system, where the "real" transaction executes. Because this transaction will probably try to send maps or data streams to a terminal, the AOR provides a surrogate TCTTE to intercept these transmissions and route them back to the "real" terminal in the TOR.

There is also a special routing transaction called CRTE which allows an operator to explicitly connect to a remote system. Once connected, the operator can execute transactions on the system. The connection remains until the user specifically cancels. Because the connection is explicitly created by the user, PCT entries associating the transaction code with the DFHCRP program need not be defined in the TOR. This can be used to avoid conflicts with system codes such as CEMT, and for debugging remote applications.

**178  Chapter Nine**

### 9.4.3. Asynchronous processing

Asynchronous processing consists of two or more transactions which execute independently and communicate by dropping off and picking up messages. It is similar to the procedure that we may use in everyday life when two people try to communicate by leaving messages on each other's telephone answering machines rather than talking to each other directly.

In CICS, the process starts when one task initiates a transaction in a remote region, optionally passing data to it. The remote transaction, once started, can then retrieve the data. If it wishes to, the remote task can even start another transaction in the local region. The tasks may complete at any time, on their own terms, without any communication. This type of communication is ideal for inquiries that do not require synchronized update or recovery. Although it is usually referred to as a separate facility, asynchronous processing is actually a subset of Function Request Shipping, and sometimes of DTP.

In the Function Shipping style, Interval Control START (or START FROM) requests are shipped back and forth. The remote transaction can use the RETRIEVE command to collect any passed data. Alternatively, the data can be sent via a SEND LAST command (which is actually a form of DTP). In this case, the remote transaction would use the RECEIVE or EXTRACT ATTACH command to get the data. If there is any doubt about it, the remote transaction can examine the EIB or use the ASSIGN command to determine how it was started.

### 9.4.4. Distributed Transaction Processing (DTP)

DTP allows a transaction in one CICS to communicate synchronously with a transaction running in a different CICS region. Unlike asynchronous processing, this is a direct task-to-task communication facility that can take place over MRO or ISC links. Because the communication is direct and synchronous, applications may take advantage of full and automatic shared syncpoint processing, which uses the two-phase commit protocol.

Distributed applications are usually divided into pairs of transactions, half of each pair on each system. In a typical conversation, one task (the front end) controls and commands the other (the back end). When the front end of a DTP application wants to communicate with the back end, it first acquires a session to the remote CICS by issuing the CICS ALLOCATE command, then initiates the back-end task with the CONNECT PROCESS command.

An initial data stream can be sent with this command by using the Process Initialization parameter (PIP). Alternatively, if the LU6.2 protocol is not being used, the first SEND or CONVERSE of the front end starts the back end. Communication then takes place as the partners use the SEND and RECEIVE commands. To end the conversation, the partner in control (the one in SEND state) issues a FREE command. Each partner is then free to continue or end its own task.

All this communication uses SNA half-duplex flip-flop protocol, which means that only one end can be in SEND state at any given time. The front end always starts in SEND state, and the back end always begins in RECEIVE state. This is similar to the protocol we use when we speak on the telephone. The caller always starts in SEND state, the call recipient in RECEIVE state.

Throughout the conversation, one party is always sending while the other receives. The listener receives control only when the speaker relinquishes it. While it is true that the listener can interrupt the speaker, this is usually regarded as a protocol violation. In fact, when two parties are in SEND state at the same time (possible with full-duplex protocol), this is usually the result (or cause) of a misunderstanding.

The MRO or ISC session used here by the front end is an alternative facility (the principal facility is the task's terminal). The principal facility for the back end is the MRO or ISC link. Because the CICS commands map almost directly into the appropriate SNA LU6.2 commands, this is essentially a command-level facility. No special macro-level facilities are provided.

Because each partner in this relationship is coded by the application programmer, much more flexibility is offered in this facility than in the ones previously discussed. A remote browse DTP back-end program, for instance, can return only selected records, saving valuable transmission overhead.

This technique is particularly important in distributed DB2 systems, as SQL requests cannot be directly shipped. This also implies, however, that DTP is not intended to be retrofitted to existing applications. Applications in this environment are specifically designed to converse with one another.

## 9.5. Types of Intercommunication

ISC is designed to provide communication between systems on separate computers, but it can (if desired) be used within a CPU. MRO facilitates communication between CICS regions running on the same system. Both modes of communication, however, are controlled by components of the Terminal Control modules in CICS. Whichever type of link is being used, there are distinct layers of program code which control the flow.

**180  Chapter Nine**

The application layer does not interface directly with the access method (such as VTAM). Instead, the program makes a request by using CICS commands. CICS modules then issue specific Terminal Control (DFHTC) requests. The layers implemented within CICS Terminal Control are designed to interface with the access method. These layers are the function management layer, which identifies the type of LU6.2 communication, and the data flow control layer, which directs the course of communication. These layers operate similarly in all types of request, and are concerned more with passing the request than with implementing it.

### 9.5.1. Intersystem communication (ISC)

ISC requires a network management system, VTAM, to pass data streams containing SNA LU6.2 protocol commands and data. Recall from our Terminal Control discussion that SNA is concerned with communication between LUs. An LU can represent an application (such as CICS), a terminal (a 3270, for example), or another application. A type 6 logical unit (LUTYPE6) represents an application, and the communication between two applications is called an LU–LU session.

LUTYPE6 is the protocol which CICS uses to implement IBM's SAA (System Application Architecture) APPC standard. Before LUTYPE6, applications emulated terminals to communicate with CICS, or used Extrapartition Transient Data.

The original program-to-program LU protocol was called LUTYPE6, and was later enhanced. To distinguish between the older and newer protocols, the older one was renamed LU6.1, while the newer one became LU6.2. LU6 or LUTYPE6 is often used generically when referring to either protocol. There are distinct differences, however. LU6.2 enhancements provide additional tools to control program communication more directly.

ISC links allow CICS to communicate with any program, CICS or otherwise, which understands the LU6 protocols. APPC provides a well-defined application programming interface. CICS implements this interface in mapped conversations. Using the mapped conversation technique, CICS only passes user data to and from the API (application programming interface). The GDS (generalized data stream) header is removed, as is the application's responsibility for dealing with it. This facility uses normal EXEC CICS commands, and is similar to LU6.1.

Unmapped, or "base," conversations present the program with the GDS headers, which contain data length and type information. This facility is most often used with device-level products, which might not support mapped conversations or may not have an application programming interface open to the user. This facility is implemented with special `EXEC CICS GDS` commands.

LU6.2 also provides conversation partners with several levels of synchronization. A Level 0 session provides no synchronization. Level 1 allows partners to use a private synchronization level. Level 2 gives the effect of full CICS syncpointing, including rollbacks, and is the standard (and safest) conversation level. This means that a syncpoint in one region will cause a syncpoint in the other.

There are a few intercommunication strategies available within the framework of ISC. In one scenario, the communication can take place within a single processor. This intrahost ISC takes place via the application-to-application services of VTAM or TCAM. This communication looks the same to ISC as remote processing.

Another environment might be two physically adjacent processors. In this case, they may be connected by 37XX controllers with a multi-channel adapter. Starting with VTAM 2.1, however, a more common arrangement is to use direct channel-to-channel communication. If the processors are physically remote, the connection can be made with 37XX units running the Network Control Program (NCP) and remote network links. Implementing any of these environments requires coordination with network support to define communication links.

### 9.5.2. Multiregion operation (MRO)

MRO support is provided by the CICS interregion communication (IRC) modules and by portions of the Terminal Control facility, and is limited to CICS regions running in the same host computer. All four ICFs are supported—Function Request Shipping, Transaction Routing, Asynchronous Processing, and DTP. There are some restrictions to DTP, however, which do not exist on an ISC link.

MRO supports only communication between CICS regions, except for IMS batch connections. IRC is also used to support shared DL/I and Data Dictionary. Like ISC, MRO passes data in an LU6 format. Unlike ISC, however, it does not require any special networking facilities. Instead, it uses either MVS XMS or the CICS Interregion Program.

This program (DFHIRP) resides in the MVS LPA or DOS SVA, and is invoked via the CICS type 2 SVC. It establishes the intersystem connections and passes requests and data between them, using storage in the CSA. SRB scheduling is used to pass control. The more common alternative, however, is XMS, which does not require CSA storage for data transfer. The XMS instructions PC (Program Call) and PT (Program Transfer), along with ECB posting, pass control back and forth between programs using the MRO link. In this case, DFHIRP is used only to open and close the links.

## 9.6. Resource Definition

Although many of the facilities are transparent, or at least relatively simple to implement within an application, the links that they use must be defined ahead of time by the system programmer. This involves coding definitions in the TCT, as Terminal Control manages much of the communication. Before defining the connection, we must know the CICS APPLID of the systems to be connected. This is the one- to eight-character name by which each CICS is known to intercommunication facilities.

For ISC, CICS's VTAM network name can be found by looking at the VTAM `VBUILD TYPE=APPL` label. In an MRO session, the APPLID is the logon name, used when IRC opens the session. There are several ways to establish the CICS APPLID. If nothing at all is coded in any table, the default will be DBDCCICS. To specify an APPLID, use the `APPLID=` parameter of the `DFHTCT TYPE=INITIAL` macro. This value can be overriden by coding the `APPLID=` parameter of DFHSIT. Finally, all values can be superseded by using a startup override (on the job card) of `APPLID=`.

The CICS SYSIDNT is a one- to four-character "private" name by which a remote region will be known to the local region in which it is defined. The default is CICS. It can, however, be coded in the `DFHTCT TYPE=INITIAL` macro's `SYSIDNT` parameter. This parameter also exists in the SIT, which overrides the TCT definition. Like APPLID, it can also be specified as the startup override SYSIDNT.

TCP handles much of the intercommunication links for CICS, and because of this, the TCT defines MRO and ISC connections and sessions. All remote connections are defined on a `TYPE=SYSTEM` macro and are related to the system via the `NETNAME` parameter.

These entries serve as the anchor for all link sessions. Other resource tables point to these anchors via the `SYSIDNT` operands. Link session TCTTEs require `TYPE=TERMINAL` definitions, which are related to the TCTSE (TCT system entry) via the `SYSIDNT` operands. Some of these entries are used when initiating an intersystem request, while others are needed to receive a request.

A Send session is used when that system first initiates a request, and a Receive session is used when the system first receives the request. Once either type of session is allocated for request processing, it handles all the send and receive processing, regardless of whether it was originally a Send or Receive session. Remote terminals also require a special TCT entry, `TYPE=REMOTE`. These entries are related to their TCTSE entry, also by the `SYSIDNT`, and are resolved to abbreviated skeleton entries and a model entry.

Chapter

# 10

# Temporary Storage

## 10.1. Introduction

Temporary Storage Control, which is used to store data temporarily or
to pass data between programs, is sometimes termed the scratchpad facility of CICS. Despite this humble name, temporary storage queues
are widely used within CICS, both internally and by application programs. This chapter takes a look at the uses of temporary storage, and
its internals, explaining:

- The two types: MAIN and AUXiliary

- Internal uses of TS queues

- How to define the AUX temporary storage data sct

- Processing a `WRITEQ` TS command

- The TSIOA, TSUTEs, and TSGIDs

- Control areas for AUX temporary storage

- Defining the Temporary Storage Table (TST)

## 10.2. Overview

The CICS temporary storage facility allows applications to store data
temporarily in main storage or on DASD. These data are stored, retrieved, or released by referring to a unique 8-byte symbolic name.
Although temporary storage can be organized into single records or
into groups, the single-record facility preceded the group organization,
and is available to macro-level programs only. CICS management modules themselves use this type of temporary storage quite frequently.
Message groups, or sets, were designed for terminal paging, and can be

183

**184    Chapter Ten**

used when a program needs random or sequential access to multiple records. These message sets are commonly referred to as queues. The records within each queue are called items, and are referred to by relative position number. In other words, each queue has a name, and each item within the queue has a number, just like pages in a book.

Temporary Storage (TS), like many other CICS resources, can be protected against concurrent update integrity problems. If a TS queue is to be updated by multiple tasks, the Temporary Storage Program enqueues upon it by using the `DFHKC TYPE=ENQ` macro. TS queues survive the end of a task, and actually remain intact until they are explicitly purged by the application. When the queue is released, the disk or main storage it occupied is also freed. Until it is deleted, however, the data can be retrieved by the task which created them, or by any other task, as long as the application knows the queue's unique eight-character name. Because this storage is durable between tasks, it is often used for terminal paging, for data accumulation, or for passing data from one task to another.

Another consideration is the fact that MAIN storage cannot be recovered by CICS facilities in the event of a system failure. We said earlier that these queues can reside either on DASD (AUXiliary) or in virtual (MAIN) storage. If an application will only be storing small amounts of data for a short period of time, MAIN will probably perform best. To allow programmers to use only MAIN storage, just code `TS=(,0)` in the SIT. Large queues of long-term data are usually held better in AUX storage. To use the TS AUX facility, the system programmer defines a single VSAM data set to hold all the queues. This data set should, of course, be large enough to hold all the anticipated concurrently used AUX TS queues. To facilitate faster operations against AUX TS queues, CICS can use VSAM subtasking.

## 10.3.  Internal Uses of Temporary Storage

In addition to its use by applications, the TS facility is exploited by several CICS management modules. If an application issues a BMS terminal page-building command, BMS uses temporary storage to save screen data to facilitate browsing. In practice, however, most developers prefer to use TS directly for this purpose. When the VTAM message recovery options are used, CICS uses predefined recoverable queues to reestablish message sequences during emergency restart after a system failure. (For more information on this facility, see Chap. 5, "Terminal Control.")

CEDF users invoke TS indirectly during a debugging session. CEDF, being pseudoconversational, uses TS queues to communicate between task iterations and to develop a trace of the user task's execution. The

CICS intercommunication modules store work in the local region (local queueing) when the target system is not available. All of these facilities use auxiliary temporary storage. If the dynamic log fills, CICS will spill the records to temporary storage until the logical unit of work completes. Dynamic log overflow can be controlled by the system programmer by coding `DTB={MAIN|AUX}` in the SIT. The default is `MAIN`.

## 10.4. The Auxiliary Temporary Storage Data Set

To allow the use of auxiliary temporary storage (AUX TS), the system programmer defines a single nonunique VSAM ESDS data set. (A nonunique VSAM data set resides within an already catalogued VSAM space.) Each control interval defined will contain a number of temporary storage records. The size of each record is rounded up to a multiple of 64 or, if the CI is larger than 16 Kbytes, 128 bytes. Once purged, a TS queue frees up its space, making it available to handle other requests. The AUX TS is defined using standard Access Method Services (AMS) statements and looks something like the example in Fig. 10.1.

In this example, we have defined a data set containing 200 CIs of 4 Kbytes. Although it is tempting to define a secondary allocation on the `RECORDS` parameter, it was not always a good idea. Prior to release 1.7, CICS tried to get the secondary allocation not when it needed it, but during initialization. This meant that the size of the data set increased

```
//CICSJOB JOB job card info
//DEFINETS EXEC PGM = IDCAMS
//DDNAME DD DISP = OLD, UNIT = 3380, VOL = SER = volume
//SYSPRINT DD SYSOUT = *
//SYSIN DD *
DEFINE CLUSTER -
(RECSZ (4096, 4096) -
RECORDS (200) -
NIXD -
CONTROLINTERVALSIZE (4096) -
SHAREOPTIONS (2) -
NAME (auxts.dataset.name) -
VOL (volume) -
FILE (DDNAME)) -
CATALOG (catalog name)
/*
//
```

Figure 10.1 Defining the AUX TS data set.

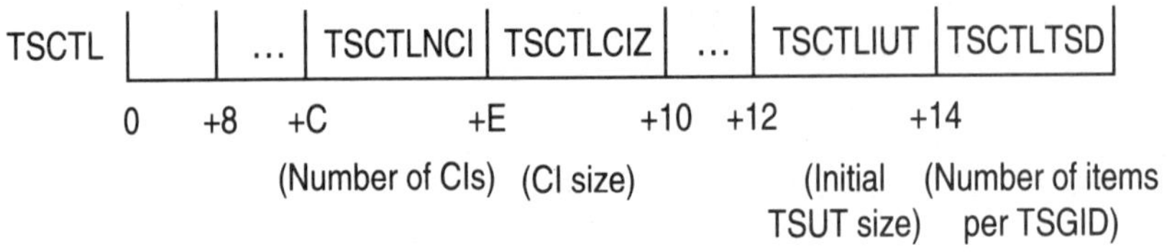

**186 Chapter Ten**

| TSCTL | | | ... | TSCTLNCI | TSCTLCIZ | ... | TSCTLIUT | TSCTLTSD |

0     +8    +C         +E          +10  +12           +14

(Number of CIs) (CI size)           (Initial    (Number of items
                                    TSUT size)   per TSGID)

**Figure 10.2** The Temporary Storage Control record (TSCTL).

at each execution. Starting with release 1.7, CICS initializes only the first extent, then initializes the additional extents as they are needed during execution.

Let us take the case of a very large system which wants to spread its auxiliary temporary storage over several volumes. The IDCAMS define cluster job stream must contain the "number of volumes" parameter in the UNIT parameter, e.g., UNIT=(3380,3), and must also have the matching volume serial numbers in the DD card's VOL parameter (in the same order as the IDCAMS VOLUMES parameter). When the job runs, cluster space will only be allocated on the first volume. After CICS starts up, the second and third volumes will show allocations only after CICS exhausts all the space allocated on the first volume.

Because temporary storage uses a first fit algorithm, the first pack will tend to be accessed much more frequently. In order, then, to spread access out across volumes, make the primary allocation for the volumes well below the TS usage high water mark (printed in the CICS shutdown statistics). After the AUX TS data set is created and CICS starts up, CICS formats the data set and writes a temporary storage control record (TSCTL) at the beginning of the first CI (see Fig. 10.2). At subsequent startups, it will reference this record to avoid having to reformat each time. This control record contains information such as the number of control intervals and the size of each one, the initial size of the Temporary Storage Unit Table (TSUT), and the number of items which can be held in each temporary storage group identifier (TSGID).

Generally speaking, a CI size of 2 to 8 kbytes will produce the best results, but to be more precise in our estimates, let us look at the actual storage requirements of a TS record. In addition to the actual data being stored, each record needs 24 bytes for a temporary storage record prefix (TSCI). This field contains an SAA (CLASS=TEMPORARY STORAGE), the 8-byte DATAID (field TSID), the item number (field TSIRN), and the length of the entire temporary storage record, including the prefix (field TSIDLEN), as shown in Fig. 10.3.

If the storage is recoverable, and is being used in a START command (EXEC CICS START TRANSID...FROM), another 32 bytes are needed.

## Temporary Storage

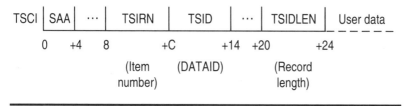

**Figure 10.3** The Temporary Storage record prefix (TSCI).

When BMS uses temporary storage, it will need a record as large as the 3270 buffer (1920 bytes for a standard 24 × 80 screen). If the system is using AUX TS for dynamic log overflow, leave enough room for the largest anticipated dynamic log record.

VSAM does not require storage for each record, but does need 64 bytes from each CI to store control information. If the CI is larger than 16 Kbytes, it needs 128 bytes. To conform to VSAM sizing requirements, the CI should be a multiple of 512 bytes for CIs up to 8 Kbytes, or a multiple of 2 Kbytes for large CI sizes.

The actual number of CIs that will be needed is a function of the anticipated frequency and size of TS requests, of course. For instance, if an application expects to generate 30 transactions/s with a throughput of 2 s, and each one holds five stored screens (at 1920 + 24 bytes each), this portion of the requirement mandates 300 records of 1984 bytes (1944 rounded up by 64) each. A 4-Kbyte CI will hold two of these records (plus 64 bytes of VSAM control information), leaving us with a requirement of 150 CIs, or about one cylinder of a 3380. Remember of course, that this figure is for one application only, and does not take into consideration system needs or future expansion. In reality, we would probably allocate at least 10 cylinders (about 1500 records) for a system with this activity.

### 10.5. Processing a WRITEQ TS Command

A temporary storage queue is created automatically when an application writes the queue's first record. When a program requests the service EXEC CICS WRITEQ TD('TSQUEUE1'), the Temporary Storage Program (DFHTSP) checks to see whether or not the queue already exists. If it does not, TSP creates the queue (TSQUEUE1 in our example) and writes the first record (item number 1) to the queue, returning that number to the program. Let us look more closely at how the queue is actually created.

#### 10.5.1. The TSIOA

When the request is made, the EXEC Interface program DFHETS (EXEC Temporary Storage) issues a DFHTS TYPE=PUTQ macro, and

**188 Chapter Ten**

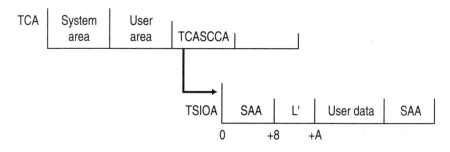

**Figure 10.4** TCA—TSIOA addressing.

places the program's data in a Temporary Storage input-output area (TSIOA) which is addressed by the TCASCCA field task's TCA. The TSIOA (see Fig. 10.4) contains an SAA, a halfword containing the (binary) length of the data, and the actual data to be stored.

### 10.5.2. TSUTEs and TSGIDs

Each temporary storage queue is represented by an entry in an area called the Temporary Storage Unit Table (TSUT). Before TSP can create a queue, it must locate an available entry (TSUTE). If there are no entries available, TSP allocates a new TSUT. These tables are created dynamically on an as-needed basis. If one fills up, TSP allocates another, and chains it off the previous table from the TSUTFC field. Backward chaining is maintained through the TSUTBC field. The TSUTs are chained from the CSA at CSATSMTA (see Fig. 10.5).

Having found (or allocated) a TSUTE, TSP places the eight-character DATAID 'TSQUEUE1' in the TSUTEID field. The actual data themselves may end up in one of various locations, depending on whether

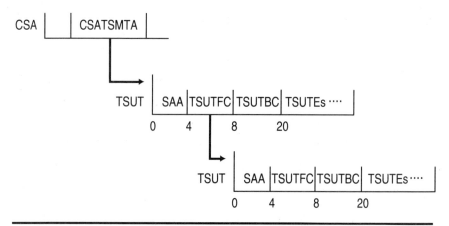

**Figure 10.5** TSUT chaining.

the request specified AUX or MAIN storage, and whether this request was for queued temporary storage (the only type available through the command-level interface) or for a single area (requested only by management modules or other macro-level programs). This single area is requested by the DFHTS TYPE=PUT macro, and is the ancestor of queued temporary storage.

If the request is for queued storage, the TSUTE will anchor a chain of TSGIDs (Fig. 10.6). In the case of a single area, the TSUTEPTR points directly to the stored data, either within VSAM or in virtual storage. The VSAM address consists of a CI number, a displacement into the CI (in segment multiples), and the data length (also in segment multiples). More about this addressing technique later.

The TSUTETC field contains one or more type codes which tell us more about the nature of the TS request. A hex 80, for instance, indicates that this TSUTE describes a message set. Hex 40 means that the request was for AUX storage, while X'20' shows a MAIN request. These codes are combined by logical OR operators, so that 1 byte may have several codes. If we were to find a hex X'C0', we could break it down to X'80' and X'40', telling us that this TSUTE represents an auxiliary message set. Other codes indicate that the queue is waiting for session recovery (X'10') or was originated by BMS.

If the queue is being written by the Interval Control Program (as a result of a START WITH DATA command), this field will be flagged with X'02'. To protect the queue while it is being changed, TSP locks it by setting a flag of X'04' in this field. The TSUTEQEA field contains the entry's queue element address (QEA). During recovery, it is used by the

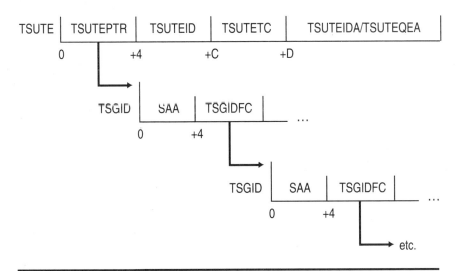

**Figure 10.6** TSUTE/TSGID chaining.

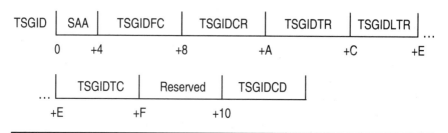

**Figure 10.7** TSGID contents.

Temporary Storage Recovery Program, and is referred to as the TSUTEIDA field.

If the request is for queued data (DFHTS TYPE=PUTQ), TSP allocates a TSGID area for items within the message set. The TSGID contains a series of 4-byte entries, one for each item in the queue. The system programmer specifies the number of items in each TSGID by coding the TSGMGSET parameter in the SIT. The default (and minimum) is 4, while the maximum is 100.

The first TSGID, allocated when the queue is created, holds the first few items and is called the parent TSGID. The parent is addressed by the TSUTEPTR field of the TSUTE. Items which are written later on are placed in child TSGIDs which are chained back to the parent through the TSGIDFC field.

Each TSGID entry contains the virtual storage or VSAM address of the item being stored. Between the chain field (TSGIDFC) and the item pointer itself (TSGIDCD) is a set of counters and indicators. TSGIDTR and TSGIDLTR contain the number of physical and logical items held within the logical queues. The logical count is used for recovery purposes, when the queue is specified as protected in the Temporary Storage Table (TST). TSGIDCR contains the current record number. The type code (TSGIDTC) is set to X'80'. Figure 10.7 shows the contents of the TSGID.

The TSGIDCD field contains the address of the actual temporary storage data for the given item represented by the TSGID. If the queue is being held in MAIN storage, this address points directly to a subpool 05 address. In an XA system, this may be a 31-bit address. If, however, this is an AUX queue, things get a bit more complicated.

## 10.6. Auxiliary Temporary Storage Control Areas

CICS stores all AUX queues on a single VSAM ESDS data set. Instead of accessing it via the VSAM record interface, however, CICS uses CI processing and organizes the space in its own way. The CSA points to a temporary storage common area (TSMAP), shown in Fig. 10.8, which

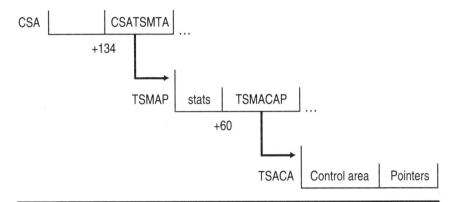

**Figure 10.8** TSMAP addressing.

contains statistical and control information. The TSMACAP field addresses the auxiliary control area, which contains more control information, and pointers to TS buffer and VSAM control areas.

Let us take a look at a few of the TSMAP fields, as shown in Fig. 10.9. The first 12 fullwords contain numbers which reflect the amount and type of temporary storage activity which has taken place. The first field, TSMSTA1F, indicates how many nonqueued records have been added with the DFHTS TYPE=PUT macro. These macros are generally issued only by management code. The next field, TSMSTA2F, shows how many DFHTS TYPE=PUTQ macros or WRITEQ TS commands have been issued. TSMSTA3F keeps track of the current number of TS queues and nonqueued records. If at some point extra TSGID extensions must be created, TSP creates them, and increments the counter at TSMSTA4F.

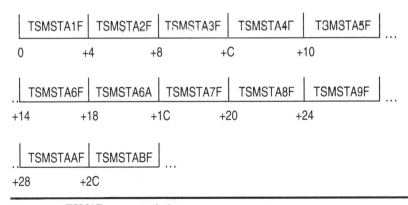

**Figure 10.9** TSMAP usage statistics.

**192  Chapter Ten**

The number of records (queued or nonqueued) written to MAIN storage is stored at TSMSTA5F. Fields TSMSTA6F and TSMSTA6A keep further track of MAIN storage by keeping a record of the high water mark and current use of virtual storage by Temporary Storage, respectively. AUX records (queued or nonqueued) are counted in TSMSTA7F. If there have been any suspensions, compressions, or I/O errors, they are recorded in TSMSTA8F, TSMSTA9F, and TSMSTAAF, in that order.

There was a time (before CICS 1.6) when an AUX TS record had to fit into a single CI. This meant that if even one program wrote one single record to AUX TS of, say, 31,000 bytes, the system programmer had to define a CISIZE of 32 Kbytes for the AUX TS data set. Needless to say, this hurt temporary storage performance in general. Now, an AUX TS record can span two or more CIs. To do this, however, the EXEC Interface must make a call for each part of the record, degrading performance. To avoid this, make the CI size large enough to handle most normally occurring records. The number of records which exceed a single CI is recorded in the TSMSTABF field.

To manage the AUX TS data set, CICS divides the CIs into segments. Each record can then be assigned to a given segment within a given CI. The number of CIs in the data set can be found in the TSMAPNCI field, while the size of the CI is stored in TSMAPCSZ. The number of segments per CI is in TSMSPCI. Another (strange) field is TSMBPSEG, which shows the number of bytes per segment as a power of 2. Figure 10.10 shows what these fields will contain (in hex, of course) if our TS AUX data set consists of 100 8-Kbyte CIs.

When CICS takes a keypoint, it quiesces all temporary storage activity via an ECB (TSMTQLB) at offset X'34' in TSMAP. This ECB is cleared when the keypoint starts, and is posted when complete. TSP checks this ECB each time it scans the TSUT.

Remember that the TSMAP points to another TS area called the temporary storage auxiliary control area, or TSACA (see Fig. 10.8). This area is dedicated to controlling the use of AUX temporary storage, and is allocated at initialization by the DFHSIH1 overlay module. The first set of fields, TSANBCA and TSANVCA, specifies the number of temporary storage buffer control areas (TSBCAs) and VSWA control areas (TSVCAs). These numbers govern the amount of concurrent AUX TS activity, and are set by the system programmer in the TS parameter of

| | TSMAPNCI | TSMAPCSZ | | TSMSPCI | TSMBPSEG | |
|---|---|---|---|---|---|---|
| ... | 0064 | 2000 | ... | 08 | 09 | ... |
| +3C | +3E | +40 | +44 | +45 | +46 | |

**Figure 10.10**  TSMAP control interval statistics.

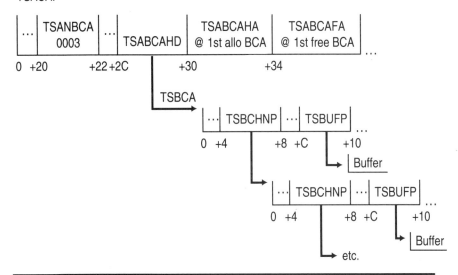

**Figure 10.11** Temporary Storage buffer pointers.

the SIT. TS=(,3,2) allocates 3 buffers (TSBCAs) and 2 strings (TSVCAs). The maxiumum number of buffers is 255, while the minimum (and default) is 3. The number of strings cannot exceed the number of buffers, and can range from 1 through 255. The default is 3.

The buffer areas are anchored in the TSACA at TSABCAHD. Each buffer area (or TSBCA) contains a pointer to the actual buffer (at TSBUFP) and to the next buffer (at TSBCHNP). The last buffer pointer contains a zero. In our system described above, with TS=(,3,2), the buffers and pointers would look like Fig. 10.11.

To satisfy a WRITEQ TD AUX request, CICS must find an available buffer. To help in its search, it maintains a couple of other pointers. TSABCAHA at offset X'30' indicates the first allocated BCA, and TSABCAHF (offset X'34') addresses the first free BCA. These two pointers are passed through the TSBNAP (allocated) and TSBNFP (free) fields at offset X'08' of each allocated or free TSBCA.

The 2-byte field TSABLKN (offset X'24') shows the number of BCAs currently locked and unavailable. If TSP needs a buffer, but they are all locked, it issues a WAIT on an ECB (TSABUECB) at offset X'50' of the TSACA. It will be posted as soon as a buffer is freed. If it specifically needs a write buffer, and they are all locked, it issues a WAIT on another ECB (TSABUEC) at offset X'68' in the TSACA, which will be posted when a write buffer is unlocked. Either of these conditions will cause a temporary storage WAIT (see Fig. 10.12).

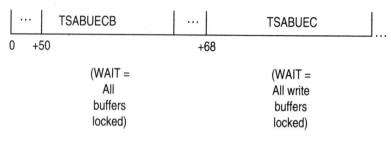

**Figure 10.12** AUX TS buffer WAITs.

A more serious temporary storage WAIT condition occurs when the data set becomes full. If this happens, TSP will try to make the data set larger by adding a new record. Because this procedure must be single-threaded, CICS controls it by using an ECB in the TSACA (TSAEX-ECB) at offset X'58'. This can eventually slow CICS to the point that it abends (or must be abended). TSP clears the ECB when it starts to extend the data set, and posts it when it is finished.

The buffer control area itself keeps track of its buffers' address and use (see Fig. 10.13). Each buffer is a copy of a VSAM CI. To manage the CIs, CICS gives each one a number, which can be found in the fullword TSBCIN field (offset X'14') of the TSBCA. TSBNASP (offset X'10') points to the next available segment within the buffer.

The status of the buffer is monitored by four flags in the TSBFLAGS field (offset X'02'). If the buffer has been updated, but has not been written yet, the first bit (TSBTBW) is set (X'80'). The next bit, called TSBLOCK (setting X'40'), indicates that the buffer is locked and cannot be used by another concurrent request. If this bit is set, the TSBLTCA field at offset X'20' contains the address of the TCA for the task

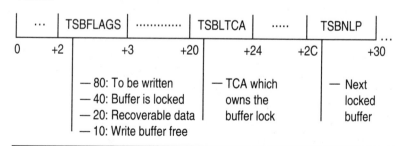

**Figure 10.13** TSBCA flags.

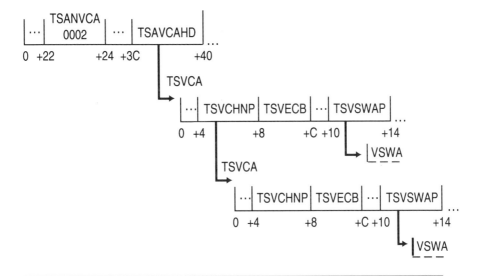

**Figure 10.14** Temporary Storage VSWA pointers.

which owns the lock. The TSBNLP field will address the next locked buffer (if any). The third bit (X'20') is set if this buffer is being used to satisfy a TS write to a recoverable queue, and is called TSBRECOV. The fourth (and last) bit shows that the write buffer is free. The mask for this setting is X'10' and is also known as TSBWBUF. The last 4 bits of this byte are unused.

The temporary storage VSWA control areas (TSVCAs) are mapped in very much the same way as the TSBCAs. The TSVCA chain is anchored in the TSACA at TSAVCAHD, and passes through the TSVCHNP field of each TSVCA. When TSP makes an I/O request to VSAM (and VSAM subtasking is not being used), it waits on the ECB at TSVECB (offset X'08'). The actual VSWA for each control area is addressed by the TSVSWAP field. If VSAM subtasking is in effect, TSP issues a WAIT on VSWAECB at offset X'70' in the VSWA itself. Our TS=(,3,2) configuration would look like Fig. 10.14.

Each TSVCA (Fig. 10.15) represents one VSWA, and has a flag field (TSVFLAGS) which is set when the VSWA is locked, is in the middle of an I/O operation, or is unused. Unlike buffer areas, which indicate the CI number, the TSVCA holds the RBA (relative byte address) of the associated VSAM data. TSVRSA is a register save area used by VSAM while performing the I/O request.

If all the strings are in use and TSP needs another, it issues a WAIT on an ECB in the TSACA (TSAVUECB) at offset X'54'. This condition

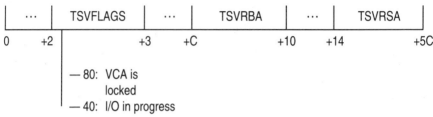

Figure 10.15  TSVCA fields.

causes a temporary storage WAIT, which will end when a string becomes available and TSAVUECB is posted.

Each CI in the AUX TS data set is represented by a corresponding byte in the temporary storage byte map (TSBM). This concept is similar to the PAM used by the SCP. Each byte shows how many segments are available in the CI. The byte map shown in Fig. 10.16 starts at offset X'20' of TSBM, which is addressed by the TSACA.

During initialization, CICS allocates a temporary storage request element block (TSREB) from the Shared subpool (Fig. 10.17). This control block holds two other control elements, TSQEs and TSREs, which are allocated for AUX TS requests. The TSREB is addressed by the TSACA at TSAREBHD. There are 512 bytes available for TSQE and TSRE storage. The amount of storage currently available is stored in the TSREBLEN field. If there is none available, TSP will dynamically allocate another TSREB and address it from the previous TSREB's TSREBCHN field.

CICS allocates a temporary storage queue element (TSQE) from the TSREB for each active AUX TS queue (Fig. 10.18). These elements are created when TSP receives requests to write to a new queue, and are deleted when all requests against the queue have completed. In the case of recoverable queues, however, the TSQE will not be deleted until the application issues a syncpoint request or the task ends. It is possi-

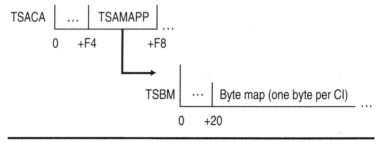

Figure 10.16  Temporary Storage byte map.

# Temporary Storage 197

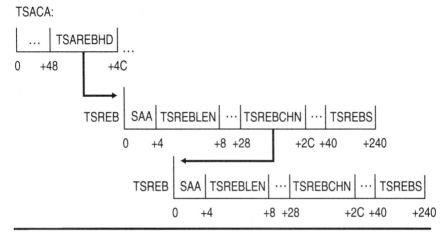

**Figure 10.17** TSREB chaining.

ble, of course, for a new request against this queue to come in before the LUW completes; in this case the TSQE will not be deleted.

To find the currently allocated TSQE for a particular queue, look at the TSUTEQEA field of the queue's entry in the TSUT. TSQEID (in the TSQE) identifies the queue's DATAID. If the TSQE is associated with a task or terminal, the task's TCA (or the terminal's TCTTE) is addressed at TSQEOA. When a request is in progress against the TSQE, TSP sets the high-order bit of TSQERIP. The TSQECHNP anchors the chain of TSREs associated with the queue.

The other type of element held in the TSREB is the temporary storage request element (TSRE), shown in Fig. 10.19. TSP allocates a TSRE for each request against AUX TS, and frees it when the exit completes. The first TSRE is addressed by the TSQECHNP field of the TSQE (see above). Further request elements are chained through the TSRE's chain pointer (TSRECHNP). If there are no further requests active, this field addresses the next free request element. TSREQID contains the DATAID, while TSRETCAA points to the TCA of the task making the request. TSRETYPE indicates the type of

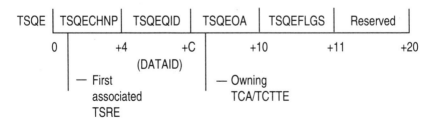

**Figure 10.18** TSQE fields.

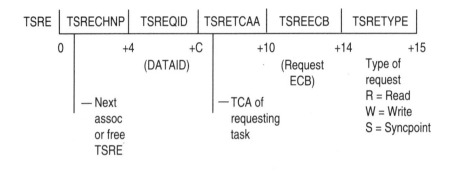

Figure 10.19  TSRE fields.

request. Temporary storage requests against a given queue are single-threaded. To enforce this, CICS uses an ECB (TSREECB) in the TSRE which is waited and posted when an operation starts and ends. This is a common cause of temporary storage WAITs. The fact that a TS queue is a single server resource can cause major performance problems.

The first flag byte (TSREFLGS) indicates whether the request is currently active and whether a restart of the request is active (see Fig. 10.20). The next four flags are used for exception processing. TSRECFLG indicates that the temporary storage request was cancelled. The next flag, TSRECTYP, shows whether the request was cancelled because of a WAIT, suspension, or I/O problem. The address of the cancelling ECB is in TSRECECA, while TSRECABC holds the abend code associated with the cancellation.

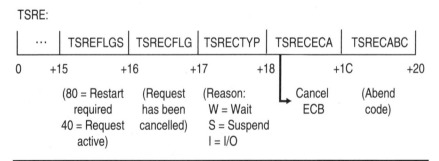

Figure 10.20  TSRE flags.

## 10.7. Defining the Temporary Storage Table (TST)

Temporary storage queues are usually created dynamically when an application writes a queue's initial record. These queues need not be defined on the TST. There are, however, three cases where the system programmer will need to predefine the queues to CICS via the TST: when the queues are protected resources and need CICS recoverability, when they exist on a remote system, and when security checking is required. In the first two cases, TST-defined queues must reside on auxiliary storage.

The first TST macro, DFHTST TYPE=INITIAL, defines the control section. As usual, the suffix (which determines the last two characters of the load module's name) is coded in the SUFFIX=xx parameter. This suffix is reflected in the DFHSIT TST=xx parameter. Other parameters available here are TST=NO|YES. TST=NO means that there is no TST, while YES tells CICS to look for an unsuffixed DFHTST. The TST TSAGE=n parameter applies to recoverable TS queues. TSAGE defines the age limit that the Temporary Storage Recovery Program (TSRP) will use during an Emergency Restart. The mininum number of days is 0 (the default), while the maximum is 512.

To make an auxiliary queue eligible for Dynamic Transaction Backout (DTB) or Emergency Restart recovery, it must be defined with a DFHTST TYPE=RECOVERY macro. (The word ENTRY can be used instead of RECOVERY, if you wish.) The only parameter for this entry is DATAID=(character-string,character-string,…). Each TYPE=RECOVERY macro can contain one DATAID parameter, and each DATAID parameter can specify several character strings, up to the limit of assembler macro coding limits. The character string can be the name of a particular queue or the first few characters of that name.

Suppose, for instance, that we have transaction UPDT which runs at terminals T001, T002, and T003, and that UPDT requires a protected TS queue. One standard naming convention for these queues specifies that the transaction name and terminal name be concatenated. In our case, this results in the queues UPDTT001, UPDTT002, and UPDTT003. We could, of course, specify each of the three in the DATAID parameter, but this would limit our transaction to these three terminals only. If terminal T004 was added to the system, the system programmer would have to add UPDTT004 to the TST. An alternative would be to code one recovery entry with DATAID=UPDT*, which will protect all UPDTxxxx TS queues.

BMS uses queues starting with the characters ** and $$. If IC START with data commands is being used, CICS generates queues starting with DF. Our resulting TST entry now looks like this:

## 200 Chapter Ten

```
DFHTST TYPE=RECOVERY,DATAID=(**,$$,DF,UPDT*)
```

To define a queue as remote, code a `TYPE=REMOTE` entry. The `DATAID` parameter is coded the same way as it is in a `TYPE=RECOVERY` entry. `SYSIDNT=` should contain the name of the remote CICS system (or region) which owns the actual temporary storage queue. This name should match the `DFHTCT TYPE=SYSTEM SYSIDNT` macro which identifies the system. If the name of the queue in the remote system is different from the one specified in the `DATAID` parameter, code that name in the `RMTNAME` parameter. One limitation here is that the length of the name given in this parameter must be the same as that of the one specified in `DATAID`.

The purpose of this parameter is to allow an application to access a TS queue in the remote region which has the same name as a queue in the local region. Recovery for remote queues can only be specified in the TST of the region which owns the queue. To provide security for specific queues, code a `TYPE=SECURITY` macro. This macro assigns an RSL (resource level) number which is used by the internal security mechanism, e.g., CICS "native" security or OMNIGUARD. It has no effect on external security mechanisms such as RACF or Top Secret.

The `DATAID` specifies the queues to be protected. Good candidates here are queues which can be browsed with the CEBR transaction. This transaction allows operators to browse queues directly and without using an application transaction. The RSL parameter will contain a security level (from 0 to 24), which CICS will check against the operator or terminal's security definition. If the number 0 is coded (the default), transactions defined with `RSLC=YES` will not be allowed to access the queue. `RSL=PUBLIC` will allow any transaction to access the queue. To declare the end of the TST, code the `DFHTST TYPE=FINAL` macro.

Chapter

# 11

# Interval Control

## 11.1. Introduction

Many events which occur in CICS are time-ordered. The Interval Control Program (ICP) controls and schedules these events, and is responsible for maintaining the CICS internal clock and synchronizing timed tasks with each other, with CICS terminal services, and with time-related data. In this chapter we will explore the IC services available to the application and how they may be used. Then we cover some ICP internals. Topics include:

- Time of day services
- Task initiation: WAIT, POST, START
- Cancelling an Interval Control request
- Interval Control data areas
- Request handling logic
- ICE expiration analysis

## 11.2. Time of Day

ICP maintains three internal time of day (TOD) clocks within the CSA (common system area). The first of these clocks is a fullword located at CSACTODB, which reflects the time of day in hundredths of a second. This clock is updated during the Task Control dispatch scan and during binary requests for the time. This request is issued internally by CICS programs via the DFHIC TYPE=GETIME,FORM=BINARY macro.

When the Task Control Program regains control from CICS (after it issues its MVS WAIT macro), it gives control to ICP. At this point, ICP

**202   Chapter Eleven**

updates another clock located at CSATODP. This is a 4-byte decimal clock (DS PL4) that stores the request in the format HHMMSSt+, where "t" is tenths of a second and "+" is a valid positive sign. Thus the hexadecimal number 093456C represents the time 09:34:56. This clock is also updated when an application program requests the time of day in a decimal format with the CICS ASKTIME request. The ASK-TIME command also updates the application fields EIBDATE and EIBTIME.

One additional clock is CSATODTU, which is saved in a fullword. This clock is more likely to be accurate than either of the above, as it is updated when either CSACTODB or CSATODP is set. This value is hard to manipulate, however, as it stores the time value in 1/300s of a second. This is the same format used by the operating system clock.

### 11.3.  Task Synchronization

ICP services can be used to synchronize task execution. The EXEC CICS DELAY command allows any application to suspend itself for a given period of time. The macro equivalent of this command is DFHIC TYPE=WAIT. Remember that the task is suspended after this command and cannot perform any actions.

The EXEC CICS POST command (or DFHIC TYPE=POST macro) gives the application a 4-byte time ECB, initialized to binary zeros, stored in the TCA at TCAICTEC. When the interval of time has expired, byte 0 is set to X'80' and byte 1 to X'40' (this provides compatibility with both MVS and DOS WAIT/POST conventions). The ECB can then be tested at intervals, or, as an alternative, the task can suspend itself with the WAIT EVENT command. The difference between DELAY and WAIT/POST EVENT is that the task can continue processing after the POST. This ECB can also be used as the ECB referred to in the EXEC CICS WAIT EVENT command or DFHKC TYPE=WAIT macro.

The timer ECB is held unaltered until one of four events occurs:

1. The interval has elapsed or the time has been reached.
2. The task issues a subsequent DFHIC TYPE= WAIT, POST, INITI-ATE, or PUT. (The command equivalents are EXEC CICS DELAY, POST, START, and START FROM.)
3. The task issues a DFHIC TYPE=CANCEL (EXEC CICS CANCEL) against the POST specifying the request id (REQID) assigned by the system to the original request.
4. The task terminates.

There are some limitations to this service. Time expiration is determined during the dispatch scan via a call from KCP to the Interval Control expiration analysis routine. Because of this, the task must give up control before the timer ECB is tested. (If the task does not give up control, CICS will never have a chance to see whether or not the interval has expired or the time has been reached.) In addition, only one current POST may exist for any given task. Any WAIT (DELAY), POST, INITIATE (START), or PUT (START FROM) request supersedes and cancels a previously issued POST.

## 11.4. Task Initiation

The most common application use of IC is the START command (DFHIC TYPE=INITIATE). With this request, one task can request the initiation of another by either time or interval. This technique was commonly used in DB2 applications (prior to dynamic plan allocation and incremental binds) to effect a plan switch (in DB2, plans are associated with transactions, not programs). The specified TRANSID is validated by a call to the Table Manager (TM), and control is returned to the program. When the interval passes or the time is reached, the new task is started. As an option, the starting task may specify that the new task may be associated with a terminal. If that terminal is the same one associated with the starting task (as is usually the case), that task must end before the new one may begin. Remember that the new task will be operating under a different LUW from the old one, so that the two tasks should not issue dependent shared updates. Dynamic transaction backout will not cross a START command.

One interesting option in the START function is the ability to pass data to the new task with the DFHIC TYPE=PUT macro or the START FROM command. Using this facility, the original task can make one record available to non-terminal-oriented tasks. Time-ordered data are available to terminal tasks. If the new (STARTed) task is in command level, it can get these data with the RETRIEVE command. Macro-level programs can find the addresses of the data in ICADDR. For terminal-oriented tasks, the first PUT or START FROM causes task initiation. Subsequent PUTs or STARTs store data to be retrieved by the initiated tasks. Interval Control uses Temporary Storage to pass these data, which have a standard variable-length format (llbb). If there is not enough room in auxiliary TS, the starting task will receive the IDERROR condition.

When a PUT request expires, the initiated task can RETRIEVE PUT (macro) or START FROM (command) data with the GET macro or RETRIEVE command. The records are presented in expiration time sequence. When a record is read, it is destroyed. Internally, the interval

**204   Chapter Eleven**

control REQID is used as the temporary storage DATAID. After the last record is RETRIEVED, the task will receive the ENDDATA condition (command) or can detect the EOD (End of Data) condition in the TCAICTR field (macro).

## 11.5.  Cancelling an Interval Control Request

To cancel any Interval Control request, a task can issue the EXEC CICS CANCEL command or DFHIC TYPE=CANCEL macro. This request cancels any previous DELAY, POST, or START. A DELAY can only be cancelled before it expires, and only by a task other than the one which issued the DELAY. (This is because the task which issued the DELAY has been suspended. By the time it is running again, the DELAY has already expired.) Because the DELAY was issued by another task, the cancelling task must specify the REQID associated with the original DELAY request. After the DELAY has been cancelled, the delayed task becomes dispatchable again.

When a POST is cancelled by the originating task, the REQID is not needed. The POST ECB is posted just as if the time had expired. To cancel a START request, the REQID must be specified. The cancellation will take effect, however, only if the time or interval has not yet expired.

## 11.6.  Interval Control Data Areas

The most important Interval Control area is the Interval Control element (ICE), which represents a time-ordered request. (See Fig. 11.1.) The ICEs are chained to the CSA in time expiration sequence from the CSAICEBA field of the CSA. Each ICE points in turn to the next ICE via the ICECHNAD field. Because each request is associated with a particular task, the ICE's ICETCAAD field addresses the associated task's TCA. The next field, ICETRNID, provides the task's transaction code or, for a WAIT, the ECB associated with the request (ICETECA). The next field, ICETYPE, identifies the type of request as follows:

X'20'   WAIT/DELAY
X'30'   POST
X'40'   INITIATE/START
X'50'   PUT/START FROM

The ICEXTOD field indicates the ICE expiration time, while ICERQID contains the request id (REQID).

## Interval Control    205

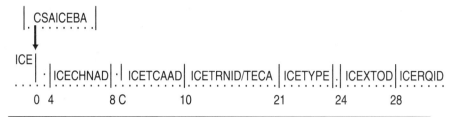

Figure 11.1   The Interval Control area.

### 11.7. Request Handling Logic

When a task issues an Interval Control request, either through a macro or through a command, the type of request is set in the TCA at TCAICTR. Control is passed to the ICP, which saves the program's registers in the task's TCAICRS field. If an interval control exit is coded, Interval Control links to it. In general, ICP calls the storage, task, and temporary storage programs to perform services. SCP is called to GETMAIN and FREEMAIN ICE storage. This ICE is used to track time-dependent requests. KCP performs a KC SUSPEND for IC WAIT requests, a KC WAIT in response to an IC POST, and a KC LOCATE to validate a transaction specified in an IC START command. Temporary Storage performs PUTs and GETs to acquire storage for IC START FROM and RETRIEVE requests. If there are any errors in the processing, ICP sets a negative return code in the task's TCA. The EXEC Interface will cause a condition to be raised in the application program.

Let us look at these requests a little more closely. A START command becomes a DFHIC TYPE=INIT macro. If the command specifies the FROM option, it becomes a DFHIC TYPE=PUT macro. ICP verifies the specified transid by issuing a DFHKC TYPE=LOCATE macro. If the transaction specifies a terminal, ICP issues a DFHTC TYPE=LOCATE to force Terminal Control to verify its existence. If not, ICP simply clears the task's TCAICTID field. If all has gone well, an ICE is created and initialized. If this is a START FROM command, ICP issues a DFHTS TYPE=PUT macro to Temporary Storage to hold the data in auxiliary storage with a class of IC. This is a conditional request, so if there are any problems, the task will not be suspended.

The RETRIEVE command becomes a DFHIC TYPE=GET macro. When ICP receives this macro, it determines whether the requesting task is associated with a terminal. If it is, ICP searches for an automatic initiate descriptor (AID; see Chap. 12, "Transient Data") by using the DFHAL TYPE=ICP1 macro. If no terminal is involved, this step is skipped. If the task is defined with DTB, ICP saves information about

**206   Chapter Eleven**

the ICE (or AID) in a deferred work element (DWE). This is so that the information can be re-created later, as ICP is now going to issue an SCP TYPE=FREEMAIN against the ICE (or AID). The next step is to actually retrieve the date by reading from temporary storage to the user error. If this read fails, ICP will try one more time before setting a negative response.

When ICP receives a WAIT request, it creates and chains the ICE, then issues a DFHKC TYPE=SUSPEND for the task. After the WAIT interval expires, it frees the ICE. In POST processing, ICP creates the ICE, clears out the timer ECB, then chains the ICE, before issuing a DFHKC TYPE=WAIT,DCI=DISP macro. ICP checks to make sure that this is not a Journal Control task before issuing the WAIT macro.

It is possible to CANCEL an Interval Control request. If the REQID is not supplied, ICP assumes that a task is cancelling its own request. First, it clears the task's TCA ICE address, then it unchains the ICE. If the CANCEL is for a PUT macro (START FROM command), ICP calls Transient Data to perform the automatic transaction initiation (ATI) release routine.

If the REQID is specified, the requesting task is trying to CANCEL a request that it did not originate, and the procedure is quite different. If the request was a protected START FROM command (PUT, DEFER macro), ICP searches the DWE list for a PUT DWE with the given REQID. If one is found, the DWE is unchained and released. This is done because the ICE was never created. Because the request was protected, ICP had made a notation in the DWE to create the ICE later, when the requesting task reached a syncpoint. For other requests, the ICE chain is searched for an ICE with the given REQID, and the ICE is cancelled.

During all this processing, ICP does not actually ever WAIT for an event to complete. It does, however, pass control to KCP in response to a DFHIC TYPE=POST macro, to allow a task switch. It does this by issuing a DFHKC TYPE=WAIT,DCI=DISP. As we will recall from our discussion of KCP, this is not really a WAIT, as KCP has shifted control to its own TCA at the time. The WAIT macro simply returns to KCP, which called DFHICP in the first place.

### 11.8.   ICE Expiration Analysis

When the Task Control task (the mighty KC) receives control from the operating system, the first thing it does is to check and see whether any requests have expired. It does this by branching to the ICP via the DFHIC TYPE=EXPYANAL macro. The first step this routine takes is to determine if any unusual conditions exist. If CICS is SOS (Short on Storage), at MXT (Maximum Tasks), or in the process of shutting down, the routine is bypassed. Normally, however, it will examine each ICE, looking for those whose time has come and performing different actions for each expired ICE, depending on the request it represents. One thing all the processes have in common is that an expired ICE is unchained.

For a WAIT request, the suspended task is resumed. A POST ICE causes the associated ECB to be set to complete. If the ICE has been cancelled, it is unchained, and if it is a PUT ICE, the associated temporary storage area is freed. If the request is associated with a terminal, the ICE is unchained, and a DFHKC TYPE=SCHEDULE is issued to begin the process of associating the task with its terminal (when and if that terminal is free). A PUT ICE initiates a DFHKC TYPE=ATTACH macro to begin execution of the requested task.

Chapter

# 12

# Transient Data

## 12.1. Introduction

In earlier CICS, destinations functioned primarily as aliases for standard report printers, but today automatic task initiation (ATI) has become a key consideration in good system design. Internal and external destinations are discussed, with attention paid to the Transient Data Program's ability to communicate with file access methods not supported by the File Control Program interface.

Topics covered in this chapter are:

- Typical uses of intra and extra destinations
- How automatic task initiation (ATI) works
- The mechanisms of physical and logical recovery
- How to define TD destinations in the DCT
- Sample table entries to define a 3270 printer queue
- Transient Data services flow
- DWEs, AIDs, and ICEs
- Transient Data user exits

## 12.2. Transient Data Overview

Transient Data (TD) is a generalized queueing facility through which we can store data for later CICS processing or for off-line processing. We can move data from destinations which are either inside or outside CICS. Before MRO or ISC was available, people sometimes communicated between CICS regions by sharing a common TD queue. This was

**210  Chapter Twelve**

done by setting up a QSAM data set, which was defined in each region as an extrapartition destination. Each CICS would continually check the data set.

What are some differences between transient data and temporary storage queues?

- You do not need to predefine a temporary storage queue, whereas each transient data queue must be defined in the Destination Control Table (DCT).

- Items from a TD queue are read sequentially and destructively, as opposed to TS queue items, which may be read randomly or sequentially, and which remain on the queue until specifically deleted.

- TD queues reside on disk or tape, while TS queues can reside on disk (TS AUX) or in main storage (TS MAIN).

- TD queues may be used to communicate outside the CICS region (extrapartition) as well as within CICS (intrapartition).

- TD queues often contain more than one record, while TS queues of more than one record are used only when direct access or repeated access is necessary.

A TD queue can do these things a TS queue cannot:

- Start a CICS transaction

- Generate a batch job (JCL) to be run outside CICS

- Write to tape (journal)

The Transient Data Program also provides support for sequential files, which can be important since the File Control Program offers no support for non-VSAM sequential files. However, there is a performance consideration, since processing a QSAM file causes the CICS region to wait for the completion of an I/O.

### 12.3.  Intrapartition Destinations

After 1.6, queues of data are held in direct-access VSAM data sets. CICS transactions can access intrapartition destinations. These records are variable-length, and the space is reusable. When REUSE=YES, the Transient Data Program (DFHTDP) controls reusability. When REUSE=NO, the application can control it, by issuing purges. REUSE=NO means that the read is not destructive. Applications can issue TD macros that do not cause a destructive read, but in macro level only. (This is an old feature, not available in command level.)

### 12.3.1. Typical uses

Some typical uses of intrapartition TD are:

- Serial processing of transactions, such as one in which order numbers are assigned
- Batching of input data to be processed asynchronously
- Routing data or message switching
- Control of file updates.
- Starting tasks via ATI
- Printing via ATI

For high-speed data entry, the data can be entered onto a queue which is processed separately, without tying up the operator's data entry terminal. We can control file updates in a similar manner. Our application might have a very busy transaction whose purpose is to update a file. We do not wish to tie the transaction up with a lot of File Control requests. So instead, we will write to a TD queue. And later, another transaction will read the queue, perhaps when 20 items have accumulated, and do file updates. This eliminates a lot of file overhead up front. The writer task reads the queue and writes to a file. We can even associate it with a file in the DCT (DESTFAC=FILE), although this feature is not used often. Automatic task initiation (ATI) is accomplished through use of intrapartition destinations defined in the DCT.

### 12.3.2. Recovery

Intrapartition destinations can be recovered after a system abend by reconstructing the DCT from log records written before the abend. This is performed automatically by Emergency Restart and DTB. There are two types of recovery: physical, which is systemwide, and logical, which applies to a unit of work on the task level.

How is recovery accomplished? The system log has pointers to the DCT, which has pointers to the actual space on the DFHINTRA data set. Those pointers are logged for each entry after the first write and after every GET and PUT. For physical recovery, the DCT entry input pointers are restored from the system log where the GETs and PURGEs were recorded. The first PUT to an empty queue is always logged.

The TDP recovery program reads the queue forward and sets the output pointer to the end of the queue. For logical recovery, the queue is restored to the way it was at the last syncpoint. The same mechanism of pointers applies, but in a different context. When we want to back out something that we have written, what really happens? We have

## 212 Chapter Twelve

written a record, and have done physical I/O. But to back it out, the deferred work element (DWE) just moves the pointer back. See Chap. 13, "Recovery/Restart Facilities," for a more detailed discussion.

### 12.4. Extrapartition Destinations

An extrapartition destination can be DASD, tape, or printer. Disk data sets are sequential and processed under QSAM, are fixed or variable in length, are blocked or unblocked, and are nonrecoverable. Each extrapartition destination is defined in the DCT with a TYPE=EXTRA macro. This is in turn associated with a TYPE=SDSCI macro, which provides data set control information and generates the necessary data set control blocks (DTFs and DCBs).

#### 12.4.1. Typical uses

Extrapartition transient data has many uses, some of which are:

- System statistics
- Transaction error messages
- Data that can be applied off-line
- Message queueing
- Journaling
- Batch job submission via internal reader
- Data input (sequential data created by non-CICS programs can enter CICS as extrapartition destination data sets)

#### 12.4.2. Batch job submission via internal reader

We can define the internal reader as an extrapartition destination by using a destination of SYSOUT=A, INTRDR. This lets us submit JCL to the internal reader, and most of the old JES job submission packages and programs worked this way. For example, if we needed to write out 30 pages of something, we defined the internal reader and wrote some JCL to it, and JES picked it up and started a batch job. This was a way to offload the work to JES or POWER. For volume printing, offloading was preferable to using the intrapartition facility for printing within the CICS region.

### 12.5. Indirect Destinations

Indirect destinations take things one step further. An indirect destination is a pointer, or reference to another queue. Both intra- and extrapartition destinations can be referenced indirectly. This provides flexibility in programming maintenance, since DCT entries can be changed without recompiling programs. We can point to an entry from other entries, so that if we change an entry, all we need do is change the indirect destination in the DCT.

In other words, there is one DCT direct entry pointing to another DCT indirect entry, so if our program says WRITE to PRNT and we have a new standards manual that says PRNT is now spelled RPNT, we can keep PRNT and point it to the new DCT entry called RPNT. This becomes an indirect reference. We write to PRNT, which just points to RPNT. In addition to allowing this kind of substitution, TYPE=INDIRECT also allows several TD queues to be merged into one physical destination. The DCT entry TYPE=INDIRECT is always associated with another entry, which is either a TYPE=EXTRA or TYPE=INTRA destination.

## 12.6. Automatic Task Initiation (ATI)

Intrapartition transient data is one of the CICS mechanisms that enable automatic task initiation (ATI). Destinations, transids, trigger levels, and terminals are specified in the DCT. An entry is defined in the DCT for an intrapartition destination with a trigger level and transaction id. When data are sent to the queue, and the number of queue entries reaches a predefined level, a transaction will be initiated. The ATI transaction may be associated with a terminal (or printer), and it is able to process data on the queue that initiated it.

ATI allows the transaction to be initiated immediately, or when its associated terminal (if any) is free. By using the trigger and ATI, an application program can start tasks, switch messages to terminals, and write reports to printers, perform deferred database update, write statistics, etc.

### 12.6.1. Printing via ATI

Let us discuss how to make use of ATI to write to a 3270 printer. The 3270 printer is defined as a terminal in the TCT. Why not just use a SEND or WRITE command? One problem is that other people can do this too, contributing to a tower of Babel effect. The other problem is that a SEND command is issued to a specified printer.

The SEND goes to the principal facility associated with the task, the principal facility being the TCTTE pointed to by the task's TCA. Even though we cannot simply send to a printer, we can get another task to do it for us; Transient Data gives us this facility. We can set up a DCT entry and associate it with the transaction id of the printer task. In addition to the DCT entry, entries in four other tables are needed.

## 214 Chapter Twelve

DCT entry:
     DFHDCT  TYPE = INTRA, DESTID = T032, DESTFAC = TERMINAL, TRANSID = L86P

PCT entry:
     DFHPCT  TYPE = ENTRY, TRANSID = L86P, PROGRAM = DFHTDWT$

PPT entry:
     DFHPPT  TYPE = ENTRY, PROGRAM = DFHTDWT$

TCT entry:
     DFHTCT  TYPE = TERMINAL, TRMIDNT = T032

FCT entry:
     DFHFCT  TYPE = DATASET, DATASET = DFHNTRA

**Figure 12.1**  Sample table entries for a printer destination.

Figure 12.1 shows the various table entries and how they are tied together. The DCT entry defines the destination facility as a terminal, the destination identification as T032, and the transaction identification as L86P. T032 is the 3270 printer, which is defined as a terminal in the TCT. L86P, which is defined in the PCT, is the transaction that will be initiated. DFHTDWT$, which is the program invoked by L86P, is defined in the PPT. The FCT entry names the data set DFHNTRA, which is the VSAM data set that will contain all the intrapartition queues.

If the destination facility (DESTFAC) is a terminal, TDP sets a bit in TCTTE to initiate the task. If the DESTFAC is a file, TDP asks KCP to attach the task, and there is no terminal involved. Either way, the new task then issues GETs to deplete the queue. If you do not specify TRMIDNT on the DESTFAC parameter of the TYPE=INTRA macro, it defaults to the value of DESTID, as in the above example, where the queue name and terminal id are the same. For the rest of this discussion we will refer to a DCT destination that we will call PRNT. We will associate it with a transaction called SEND.

The name of the destination, PRNT, is the name of the entry in the DCT, the DESTID. When we do a WRITEQ TD we specify PRNT, and we associate it with the transaction SEND. SEND is going to issue a Terminal Control WRITE or an EXEC CICS SEND or SEND MAP. To which terminal does the transaction SEND issue the TC WRITE? To the terminal associated with PRNT. In the TCT we define an entry called PRT1. The DCT entry is associated with the terminal PRT1 by specifying TRMIDNT on the DESTFAC parameter. So when we write something to the queue PRNT, we want Transient Data to start the task SEND, making PRT1 its principal facility and loading its address in the TCA facility control area address (TCAFCAAA). When there is no principal facility,

|  | DCT entry | Where defined |
|---|---|---|
| Destination name | PRNT | DCT |
| Trigger level | 3 | DCT |
| Transaction id | SEND | PCT |
| Associated facility | PRT1 | TCT |

**Figure 12.2** DCT values.

the TCAFCAAA is X'00'. If we also want this transaction to start every time there are three records on the queue, we can associate a trigger level of 3 with PRNT. What we have, then, is shown in Fig. 12.2.

### 12.6.2. Trigger levels

Often, a trigger level of 1 is used to initiate a task which reads a queue, moves the data from the queue into a TIOA, and then issues a TC WRITE or the command-level equivalent. The danger of putting more than 1 in the trigger level is that if we had 3,987 writes to the queue, we might miss one. It is possible to set it up so that the transaction will read to QZERO. What will that save us? If we do 9,000 writes and the trigger level is 1, how many attaches is TDP going to issue? Up to 9,000. If this is a heavy transaction, and it usually is, reading to QZERO could save attach overhead.

What happens when there are three items on the queue and the trigger level is zero? Will Transient Data attach the task? The answer is no. Many shops experience big bottlenecks with hanging ICEs waiting for these things. But you can zap the trigger level to zero (using CEMT or the Intertest CORE transaction, for example) in order to prevent the attaching of tasks temporarily and clear bottlenecks.

A better way might be to write a program that can be used to clear the queue to zero. You can use Interval Control to close and open the gates for particular time spans. For example, you could create a transaction that closes down specified DCT entries for a period of minutes. What we are doing is temporarily preventing the initiation of print tasks. A suggested techique is to single-thread and read to QZERO. We can achieve single threading either by issuing an explicit enqueue or by class MAX TASKing it (CMXT in the SIT in conjunction with TCLASS in the PCT). It makes sense to single-thread, as a transaction will be faster than a CICS printer.

Using the Transient Data ATI facility for printing is not always the right solution. There is very little recovery, and no reprint facility. It was designed to send occasional screens of data to the printer. When broadcasting to a whole network or doing volume printing, we need something more sophisticated, for example, offloading the work to JES or POWER.

### 12.6.3. AID chains

An automatic initiate descriptor (AID) is created for each ATI request and keeps information needed by the task. It is added to an AID chain (Fig. 12.3), sequenced by a symbolic task id within a symbolic terminal id, and remains there until the task initiates or until it retrieves data, if there are data. AID chains look suspiciously like ICE chains. In fact, they are really the same control block, and ICEs melt into AIDs when they expire. The CSA points to an AID chain, which is chained the same as an ICE and has the same SAA as an ICE.

So what is the difference between an AID and an ICE? The difference is that with Interval Control to the terminal we have to wait for the time to expire and the terminal to become available, while in Transient Data we just have to wait for the terminal to become available. So in Interval Control we start with an ICE, and when the interval expires, that ICE essentially becomes an AID. There is a little difference here though: AIDTYPE says that it was initiated by TDP. AIDSTATI says that it was an ICE. The CSA anchors the AID chain. The TSTTE for PRT1 points to the AID. And the DCTE for PRT1 is also chained to the AID. If this was not associated with a terminal, we would not be talking through a TCTTE.

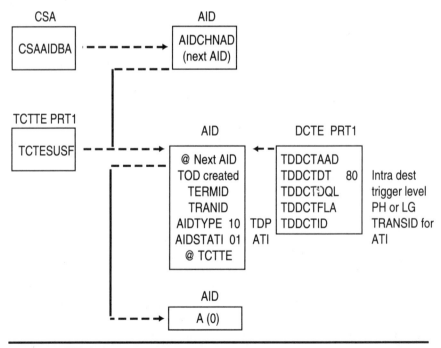

**Figure 12.3** AID chain.

## 12.7. Transient Data Services Flow

Figure 12.4 shows the flow of Transient Data services. The application supplies two items: the type of request, which goes into TCATDTR, being put there by DFHETD, and DESTID, in TCATDDI. The Transient Data Program looks through the DCT, looks to see that the DESTID and the request are valid, then looks to see if the request is extrapartition; if it is, it issues a QSAM request and exits. If it is intrapartition, a KC enqueue is issued. KC will enqueue on the DCT and the VSAM control blocks associated with this particular destination. At this point the enqueue is on the character string, which is the name of the DESTID, that is, the name of the queue. The ENQ remains for the duration of the request, after which a DEQ is issued.

Now we look to see if there is any recovery defined for this destination. Recovery associated with the VSAM control blocks associated with this destination is mechanical, and not of concern here. TD will ENQ essentially on the name of the entry, whether or not recovery is generated. If there is logical recovery, it will enqueue on the end of the queue. This means that if we have six records there, TD will enqueue all the way out, so that nobody can read anything. This creates a DWE, or something we are not going to do yet.

If recovery is physical, we log the DCT entry. If there is a system crash now, all we are interested in is putting the DCT entry back the way it was after the last successful TD operation. If recovery is logical, we want it to go back to the way it was at the end of the last logical unit of work, so we create the DWE.

The KC ENQ to end of queue goes away at the end of the LUW. The DWE processor will kick it off later. At the end of the LUW, the Syncpoint Program (SPP) will call the Transient Data DWE processor. The DWE processor will perform the actual operation of backing out the I/O. If recovery is logical, we back out in-flight tasks and back out the changes they have made on logically recoverable resources. If recovery is physical, DTB does not even touch it; we do not get a dynamic log record; nothing happens. The only time there will be recovery for physically protected queues is during Emergency Restart. If we are using physical recovery with a task using DTB, be aware that the queue may or may not be logically recoverable, and realize what the ramifications are.

Next we do a Storage Control GET for an input area. In the DCT there is a map of the disk area. (You can look it up in the OSI handbook or CICS data areas.) We look to see if this is an ATI type of request. If it is not ATI, we exit. If so ATI, is it associated with a transaction? If so, is the transaction associated with a terminal? If not, then issue a KC ATTACH, and we finish.

## 218 Chapter Twelve

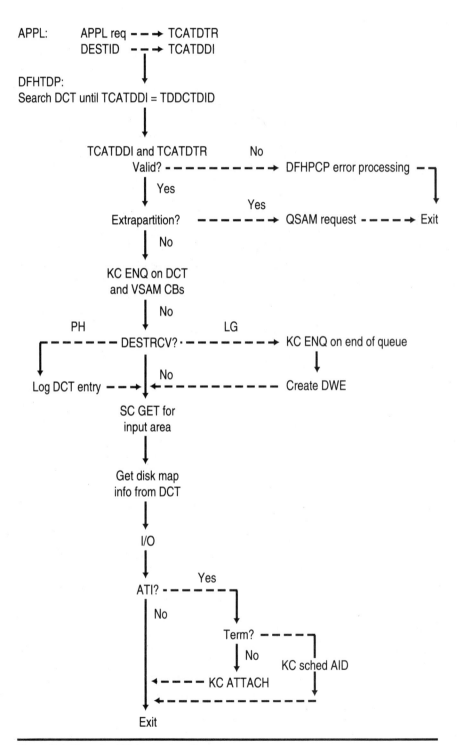

**Figure 12.4** Transient Data services flow.

If the ATI request is associated with a terminal, then issue a KC Schedule AID. This is the same thing done by Interval Control when a specified time elapses. It is the same macro, and what it does in this case is hang an AID off the TCTTE. The KC Schedule AID performs the following:

1. Hang the AID off the terminal.

2. Ask Terminal Control if the terminal is available.

3. If the terminal is available, ask Terminal Control to issue an `ATTACH`.

What we have is Task Control issuing a Terminal Control macro which asks Terminal Control to go into dispatch logic so that it can issue an `ATTACH` to Task Control! It seems convoluted, but it has a good purpose, as it makes things pretty bulletproof. If the terminal is not ready, an AID pending bit is set, and Terminal Control, whenever it gets control as a task, looks to see if there are any AIDs hanging off this TCTTE. If there are, and the terminal is free, Terminal Control issues an `ATTACH` for the transaction named in the AID.

What is illustrated here is that all the basic CICS ground rules apply: Each task performs only its special function, and every control program performs its special functions and directs requests for other services to other functions; therefore when Task Control wants to do something with the terminal, it issues a Terminal Control request, even if that will only drive a Task Control request over a Terminal Control request.

## 12.8. Transient Data Facilities

The three basic facilities available to the application are `READQ TD`, `WRITEQ TD`, and `DELETEQ TD`, or the `DFHTD TYPE-PUT`, `TYPE=GET`, and `TYPE=PURGE` macros. Normally a read is destructive and the pointer to the record is erased after it is read. You can specify that you do not want destructive read in the DCT. In this case it is up to the application to issue the purge.

## 12.9. Transient Data User Exits

User exits allow you to effectively install a user modification without really doing so, that is, without changing IBM code. To use the facility, you simply write a program, define it in the processing program table, and enable it. There are three user exits within the transient data program:

- *XTDREQ:* Before the type of request
- *XTDIN:* Before processing an input request
- *XTDOUT:* After the DCT entry is found, but before output

In all of these exits, R3 points to the DCT entry. The only exit taken for extrapartition destinations is XTDREQ.

Chapter

# 13

# Recovery/Restart Facilities

## 13.1. Introduction

With the knowledge of CICS internals at your disposal, you should now begin to explore recovery options from the point of view of the application, keeping design considerations in mind.

Topics include the types of recovery available, both logging and journaling, how the Journal Control Program works and how it is generated, how to customize with user-written code, and how to approach the definition and implementation of standards and procedures. At the end of this chapter you will be able to:

- Describe how CICS recovery facilities work and the different types of initialization available

- Generate the programs and tables required for recovery/restart

- Define data sets for recovery/restart

- Understand the purpose and possibilities of user-written code to tailor and expand recovery/restart

- Review or define application standards to make them consistent with recovery conventions

- Develop operating standards and procedures for recovery/restart

## 13.2. A Recovery Philosophy

This chapter is written with the philosophy that recovery is not something to be added on at the end of a project, but something that should

**222 Chapter Thirteen**

be designed in at the start. Where recovery is concerned, people often try to build the basement before the house: they add recovery on later, and end up with something that is a little makeshift. Too often we see a version of this scenario: an attempt is made to "fit" an application into CICS, first getting it to communicate somehow, then adding on a little recovery, and finally trying to get response time down.

The best recovery is thought of at application design time. As such, it is a subject of interest in both the systems and applications areas. The question we might need to be asking is: Can we fit the people who know how CICS works into the design phase (and even into the requirements phase when performance is a requirement)? We might also hope that there is evolving a breed of system designer who is keenly aware of how CICS works, how CICS communicates with the host and other systems, what resources are available and how they are recovered, and how solutions can be programmed to run well in the CICS environment. More and more systems programmers are being called upon to participate in design sessions. Conversely, if the application programmer understands the impact of recovery, a better application—one that works with CICS, not against it—will be written.

Another area of great importance is proper design and implementation of recovery procedures. Not only is the design of procedures important but also the clear communication to the operations area of how these procedures must be carried out. Both regular and on-off emergency types of backup/recovery procedures must be set up so that they are understood and can be carried out correctly. Needless to say, they should be tested with dry runs.

### 13.2.1. Restart and recovery objectives

What are the objectives of restart/recovery? First, to be able to recover from task-related errors and, if this is not possible, to back out changes to protected resources such as files, databases, temporary storage, and transient data. The other objective is to recover from system-related errors, and if CICS must terminate, to control the termination in order to allow recovery during restart. In general, the idea is to try to contain a failure so that it will affect only one end user, one database, one application.

Some characteristics of errors are that they tend to occur randomly, they should not normally occur, and they may cause the task or CICS itself to terminate. An error may occur within an application; in CICS; in the operating system, access method, or database; or in the CPU itself or peripheral hardware. In some cases recovery code may not even have a chance to be executed, if it is beyond the control of CICS. That is why the topic in this chapter is called recovery/restart, not just recovery.

## 13.3. Types of Recovery

Within CICS there are two types of recovery, backward and forward. Backward recovery reverses updates to a recoverable resource, returning the resource to its status before the error. This requires that the contents of the resource, the before-image, be recorded before any update. CICS code exists to perform this function. Forward recovery allows the reconstruction of a file or database if it becomes unusable. This requires that the updated resource, or after-image, be recorded after the change. The resource can then be restored by merging the after-images with a previously recorded backup copy.

As an illustration of forward recovery, suppose we take a weekly or daily backup of a file on Monday night, then Tuesday at 2:00 p.m. the pack gets clobbered for whatever reason—maybe the VSAM catalog was destroyed. We use the backup copy to re-create the file the way it looked Monday night, then we run through the journal, applying the records as they occur sequentially in time, until finally we have recovered to where we were before the pack died. For standard access methods, this can get pretty tricky if you extend the concept to recovering 20 interrelated files.

There are packages now on the market, as well as a product from IBM called CICSVR, which provide forward recovery from user journals. This will be covered in Chap. 15, under new products and changes pertaining to recovery that have recently become available.

Again we need to assess the value of building in recovery over adding it on, perhaps thus making a much stronger case for using a database. However, this being the real world, it is often too late for such a choice, and we may have to retrofit recovery to an existing VSAM application.

Another consideration is on-line versus batch forward recovery: it may make sense to do it off-line, which is the way CICSVR does it. This is usually a very time-pressured situation. When a system comes down, most shops have requirements that CICS must be back up within a certain time period.

In contrast, backward recovery does not reconstruct, it backs out. For example, if a task updates two files, we do not want to update one file and not the other, so if the task abends before the second update, we need to back out the first.

The mechanism used for backward recovery is called logging, and that for forward recovery is called journaling. There is sometimes confusion in the way that IBM discusses journals and logs; for example, sometimes a journal is described as "keeping log records." It is not always clear-cut, and could have been done better, but keep in mind that CICS was not designed originally with recovery/restart in mind. This

## 224 Chapter Thirteen

was added on later, which provides our first example of the problems with add-on recovery.

In summary, backward recovery reads backward through the system log, applying before-images. It is automatically performed by CICS. Forward recovery reads forward through a user journal or file, applying after-images. It must be performed by a utility, and is not automatic.

### 13.3.1. Recoverable resources

In order to be recoverable, a resource must be defined as protected. Resources that may be protected include CICS files, Transient Data intrapartition queues, Temporary Storage auxiliary queues, databases, and VTAM messages.

Transient Data intrapartition queues may be protected with either physical or logical recovery. Logical recovery means that DTB or Emergency Restart backs out the TD intra destination to what it looked like before a logical unit of work (LUW) was interrupted. Physical recovery means that Emergency Restart will restore the destination to the way it was when CICS came down. Thus the place of restoration would depend on the type of recovery defined for the queue. If physical, the restoration would be to the last record written before CICS abended. If logical, restoration would be to what the queue looked like at the start of the transaction that was writing to the queue when it or CICS abended.

To protect a Temporary Storage queue, we must define it in the Temporary Storage Table (TST). DB2 and DL/I take care of themselves. All databases are recoverable, and need not be defined as such. If VTAM messages are defined as recoverable, CICS logs the I/O messages and makes them available to the application after a system failure. If the terminal supports the STSN (set and test sequence number) command, CICS can resynchronize and retransmit messages during Emergency Restart.

### 13.3.2. Recovery facilities

Recovery facilities extend to both system- and task-related failures. However, if a system task such as Task Control, Terminal Control, or Journal Control abends, there is no recovery capability. In these cases only restart facilities are available.

CICS provides the following system recovery facilities:

- System logging via Journal Control Program (DFHJCP)
- System Recovery Program (DFHSRP) and Table (DFHSRT)
- Emergency Restart

The System Recovery Program intercepts task abends to allow CICS to continue and also cleans up before a CICS abend. DFHSRP's associated table, DFHSRT, is basically a list of abend codes that get trapped, along with the action that is to be taken for each code. At startup you see the message that ESTAEs (STIXITs for DOS) have been issued. This means that if an application gets a S0C7, as far as MVS is concerned, DFHSIP (the name by which CICS is known to the MVS dispatcher) took the S0C7. In this event DFHSRP will intercept via the ESTAE to ensure that CICS does not abend. Of course, CICS will still abend if a system task is involved.

Emergency Restart (ER) executes, as the name implies, during startup after a CICS abend. ER backs out resources that are defined as protected, resets intrapartition Transient Data and auxiliary Temporary Storage queues that are protected, and in some cases resynchronizes protected VTAM messages. The system log is the mechanism used by these facilities to perform their functions.

CICS provides the following task recovery facilities:

- CICS request error handling routines
- TEP/NEP
- Task abend exits
- DTB of protected resources
- Transaction restart

Request error handling routines are provided to the application in the `HANDLE CONDITION` command or, more recently, by interrogation of the EIB response code via DFHRESP. The latter allows writing of more structured code by avoiding the implied `GOTO` of a `HANDLE`. The Terminal Error Program (TEP) and Node Error Program (NEP) are error handlers for terminal and network problems. A task abend exit is available to the application through the `HANDLE ABEND` command. CICS provides DTB by maintaining a dynamic log for a transaction that is specified as a `DTB=YES` transaction in the PCT. Transaction restart takes place when CICS comes up after a failure, but is useful only under certain limited conditions.

## 13.4. Error Analysis

The chart in Fig. 13.1 shows the types of errors at both the task and system level, the module that detects the error, and possibly what type of error, the code or facility to perform recovery, and additional optional termination processing that is available.

226 **Chapter Thirteen**

| Error | Analysis | Recovery | Opt. termination processing |
|---|---|---|---|
| **TASK LEVEL** | | | |
| Abnormal RC from macro or command | DFHEIP, User code | HANDLE CONDITION, Processing continues | User ABEND exit, CICS DFHDBP, User DFHPEP |
| Terminal or network error | NACP/TACP | NEP/TEP, User–coded DFHSRT routines | NEP/TEP, User ABEND exit, DFHDBP, DFHPEP |
| Program check in application | DFHSRP | User ABEND exit | CICS DFHDBP, User DFHPEP |
| **SYSTEM LEVEL** | | | |
| CICS takes an OS or DOS ABEND | DFHSRP | User–coded DSHSRT routines | User–coded DFHSRT routines |
| Program check in CICS system task | DFHSRP | None | None |
| OS, DOS ABEND or WAIT state | None | None | None |

**Figure 13.1** Types of errors, analysis, and recovery.

## 13.5. LUWs and Syncpoints

An LUW may be defined as a sequence of actions that must be completed before any of the individual actions may be committed. This sequence is delineated by a syncpoint. The LUW may encompass start of task to syncpoint, or syncpoint to syncpoint, or syncpoint to end of task.

Normally a syncpoint occurs at the start and end of a task. This is called an implicit syncpoint, one that does not need to be issued. A syncpoint may also be issued explicitly in either command or macro. When would you issue it? Possibly in a long-running task with multiple updates—for instance, in a conversational program, or even in a pseudo-conversational environment, where LINKs and XCTLs allow multiple modules to be invoked without starting a new task.

When a syncpoint is issued, if there is any work that was deferred by CICS, it gets processed now. At this point the changes are committed—there is no turning back, so to speak—and the protection of the file or resource is ended. Backout will not be performed in the event of an abend after the syncpoint, even if the task is still in flight.

Each LUW has a unique name, known as the recovery token, that is stored at TCARKTN at the start of each unit of recovery. It contains the STCK value and identifies the CICS system and any other system that communicates with it.

Figure 13.2 contains two examples of LUWs. The first is pretty simple: we do a READ UPDATE followed by a REWRITE, a WRITEQ, and a RETURN, which is a syncpoint, after which the updates cannot be backed out. If CICS takes a hit between the REWRITE and the WRITEQ, the REWRITE update will be backed out. The next example is a little more complicated: the program goes through a loop. Each time it reads a TD queue record, it does a REWRITE of a record, and each time it REWRITEs, it wants that work to be committed. If there is an abend, perhaps after the READ UPDATE, the TD queue must be restored.

As a TD read is destructive, you have to be careful about whether it is physically or logically restored, or at Emergency Restart you might find yourself with one fewer record than expected. Let us say we do a READQ TD for item 999, which is then gone from the queue, as the read is destructive. We then do a READ UPDATE and the system takes a hit. Now we start back up again with Emergency Restart. If the queue is logically recoverable, the TD queue is put back the way it was before

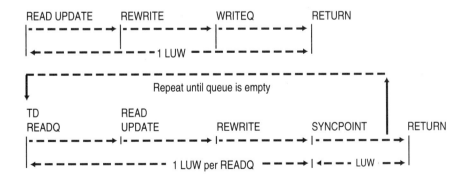

**Figure 13.2** LUW examples.

**228  Chapter Thirteen**

```
                                                              !S!
Task 1 |  - → UPDATE - → SYNCPOINT  - → READ - → UPDATE- - !Y!
                        |← - - - - - BACKOUT TASK 1 - - - - - - !S!
                                                              !T!
                                                              !E!
Task 2 |  - → RECEIVE - → READ - → UPDATE - →   RETURN        !M!
                                                              ! !
                      (PSEUDOCONVERSATIONAL)                   !C!
                                                              !R!
Task 3 |  → READ → WRITE → RETURN | TASK 4 | → READ→ WRITE- !A!
                                  |← - - BACKOUT TASK 4 - - - !S!
                                                              !H!
```

**Figure 13.3**  Backout examples.

this LUW started. We were in flight, in the middle of an LU, when the lightning hit the CPU, so the entire queue is restored. But if the queue is physically recoverable, the pointers are restored to where they were when CICS abended, and since item 999 was already gone from the queue, it is not restored.

Figure 13.3 illustrates how tasks are backed out in the event of a system crash. Task 1 issues an explicit syncpoint, and tasks 2 and 3, by issuing a RETURN, issue implicit syncpoints.

Figure 13.4 contrasts the task abend and the CICS abend in terms of when the backout occurs, what gets backed out, and how. It should be noted that in the case of a CICS abend, backout is not performed by the Dynamic Backout Program (DBP), but is performed by the Transaction Backout Program (TBP) during Emergency Restart.

|      | Task abend | CICS abend |
|------|------------|------------|
| When | During task abend processing | During Emergency Restart |
| What | Protected resources modified within the task's in-flight LUW | Protected resources modified by all in-flight LUW's |
| How  | Uses info saved in the dynamic log and deferred work elements | Uses info written to the system log during the previous CICS execution (which abended) |

**Figure 13.4**  Task abend vs. CICS abend.

## 13.6. Logging and Journaling

Figure 13.5 delineates the different types of information that are contained in system and dynamic logs and user journals. It includes a description of who writes the information and when, and also who reads it and when. Note that you can journal to the system journal, which is also called the system log, if you specify `JID=SYSTEM`. In this case you journal after-images to the same place that you normally log before-images, in effect using the system log as a user journal.

| | User journal (Journals 2 - 99) | System log (Journal 1) | Dynamic log (main storage) |
|---|---|---|---|
| Contains | AFTER-IMAGES USER INFORMATION | BEFORE-IMAGES DL/I INFO INTRA TD POINTERS TS QUEUE INFO SNA SEQUENCE NOS. SYNCPOINT RECORDS ACTIVITY KEYPOINTS USER INFORMATION, AFTER-IMAGES, IF JID-SYSTEM | BEFORE-IMAGES DL/I INFO FIRST VTAM INPUT PER LUW (FOR PROTECTED TASKS) START OF TASK STATUS OF TIOA, TCTUA, COMMAREA (IF PCT RESTART=YES) |
| Written | EXPLICITLY BY APPL COMMANDS/MACROS AUTOMATICALLY BY JCP AFTER CHANGES TO PROTECTED FILES OR DURING PROTECTED VTAM I/O | BY JCP BEFORE A PROTECTED RESOURCE IS CHANGED, AND OPTIONALLY, AFTER A FILE HAS BEEN CHANGED BY SPP DURING SYNC-POINT PROCESSING BY DFHAKP, DFHUAKP DURING A SYSTEM ACTIVITY KEYPOINT BY USER CODE WHEN JOURNAL 1 IS USED AS A USER JOURNAL | BY JCP FOR ALL DTB=YES TASKS BEFORE ANY DESTRUCTIVE CHANGES ARE MADE NOTE: EACH TASK'S DYNAMIC LOG AREA IS CLEARED AT THE START OF AN LUW EXCEPT AS NOTED ABOVE |
| Read | BY USER-WRITTEN FORWARD RECOVERY, AUDIT, EMERGENCY RESTART CODE, ETC. | BY DFHRUP DURING EMERGENCY RESTART BY USER CODE FOR VARIOUS REASONS | BY DFHDBP TO BACK OUT AN IN-FLIGHT TASK (DTB) |

**Figure 13.5** Journals and logs.

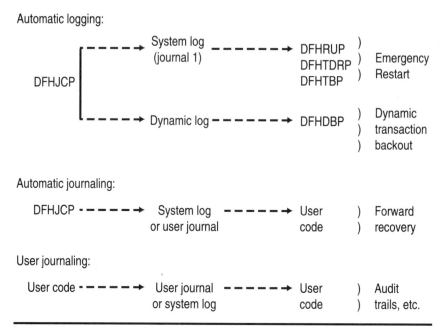

**Figure 13.6** Logging and journaling.

The Journal Control Program (DFHJCP) does both automatic logging of before-images (LOG=YES in the FCT) and automatic journaling of after-images (JREQ=RU,WN,WU,etc. in the FCT). Explicit journaling is performed when the application issues an EXEC CICS JOURNAL or the DFHJC macro. This will normally be written to a user journal (JID=nn in the FCT), to be read later as an audit trail or a history file. If you specify JID=SYSTEM, after-images will be written to the system log. This might be done for performance reasons, that is, so that fewer journal tasks are attached, or to simplify operations if tapes are used. You might get a little more efficient management of journal shiftup and journal writing.

Figure 13.6 recaps the three types of records, where they are written, and when and how they are processed.

### 13.6.1. Automatic logging

Automatic logging, as we have said, is the recording of before-images on the system log, along with syncpoints and activity keypoints, for the purpose of backout recovery. A syncpoint, to review, delineates end of task or LUW, and can be requested by CICS or an application.

At syncpoint time, outstanding DWEs are processed. A DWE saves information about an uncompleted event that must be completed before task termination. For example, a READ UPDATE causes a DWE to be created; this DWE resides on the DWE chain until the update is performed, a syncpoint is taken, or the task terminates without doing the update. If the task abends or a syncpoint rollback is requested, the DWE contains the saved information needed for backing the operation out. A syncpoint rollback may be issued by the application to back out all the changes made from the previous syncpoint.

At syncpoint time, DFHKC issues a `TYPE=DEQALL`, and the task's dynamic log area in main storage is cleared. The purpose of the dynamic log area is to record information that DBP needs to perform DTB. After the updates are committed for this LUW, the log is cleared for the next LUW for the task. Remember, DBP only needs to back out the last syncpoint or the last LUW.

Syncpoint control information on the system log is used by the Recovery Utility Program (RUP) to determine the amount of backout needed for each task. During Emergency Restart, RUP reads the system log backwards, identifies in-flight tasks, and writes information about the tasks to the restart data set. The restart data set is then read by TBP to back out updates to protected resources that were made by in-flight tasks.

Activity keypoints are records written to the system log that identify information needed for Emergency Restart. The main objective of activity keypoint records is to limit the backward search through the system log. They contain information about each task, TS and TD status, message-protected tasks on VTAM terminals, and tape volume information. The frequency of these keypoints is determined by the AKPFREQ parameter in the SIT. This parameter specifies the number of blocks written to the system log before an activity keypoint is taken. When AKPFREQ has been reached, JCP attaches task CSKP, which is associated with the Activity Keypoint Program (DFHAKP). DFHAKP LINKs to the Keypoint Processor Program (DFHKPP), which puts TCA, DCT, TCT, etc., information into buffers and logs this information to the system log (using the DFHJC macro). DFHKPP RETURNs to DFHAKP, which writes a time stamp to CSMT. DFHAKP LINKs to the User Activity Keypoint Program (DFHUAKP). DFHUAKP enables the application to write user keypoint information to the system log.

Figure 13.7 lists the various table entries associated with automatic logging.

### 13.6.2. Automatic journaling

Automatic journaling is the recording of after-images on a user journal (or the system log) for the purpose of forward recovery, audit trails, history, or other reports desired by the user. Journaling is automatic in that whenever the application requests a file operation that is specified in the journal request option (`JREQ=`) of the FCT macro for that file, FCP issues the DFHJC macro for whichever journal was specified in the journal id option (`JID=`) of the FCT macro.

**232 Chapter Thirteen**

| | | |
|---|---|---|
| DFHJCT | TYPE = ENTRY | Define the |
| | JFILEID = SYSTEM | system log |
| | | |
| DFHFCT | TYPE = DATASET, | For this file, |
| | LOG = YES | log before-images |
| | | |
| DFHDCT | TYPE = INTRA, | Intrapartition destinations only |
| | DESTRCV = LG or PH | logical or physical recovery |
| | | |
| DFHTST | TYPE = INITIAL, | AUX Temp Storage only |
| | TSAGE = 3 | recover queues 3 days old or younger |
| | | |
| DFHTST | TYPE = RECOVER, | Recover |
| | DATAID = QUEUE1 | QUEUE 1 (via Emer Restart or DTB) |
| | | |
| DFHPCT | TYPE = ENTRY | For this transid |
| | DTB = YES | back out all recoverable resources |
| | | |
| DFHPCT | TYPE = ENTRY, | This transid must run on VTAM |
| | OPTGRP = GROUP1 | VTAM info is coded below |
| | | |
| DFHPCT | TYPE = OPTGRP, | VTAM info for all transids |
| | NAME = GROUP1, | with OPTGRP = GROUP1 |
| | MSGPREQ = PROTECT | autolog VTAM I/O |

**Figure 13.7** Parameters for journaling.

Automatic journaling, then, is writing to a journal by a CICS management module. When an application writes to the journal, it is user journaling. In either case, data will not be written to the dynamic log.

Figure 13.8 shows what must be added to the FCT macro to enable automatic journaling and the journal request (JREQ) option.

| | | |
|---|---|---|
| DFHFCT | TYPE = DATASET, | For this file, |
| | JREQ = (requests) | journal after-images of these requests |
| | JID = (2 - 99, SYSTEM) | to user journals (2 - 99) or system log |

JREQ options:

| | | | | |
|---|---|---|---|---|
| RO | Read only | RU | Read update |
| WN | Write new | WU | Write update |
| ALL | RO, RU, WN, WU | SYN, ASY | Synchronization options |

**Figure 13.8** FCT parameters.

Recovery/Restart Facilities    233

### 13.6.3. Journal Control Program

Figure 13.9 shows the parameters needed to generate the Journal Control Program at system generation.

In both MVS and DOS, journaling runs as a subtask. There are as many journal tasks active as there are journals, plus one extra for communication with the subtask.

Here is a brief description of how Journal Control works. The first program to get control is the kickoff program, DFHCKOJ, which is running during startup under Terminal Control's TCA. It attaches a journal task called CSJC with a facility address of zero (TCAFCAAA=0), whose job is to wait for Journal Control's Open/Close subtask to complete.

DFHCKOJ then opens all the journals if we told CICS to open them all at initialization (JCT OPEN=INITIAL), and attaches a CSJC (Journal Control task) for each one. That's why if you have four journals you have five tasks, one for each journal and one to change the light bulb.

DFHJCBSP, the bootstrap program, initializes a CSJC task, sets up Journal Control buffers and JCT table entry pointers for the CSJC task, makes it non-stall-purgeable, and sets its priority to 255, after which the task's DCA remains. This program will not be called again for this journal.

DFHJCOCP is the Open/Close subtask (MVS or VSE), and the point of it is that the CICS TCB remains dispatchable while the journals are opened or closed. That is, it can overlap with what CICS is doing, as it is outside the region, using standard WAIT/POST logic to interface with CICS DFHJCO, which opens journal data sets, and DFHJCC, which closes journals.

The main Journal Control Program, DFHJCP, processes all DFHJC requests, and itself runs under a task named CSJC, performing output event completion processing. Some other programs are the end-of-volume processor (DFHJCEOV), the input processor (DFHJCI), which processes input requests, the journal I/O error processor (DFIIJCIOE), and the off-line disk journal formatter (DFHJCJCP).

Finally, there is the Journal Control shutdown program (DFHJCSDJ). The shutdown program gets called by DFHJCIOE for permanent I/O

---

| | | |
|---|---|---|
| DFHSG | PROGRAM = JCP | For Journal Control Program, |
| | AUTOJRN = (NO\| YES) | need YES for automatic journaling, Emergency Restart, DTB, DL/I |
| | DTB = (NO\| AUX\| MAIN) | If the dynamic log buffer is full, spill into AUX or MAIN Temp Storage |

**Figure 13.9** SYSGEN parameters.

**234 Chapter Thirteen**

errors on JOUROPT=CRUCIAL journals, by DFHJCEOV for end-of-volume on crucial journals, by DFHSTP for standard shutdown, and, if the Open/Close subtask abends, by DFHJCSP. Journal Control cannot operate if the subtask is gone.

### 13.6.4. Journal Control data areas

The Journal Control Program has various data areas that it uses for communication between itself, CICS, and the application (see Fig. 13.10). The primary one is the Journal Control area, described by DFHJCADS, which is used by the application to communicate with DFHJCP. It has an RSA (registers 14 to 11), which is used by JCP, and a communication area filled in by the application program that contains such information as the type of request, return code, journal id, volume information and user information, or the actual data that are to be written. The Journal Control I/O communication area, DFHJCICA, maps a journal's DECBs (two per journal) in the Journal Control Table (JCT).

The Journal Control Open/Close parameter list, DFHJCOCL, is the interface between the CICS Journal Control task program, DFHJCP, running under CSJC, and the Open/Close subtask, DFHJCOCP. Remember, there is a Journal Control task in CICS, and there is also a Journal Control subtask in MVS. The subtask has to communicate with the CICS task, and this is done through the Open/Close parameter list. The parameter list contains three ECBs: one for an abend, one for a request, and one saying that the request is completed. It also contains the address of the JCT entry being referred to, the address of the Journal Control area, and the address of the subtask's TCB. The record layout for the Journal Control record is in the DSECT DFHJCRDS.

Journal records are written in blocks. The llbb, a standard 4-byte prefix, specifies the length of a block and is at the beginning of each block, followed by a label record and one or more journal records. Each journal record is variable-length and contains a record prefix, made up of the llbb for the record, a user id, system prefix, user prefix, and user data.

### 13.6.5. Writing to journals

The journal request can be issued either by CICS or by the application program. When it is issued by CICS, the File Control Program (DFHFCP) initiates the request by issuing the DFHJC TYPE=WRITE macro and DFHJCP, then processes the request. What causes FCP to initiate the request? The Journal request parameter, JREQ=, on the TYPE=DATASET macro in the File Control Table.

| | |
|---|---|
| DFHJCADS | Journal Control Area |
| DFHJCICA | I/O communication area |
| DFHJCOCL | Open/Close parameter list |
| DFHJCRDS | Journal record area |

**Figure 13.10** Journal Control data areas.

When issued by the user, the request is initiated within the application with either the EXEC CICS JOURNAL command or the DFHJC TYPE=WRITE macro (Fig. 13.11). You specify which journal to write to with the journal id, JID, which corresponds to the JCT JFILEID of either a user journal or the system log. You specify the type id, JTYPEID, which is a 2-byte user id (four-character hex value in macro), to be used to identify the record type by the application that reads the journal later. You give the address and length of the user data and the optional user prefix. The two lengths cannot exceed the journal buffer size.

Journal writes may be either asynchronous or synchronous. If you specify synchronous, then you want the physical write to take place before the task gets control again, so you know that it happened. You are in effect writing out to the tape (or disk) every single journal record. Asynchronous says to put it in the buffer, to be written as a block later. If the task receives a good return code from Journal Control, it continues processing, not caring when the record is physically written.

| EXEC CICS JOURNAL | DFHJC TYPE = WRITE |
|---|---|
| JFILEID ( ) | JFILEID = |
| JTYPEID ( ) | JTYPEID = |
| FROM ( ) | JCADDR = |
| LENGTH ( ) | JCDLGTH = |
| PREFIX ( ) | PFXADDR = |
| PFXLENG ( ) | PFXLGTH = |

**Figure 13.11** Parameters for the Journal Control request.

## 236 Chapter Thirteen

---
STARTIO or STARTIO = YES
WAIT or TYPE = (WRITE, WAIT) or PUT
REQUID or value in JAECN

---

**Figure 13.12** Journal request synchronization options.

You specify this with a combination of the parameters shown in Fig. 13.12. In general, WAIT holds up the task's processing until the physical write occurs. If WAIT is not specified, the record is added to the current block, and the task's processing continues. The record (meaning the block which contains it) will be written when a STARTIO for the journal is requested, when the journal is full (or almost full), when the buffer space falls below the buffer shift-up value for that journal (BUFSUV of JCT TYPE=ENTRY), or 1 s after the last write to the buffer by this task. JCAEN or the REQUID data area will hold a unique event control number, refreshed after each successful Journal output request. Refer to IBM's Application Programmer's Reference Manual (Macro Level) for a discussion of this feature.

## 13.7. Dynamic Transaction Backout (DTB)

We define a program as eligible for DTB by coding DTB=YES in the PCT entry for that transaction. If nothing is coded for the PCT entry, the default is what is coded in the DFHPCT TYPE=INITIAL macro. If this is not coded, the default is DTB=YES. If a transaction is defined with DTB=YES, a dynamic log buffer will be created for the task when it is needed.

Each time the transaction changes a recoverable resource, a record describing the change is written to the dynamic log. At the beginning of each LUW, the log is cleared. If the task abends, DFHDBP uses the dynamic log to restore any protected resources. If it is not protected, a resource will not be restored, even though dynamic backout of the task is taking place.

The size of the dynamic log buffer is determined by the DBUFSZ parameter in the SIT. It resides in transaction storage as user class storage (8C), and if the log overflows (becomes larger than the DBUFSZ specified in the SIT), it "spills" to temporary storage. You can check your CICS shutdown stats to see how many spills have occurred and adjust DBUFSZ accordingly, starting high and tuning down. In general, it should be large enough to accommodate most of your records, with some spilling.

### 13.7.1. Deferred work elements (DWEs)

In addition to using the dynamic log, DBP uses DWEs to recover some resources. A DWE is used to delay the processing of a particular piece of work. We delay processing because we do not want it done in an uncoordinated fashion; we want everything done or we want nothing done. For example, some irreversible operations like TD PURGE and TS RELEASE or PURGE are delayed until the end of the LUW. If one of these operations is requested, the DWE holds information about the request. When the task requests a syncpoint (explicit or implicit), any deferred requests represented by DWEs are processed by a DWE processor within the appropriate control program (different management modules have their own DWE processors). The DWE chain for a task is processed at each syncpoint, and by DFHKCP before detaching the task.

### 13.7.2. Dynamic backout

When a DTB=YES task abends, DBP is invoked by Program Control. DBP first scans back through the DWE chain, looking for work to be backed out that corresponds to a DWE. For Interval Control, Transient Data, and Temporary Storage DWEs, DBP calls the management module associated with the request. In other words, DBP does not back out these DWEs itself, but delegates the work to the various DWE processors residing in the management modules.

DBP does process File Management DWEs, releasing FIOAs and VSWAs. BMS DWEs are purged via a call to a BMS routine. DL/I DWEs go to the syncpoint processor, DFHSPP. DBP then chains back through the dynamic log and issues DFHFC macros to back out file changes, calls the DL/I backout program to back out DL/I changes, and passes the first input message to a user exit; if it is a DL/I restartable transaction, the first input message is placed in a TIOA, and the TCT user area (TCTUA) and DFHCOMMAREA are reinstated. That prepares us to start the task again. However, restarting of a task is very limited, even within DL/I, and certain conditions must be met: the task must be within the first LUW, and the abend must occur before subsequent terminal input.

At the end of DTB processing, control is passed to the Abnormal Condition Program, DFHACP, and if the task is restartable, the Restart program DFHRTY is invoked. Dynamic backout can be invoked without an abend. If you want to get DBP services without abending, you can issue a syncpoint rollback.

### 13.7.3. DTB exits

There are four exits at which we can override the dynamic backout defaults:

**238  Chapter Thirteen**

- XDBINIT

- XDBINP

- XDBFERR

- XDBERR

Although we will discuss only the global interface, there is the possibility of both global and static interfaces here. The initialization exit is XDBINIT, which gets control at the entry point of DFHDBP. The three choices, indicated by the setting of the return code, are:

0  Continue DTB

4  Suppress DL/I backout

8  Suppress all backout

Maybe at this point you do your own backout, or maybe you do some of your own and then continue with DTB. At the input exit, XDBINP, a non-DL/I dynamic log record is read. You would use this exit to back out a BDAM or ESDS record, which must be done by the user, as there is no VSAM delete. Register 3 points to the record, and there are two choices, based on the return code:

0  Process the record

4  Do not process it

Database file error exit XDBFERR gets control when DBP tries to back out a record with the DFHFC macro and DFHFCP returns an error code. This could conceivably happen if a file was disabled, or if a file error caused the task abend; in this case File Control will attempt to back out the `WRITE` but cannot, since it was the file hit that caused abend. At this point we can examine the log record and determine what action to take— enable the file, or perhaps take some sort of evasive action.

The last exit, XDBDERR, gets control if a DL/I backout error has occurred. The database is closed whether you set the return code to 0 or 4, so there are no options here, but it may be useful to do some logging or some notification, or possibly take some type of damage control.

### 13.8.  User Recovery

Execution of the Program Error Program (DFHPEP), which is 100 percent user code, is the last step in abnormal termination. The PEP supplied by IBM is just a dummy program; you must link-edit your own program as DFHPEP. The following information is available to a PEP:

- ABCODE at TCAPCAC

- The PSW at TCAPCPSW if it is an ASRA

- The PCT address at TCATCPC
- The TWA

We can find out the transaction code and other information about the transaction at the PCT address. The TWA may contain information placed there by the application or by exits. You could code a PEP to determine that if a transaction is of a certain type, then it can find out what happened by looking at the TWA, and then take some corrective action.

Here are some of the possible functions of a PEP:

- Remove the cause of an error
- Disable the transaction
- Disable associated transactions
- If the transaction is critical, terminate CICS
- Record information about the error
- Send messages to the terminal or operator
- Perform cleanup

When would you use a PEP rather than some other facility for handling the error? It is really a question of timing and of the nature of the error and the application. There are some things that are better done with a HANDLE ABEND, some things that are better to do in TEP or NEP, and some that are better to do in transaction backout, because of the times at which different processes take place, DTB in particular.

You could use a PEP to disable things. For example, you might disable a file and all the transactions that use that file. This type of capability becomes important in larger systems. If you have a 20,000-terminal network, you do not want 20,000 dumps because a file took a hit. You could use a PEP to decide whether to continue or terminate a CICS region in cases where a critical resource has become unavailable. Terminating CICS if the transaction is critical may not be as bad as it sounds, especially in the MRO/ISC extended recovery (XRF) environment.

In general, you want to try to remove the cause of the error, but only if the application was designed to do this. This brings us back to the desirability of designing recovery into the application. A PEP can help you to do this. The point here is that you can anticipate some errors that are application-dependent, and a PEP allows you to take some action, ideally removing the cause of the error. Being unique to a particular system, the PEP can and should be designed right into the application. This is why the PEP is user-written rather than IBM-written.

**240 Chapter Thirteen**

In summary, we can view programming a PEP as a system programming task, but we see that the PEP is really an application function. Thus the system programmer enables application requirements.

### 13.8.1. Abend recovery strategies

Let us review the possible recovery strategies in the event of a task abend, shown in Fig. 13.13.

An abend exit is application code set up within the task that provides the opportunity to ignore the problem and continue before we hit transaction backout. Its best use is for application-unique logic, placed either in a routine performing error recovery for a single program, or in a program that serves many programs. It can back out resources that CICS will not, such as bit or byte settings in the CSA or tables modified by the application.

You will hit an abend exit if you include a HANDLE ABEND and your task abends or if you issue an EXEC CICS ABEND without a CANCEL, along with a HANDLE ABEND. The CANCEL says to cancel the abend exit. Since it is executed before DTB, anything written to a recoverable resource in the abend exit will be backed out by DTB.

The next facility available is the DTB exit. After DFHDBP gets control, if the abending transaction has DTB=YES, the initial exit XDBINIT gets control. Here you could also back out resources CICS has no control over, as in the task abend exit. The main difference here is that it is systemwide, while the abend exit is application- or task-dependent. This is an application design consideration.

Next, exit XDBINP gets control as a dynamic log record is read. At this point you can tell DBP whether or not to back out the resource, and do your own backout of VSAM ESDS or BDAM records. The last two exits, XDBFERR and XDBERR, get control only if there is a file or a DL/I error, respectively.

DFHPEP gets control after all transaction abends, except when a transaction is being restarted. Since it executes after DTB, changes to protected resources will remain intact. With each facility you can write messages to CSMT, the master terminal operator, a log file, etc. After this point, recovery must be integrated with operating procedures, and this requires coordination among all or some of the various groups in-

| | |
|---|---|
| . ABEND exit | Program level user code |
| . DTB exits | Transaction level backout |
| . DFHPEP | System level user code |

**Figure 13.13** Task abend summary.

volved, which could be the people that wrote the application, the CRT operator, the computer room operations staff, DBA people, or DASD people. There is no magic software that can fix all this: there must be operating procedures and contingency plans. However, you can minimize those by doing as much automatic work as possible.

## 13.9. Emergency Restart

Emergency Restart can be activated after a system failure. It is similar to a WARM restart in that it reconstructs the system to where it was before it came down. In the case of Emergency Restart, however, the system has crashed, so there is extra work to do in the form of backout.

During Emergency Restart, the Recovery Utility Program (DFHRUP) reads the system log backwards, identifying in-flight tasks and other recovery candidates, and writes information to the restart data set, which is then used by the Transaction Backout Program (DFHTBP), the Transient Data Recovery Program (DFHTDRP), and the Temporary Storage Recovery Program (DFHTSRP) to back out in-flight tasks and uncommitted updates to protected resources.

### 13.9.1. Backout tables

DFHRUP records summary information on the restart data set in four tables: the Transaction Backout Table (TBO), the File Backout Table (FBO), the Message Backout Table (MBO), and the DL/I Backout Table (DBO). The TBO keeps information on tasks, both in-flight LUWs and those that did not go to end of task (EOT). The FBO contains informa tion on protected files, the MBO information on protected VTAM messages, and the DBO information on in-flight DL/I transactions.

### 13.9.2. DFHTBP restart exits

There are four exits available to the system programmer in the TBP:

- XINIT
- XINPUT
- XFERROR
- XDERROR

The XINIT exit, which is given control when DFHTBP is invoked, can be used to set flags in the FBO, MBO, TBO, or DBO that can allow you to bypass processing of certain records.

**242    Chapter Thirteen**

| Access method | LOG = NO | LOG = YES, SERVREQ = NOEXTL |
|---|---|---|
| BDAM | Block held by BDAM | Record held by CICS |
| VSAM | CI held by VSAM | Record held by CICS |
| ISAM | Record held by CICS | Record held by CICS |
| Released by | REWRITE, DELETE, UNLOCK, RELEASE, EOT | SYNCPOINT, EOT |

**Figure 13.14**  Exclusive control.

## 13.10.  File Control Resource Protection

If LOG=YES was specified for a data set in the FCT, File Control issues a KC TYPE=ENQUEUE on a combination of the record id and the data set name. This enqueue remains in effect for the entire LUW.

With LOG=NO you get protection on the block level for BDAM or on the CI level for VSAM. If you say LOG=YES but with no exclusive control, CICS will give you protection on the record level. (See Fig. 13.14.) CICS protection gets control of a record with a DFHKC TYPE=ENQUEUE, which lasts for the duration of the LUW. Access method protection is more logically related to activity against a file. If I do a VSAM READ UPDATE, I will have exclusive control of the entire CI until the REWRITE is complete. The chart is set up this way in order to contrast getting control of a CI and getting control of a record. In actuality, VSAM always protects the CI, based on the share option specified for the file, whether LOG=YES or NO.

### 13.10.1.  Programming restrictions

There are some restrictions applied to files with LOG=YES. A KSDS should not be updated via RBA. Files cannot be added via Mass Insert or deleted with Generic Delete.

Files with alternate indexes should have updates performed through the base only. This is due to the way the KC enqueue mechanism is used by the FCP. CICS enqueues on an FCT name, and as there are separate data set names in the FCT for index and base, as far as CICS knows these are two separate data sets, with unique enqueue arguments. Thus the base and index could be updated simultaneously by two tasks. This is a little hole in the enqueue mechanism. Also, there is no first-task lock on an alternate index key to prevent a second task from accessing the same key before the first task's LUW has ended. Clearly, recovery can fail if the first task abends before completing its

LUW, but after the second task has performed a change. Use of explicit CICS enqueueing can reserve the AIX key until the first task's LUW completes, but it is much cleaner for most application developers to adhere to the rule that updates be performed only through the base.

The use of recovery greatly increases the possibility of transaction deadlocks, since all recoverable resources are held for the duration of the task's LUW. For users of CICS 2.1.1 and higher, there is now a major improvement in the way File Control handles exclusive control conflict (ECC) deadlocks. FCP was changed to place a deadlocked task on the suspend chain instead of the active chain. This means that the task is now eligible for deadlock timeout via the DTIMEOUT option. Also, more information is now available through the VSWA, which may be used for analysis of deadlocks.

### 13.10.2. File Control protection summary

Automatic logging, specified by LOG=YES in the FCT, means that we get before-images copied to the system log and to the dynamic log for a READ UPDATE or a DELETE. For a WRITE, the new record is copied to the system log, and the key is saved on the dynamic log.

Automatic journaling, specified by JID=nn or SYSTEM and JREQ=(WN,WU), means that after-images are written to the journal for a WRITE or a REWRITE. For a DELETE, the record key is written to the journal, to show that there was a deletion. If it was for backout, we would have had to make a copy of the whole record. But as we are just going to note that we deleted it, we do not need a copy, because when we read this for forward recovery, it is just going to tell us to delete this record from the backup copy.

Chapter

# 14

# Recovery/Restart Examples

## 14.1. Introduction

One thing we want to keep in mind is that there is a constant tradeoff between performance and integrity in any system. This is good to keep in mind as we review the various CICS components and see how they are affected by recovery/restart considerations. Since it is a key area, this chapter will provide an overview of the recovery mechanisms available to different CICS facilities, and how they are generated. The following topics will be covered:

- Transient Data recovery
- Main Storage recovery
- Temporary Storage recovery
- Interval Control recovery
- BMS recovery
- Terminal Control recovery
- VTAM message protection

## 14.2. Transient Data Recovery

To review, there are two types of Transient Data: intrapartition (TD intra) queues, which reside within CICS, and extrapartition (TD extra) queues, which reside outside of the region. Only TD intra queues are recoverable, with both DTB and Emergency Restart facilities available to them. Since CICS has no control over extrapartition destinations, no

245

## 246 Chapter Fourteen

DTB or Emergency Restart is provided, but you can provide your own recovery with user journaling or writing to your own files.

There are two types of recovery of a Transient Data queue: logical and physical. Logical recovery is task-related, and is associated with a logical unit of work, the recovery of a single task. Physical recovery is systemwide and recovers the destination by restoring physical pointers to their position at the time of a system failure.

### 14.2.1. System components of TD recovery

There are many different system components involved in the TD recovery process. During normal operations, the Transient Data Program (DFHTDP), in conjunction with the Destination Control Table (DFHDCT), processes the GETs and PUTs against the destinations.

The Journal Control Program (DFHJCP), in conjunction with the Journal Control Table (DFHJCT), logs for both physical and logical recovery (DESTRCV=PH or LG in the DCT). The Syncpoint Program (DFH-SPP) performs syncpoint processing, and the Task Control Program (DFHKCP) processes enqueue requests. During dynamic backout, the management modules that are active are the Abnormal Condition Program (DFHACP), which detects the error, the Dynamic Backout Program (DFHDBP), which performs the backout, and the Program Error Program (DFHPEP), which is user-written code to perform some type of customized recovery.

During Emergency Restart, the active modules are the System Initialization Program (DFHSIP), which starts the CICS region, the Recovery Utility Program (DFHRUP), which orchestrates the recovery, and the Transient Data Recovery Program (DFHTDRP), which performs some specialized queue recovery. The following SYSGEN parameters would be needed to generate recovery for TD intra queues:

```
DFHSG PROGRAM=JCP,
   AUTOJRN=YES,
   DTB=(MAIN or AUX)
DFHSG PROGRAM=TDP,
   DESTRCV=YES
DFHSG PROGRAM=KPP,
   AKP=YES
DFHSG PROGRAM=DBP
DFHSG PROGRAM=TBP
```

We generate the Journal Control Program, specifying autojournaling and DTB, in either main storage or auxiliary storage (AUX is recommended if this does not kill response time). Autojournaling means that DFHJCP will write a record to the journal automatically, without the application program having to do anything.

We need to generate the Transient Data Program and specify destination recovery (DESTRCV), which gives us both logical and physical recovery support. We also need to generate the Keypoint Program (DFHKPP), which is needed to perform activity keypoint processing [we have the option of doing our own activity keypoint processing via the User Activity Keypoint Program (DFHUAKP), which is LINKed to by DFHKPP]. Finally, we need to generate the Dynamic Backout Program (DFHDBP) and the Transaction Backout Program (DFHTBP).

To define the logically or physically recoverable intrapartition destinations, we must code the DCT entries as follows:

```
DFHDCT TYPE=INTRA,DESTID=queue1,DESTRCV=LG
DFHDCT TYPE=INTRA,DESTID=queue2,DESTRCV=PH
```

### 14.2.2. Physical versus logical recovery

Physical recovery is on the system level, providing no synchronization with other recoverable resources. It does not provide resource protection in the sense that there is no exclusive control of the resource on the task level, and no backout (DTB does not support physical recovery). It simply restores the pointers to the queue as they were at the time of failure, ignoring any task activity going on at that time. With physical recovery, a destructive read will not be reversed, that is, the last record read from the queue will not be presented again to any task. In contrast, with logical recovery, the LUW determines the recovery of a particular resource. With logical recovery, if nine updates were performed in the course of an LUW prior to an abend, then nine writes are backed out.

Figure 14.1 shows examples of both logical and physical recovery. In the first example, the DCT entry is defined with logical recovery, DESTRCV=LG. Let us run through this transaction, which runs from left to right, with the backout running from right to left. To start, the task is attached, or we have a syncpoint. The task then does either a WRITEQ or a READQ TD. Both of these change the queue. A Transient Data queue is not like Temporary Storage or even a file: a read is destructive, so you are always either adding (WRITEQ TD) or deleting (READQ TD) a record. In the example, the queue is changed three times, then the task abends or the system crashes. Emergency Restart or DTB reestablishes the queue to its status at the start of the LUW.

The next example is defined in the DCT with physical recovery, DESTRCV=PH. After the attach, the task adds three records before the abend or crash. DTB takes no action with physical recovery, so if the task abends, the queue remains positioned after the last WRITE. However, Emergency Restart will restore the queue to the way it looked after the last WRITE. In other words, nothing is really done at this point. When CICS comes back up, the queue will look the way it

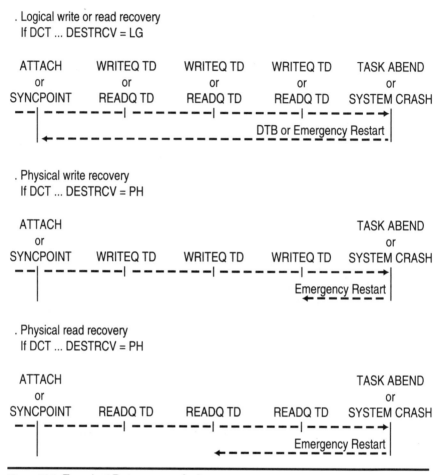

**Figure 14.1** Transient Data recovery logic.

did when CICS went down. The third example, physical READ recovery, is a little different. If the system crashes, we go back to the way the queue looked before the last READ. So the last READ is really backed out. Again, no DTB takes place with a task abend, so the queue stays the way it was after the last READ.

### 14.2.3. TD physical protection

When would you use physical recovery? In general, a physically recoverable queue is used when you want to recover everything you have got so far, regardless of what happens to the tasks. You can modify a physically recoverable queue at the beginning of DTB processing using the initial exit XDBINIT, whereas modifications to a logically recoverable

## Recovery/Restart Examples

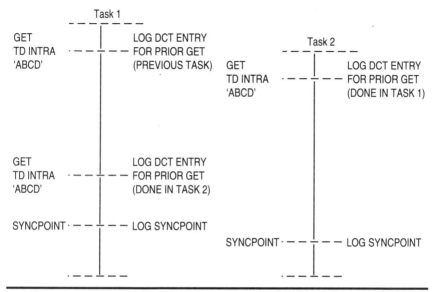

**Figure 14.2** Transient Data physical protection.

queue would be subsequently backed out. For example, you may want to write something when a task abends that you do not want backed out. You might write to a queue to trigger a transaction that runs only in the event of an abend. If the queue were logically protected, this transaction would never run.

Or you may want to write error messages that you do not want purged in a HANDLE ABEND exit. You could do this by writing to a physically protected TD queue associated with a printer which is defined as a terminal in the TCT and associated with a trigger level in the DCT. Physical protection is more durable in the sense that it will survive a transaction abend and still be recoverable, but it is important to be aware of the consequences of mixing physical recovery with DTB.

In Fig. 14.2 two tasks are each issuing TD GETs simultaneously. As you can imagine, this situation can lead to problems. Generally it is safe if a single task is allowed to READ, although multiple WRITEs are okay. The recommendation is to have only one task READ to QZERO (until the queue is empty).

### 14.2.4. TD logical protection

Logical protection is on the task level, that is, a destination being written to gets locked until the syncpoint. Protection is provided in the form of a Task Control enqueue (DFHKC TYPE=ENQ) and a DWE to update the DCT pointer for the following operations:

## Chapter Fourteen

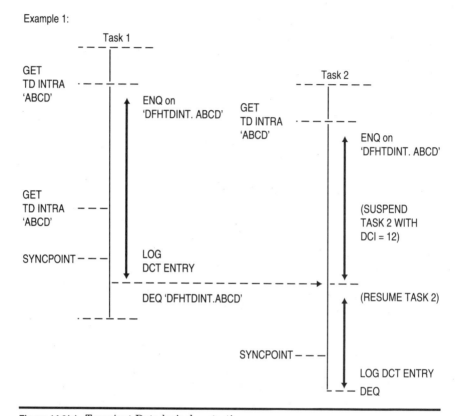

**Figure 14.3(a)** Transient Data logical protection.

```
WRITEQ TD QUEUE(queue-name) FROM(data-area)
READQ TD QUEUE(queue-name) INTO(data-area)

DFHTD TYPE=PUT,DESTID=queue-name,TDADDR=data-area
DFHTD TYPE=GET,DESTID=queue-name
```

At syncpoint, the DWE processor for the Transient Data Program (DFHTDP) will process the DWE and actually perform the necessary I/O. At this point the DCT entry is written to the system log and the ATI level is checked.

Figure 14.3 illustrates TD logical protection. In the first example, (Fig. 14.3a), Task 1 does a TD GET on TD intra queue 'ABCD', and DFHTDP does an enqueue on 'DFHTDINT.ABCD'. Task 2 also tries a TD GET, issuing an enqueue on the same argument, but is suspended with a DCI=12, as there is already an enqueue from another task. Task 1 then does another GET, being still enqueued, and then issues a syncpoint, where the DCT entry is logged and a dequeue is issued for 'DFHTDINT.ABCD'. Task 2 can now resume. The second example (Fig.

Example 2:

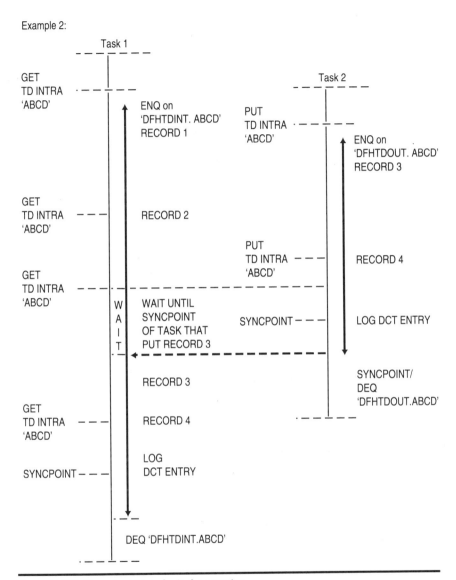

**Figure 14.3(b)** Transient Data logical protection.

14.3b) shows a different kind of enqueue element. Task 1 issues a GET for TD intra queue `ABCD`. An enqueue is created, and the task gets record 1, then GETs record 2. Meanwhile Task 2 issues a PUT to TD intra queue `ABCD`, and since records 1 and 2 exist at that point, enqueues on `DFHTDOUT.ABCD`, then puts records 3 and 4. Why does it enqueue on `DFHTDOUT` ? To ensure that nobody else can do a WRITE. Now Task 1 tries to get record 3, but DFHTDP finds an outstanding en-

**252  Chapter Fourteen**

queue for 'DFHTDOUT.ABCD', and prevents Task 1 from reading records 3 and 4, even though they have been written, since Task 2 has not committed them yet. Task 1 must wait until Task 2 does a syncpoint/dequeue.

### 14.2.5.  DTB overview

Let us review what happens during DTB. First we hit the initial exit, XDBINIT, where of course we do not really want to write anything to recoverable resources. DFHDBP sends a "DTB invoked" message out to the terminal and CSMT, which is a nonrecoverable TD intra queue used by dynamic backout. The DWEs are processed as DBP invokes the various DWE processors within the control programs. If a problem occurs, a message is sent to CSMT.

The dynamic log is processed, with an XDBINPUT exit available for each log record and a XDBFERR exit for file errors: if DBRERRCD is DBFEWA, this is your chance to mark a BDAM, or ESDS record for deletion. You can use either this exit or XDBINPUT to examine the record when backing out BDAM, or ESDS adds. XDBERR is the exit for DL/I errors. CICS closes the database at this point, but you get the chance to send messages or do some other task-related cleanup. DTB finishes up with a "DTB complete" message to the terminal and to CSMT via a LINK to DFHACP.

### 14.2.6.  DTB and Emergency Restart for TD intra queues

Now we will look in a little more detail at what happens during DTB for protected Transient Data queues. The chart in Fig. 14.4 contrasts DTB with the other forms of recovery for TD queues, showing the implications of each.

DTB extends to logically recoverable queues only, whereas Emergency Restart applies to both logically and physically recoverable queues. Dynamic backout restores the destination to its status at the start of the LUW. It adjusts the DCT GET and PUT pointers, and adjusts the queue counts. There are no specific DTB exits for TD, and remember that modifying a TD logical destination at the DTB initial exit will cause the modification to be backed out. How could you write to a logically recoverable queue, then, during abend processing and be assured that it will not be backed out? With a user routine in DFHPEP, which is invoked after DTB has taken place. ATI initiation is deferred until a syncpoint. The queue record is backed out, and if defined with DESTFAC=TERM, the task is reinitiated (otherwise the task will be reinitiated at the next PUT).

| DTB | Emergency Restart | Warm Restart | Cold Start |
|---|---|---|---|
| Logical recovery backout changes | Logically or physically recoverable queues are retained | All queues are retained | All queues are empty |
| Physical recovery No backout, last record read is not represented | Logical recovery Changes made by in-flight tasks are backed out | No backout | No backout |
| ATI: if terminal, task reinitiated, if not, at next put to queue | Physical recovery Read queue pointer is reset so that the last record is represented if the task was in flight. Write queue pointer is set to last record put. | Previous status is retained (ENA/DIS) | Status is taken from the DCT |

**Figure 14.4** TD intra backout summary.

During Emergency Restart, DFHSIP does normal cold start processing, and no formatting of the TD queue. RUP then updates the DCT based on activity keypoint records read from the system log.

For a logically recoverable resource, RUP updates the DCT based on the syncpoint sequence. For a physically recoverable queue, it reconstructs the queue based on the actual READs and PURGEs. With physical recovery, a syncpoint is taken on the very first WRITE, and on all READs and PURGEs. Why just the first WRITE? If we are writing, we are adding to the queue, and this does not get backed out. But if we are reading or purging, we are destroying what we may need to re-create.

If a DTB=YES task reading a physically recoverable queue took a syncpoint, RUP increments the read pointer to the next record. Next, RUP calls DFHTDRP to do some work specific to Transient Data, such as reading the TD intra data set for the physical end of the queue, reading and writing control records on the data set, and adjusting queue pointers. When RUP regains control, it restarts all ATI tasks associated with a terminal, but not any others. If you write to a TD queue that starts a transaction not associated with a terminal, this transac-

**254 Chapter Fourteen**

tion will not be restarted in the event of a failure, unless you write to the queue again. At this point you might want to restart the nonrecoverable ATI tasks by writing to their queues in the DFHTBP exit.

## 14.3. Main Storage Recovery Concepts

In this section we will discuss the concepts of main storage recovery, reviewing some of the material presented in Chap. 2, "Storage Control," and Chap. 4, "Program Control," from the perspective of recovery.

### 14.3.1. The storage cushion

A potential shortage of storage in the DSA is indicated when storage cushion size is exceeded. The storage cushion is actually nothing but a threshold, which is specified in the SIT.

In obsolete CICS versions, there was an area of storage in the DSA that actually was set aside, from which we could grab storage when we needed it, sort of like the reserve tank in a Volkswagen. We do not have this any more, and the storage cushion is now an Available Page Threshold, which if breached can lead to the potentially terminal Short-on-Storage condition.

When we reach or exceed the threshold, the message "system under stress" is displayed, and SCP tries to get back enough storage to avoid going into the Short-on-Storage (SOS) condition. If it is unsuccessful at this, it sets the SOS flag in the CSA +48, which puts the system into SOS mode. SCP also has an algorithm that will produce an SOS condition if the storage becomes too fragmented even if there are enough pages.

### 14.3.2. Program compression

Program compression happens when there is a potential SOS condition, during SOS, or whenever it is detected that the Program storage subpool (subpool 08) is encroaching into the other subpool areas. When the two areas meet, we have got such a fragmented situation that it becomes a potential SOS condition.

The name "program compression" is really a misnomer, because this routine does not compress programs, but rather deletes them in an attempt to free up storage. To be eligible for deletion, a program must be marked for deletion and have a use count of zero. Sometimes there is a timing problem, so that a program's delete flag is on, but its use count is not zero. It is possible for the use count to go to zero and then back up again before the program ever has a chance to be deleted. This occurs because the two things are done at different times by different control modules.

## Recovery/Restart Examples   255

Storage Control looks at the program's use count and, if it is zero, marks the program eligible for deletion (changes X'08' to X'18' in byte map 1 in the PAM) the next time around. There is no particular criterion other than use count. PCP later checks to see if the program is in use, and adjusts the program's use count in the PAM. You would think that if the use count went to zero, PCP would check to see whether the program was flagged for deletion. But it does not. When SCP regains control, it notes that PCP said that the use count went to zero, and prepares to delete the program, but first checks the use count again to make sure it is still zero, because Program Control does not tell Storage Control when the use count goes back to 1.

Program compression is nature's way of recycling the DSA by rotating Program subpool pages so that they are concentrated at the high end of the DSA. If it never occurred, programs would be loaded indefinitely. It takes place only if PAMCMPRS is set, which shows that since the last compression, at least one program's use count went to zero. It flags programs for deletion until it reaches the high address or the ideal packing point, which is the point where there are just enough pages in the DSA to hold all currently allocated nonprogram storage, and also satisfy the cushion. Loaded programs are pushed up to the high address end.

How often should program compression be invoked? It is a perfectly normal process, and can occur a couple of times a minute or an hour, or a few times a day. However, 45 times a minute all day long might signal that you are spending too much time doing program compression, which entails additional overhead to load the deleted program back the next time it is needed. SI loader does a very time-consuming thing called real I/O, so that a minimal number of compressions is natural and desirable, but too many can mean performance degradation. By looking at the CICS shutdown statistics you can see how many times SOS occurred, but not how many times program compression occurred. However, you can infer that the maximum number of times a nonresident program was loaded is the minimum number of program compressions. Also, various packages on the market can provide this important statistic. Remember, program compression may happen many times for one SOS condition, and may also happen many times without going SOS.

CICS/ESA 3.1 offers Extended DSA (EDSA), which is above the 16-Mbyte line, for DSA-constrained systems that may have been doing too many program compressions. Additionally, 3.1 offers a new least recently used (LRU) algorithm to delete programs more gradually, coupled with a new attribute that gives the user more control over how storage is compressed: only programs and maps defined as transient will be deleted when their use counts drop to zero.

### 256 Chapter Fourteen

### 14.3.3. The Short-on-Storage (SOS) condition

If program compression fails, SCP suspends tasks waiting for storage by moving them over to the suspend chain. A stall condition might now occur as a result of many programs sitting on the suspend chain. At this point CICS takes some extreme action: the storage cushion was reached, and the DSA is full. Task Control goes up the suspend chain and begins cancelling stall-purgeable tasks, testing for SOS each time, in hopes of freeing up enough storage to save the system.

SOS ends when there are no tasks on the suspend chain waiting for storage, and we have enough DSA pages to equal SCS (storage cushion size) + 1. SOS is a condition to be avoided. During SOS, all transaction initiation stops. Each time a GETMAIN is issued, SCP does a program compression. Each time a FREEMAIN is issued, SCP checks the amount of free storage, checks a bit in the PAM to see if there are tasks waiting for storage (PAMREQQI), then scans the entire chain of suspended tasks, looking for those with the "waiting for storage" bit set. It continues through the chain even if the retry for tasks already waiting has failed, a very expensive process that can also change the sequence of work, as it is a LIFO process, with the last task on the chain being the first one out.

How can SOS be avoided? Mainly by providing enough virtual storage. Remember that program compression is effective as a buffer against SOS if there are lots of Program storage pages. Other tuning techniques are proper page data set placement, loading programs in the LPA, or changing the IEALIMIT exit.

Frequently used programs are effectively resident in the DSA if they are never deleted because their use count never drops to zero. They have moved in, with toothbrush, robe, and TV, so to speak, and should probably be made resident (PPT RES=YES) in the nucleus. Only transients should be in the dynamic storage area. Increasing the storage cushion size will probably not help. Since SCS is just a threshold and not real storage, it works in reverse, so that when you increase it you increase the number of program compressions, since the threshold is reached more often. What is the correct size? One recommendation is to take the size of your largest program, add 10 percent, and round up to a page boundary. But even this is not foolproof, as there is no guarantee that the remaining storage will be contiguous, which is required for Program storage.

A task is made stall-purgeable by coding SPURGE=YES in PCT, or it can be made so dynamically (DFHKC TYPE=PURGE). What is a good stall purge candidate? Any long-running task or task that starts itself every couple of minutes, such as a message delivery task. It helps if the task is associated with a terminal so that the purge can be noted by the operator. Conversational tasks are very good candidates because they are around for a long time and tend to have a high resource utilization, which can increase drastically in a stall. They also have a tendency to be found on the suspend chain, since terminal I/O suspends the task.

Normally, a DTB=YES transaction is not a good SPURGE candidate, because of the amount of overhead needed to perform a backout. Remember, the point of purging is to free up storage by eliminating processing. In this case, if DTB is unable to complete because of lack of resources, there will be a system failure, and the transaction will eventually be backed out by DFHTBP during Emergency Restart.

### 14.3.4. Storage violation recovery

There are three subpools that are particularly vulnerable to storage violations because they are used by applications: TP, Mixed, and Isolated (Mixed goes away after CICS 2.1). For those subpools, CICS provides duplicate SAAs (Storage Accounting Areas), one on either end of the data they are describing.

A storage violation means that a destroyed SAA has been detected during the processing of a GETMAIN or FREEMAIN. To recover, the Storage Recovery Program (DFHSCR) copies the good copy of the SAA over the damaged copy. If we violate storage that does not have an SAA, we go down with a storage violation dump, which is very costly, causing the system to practically grind to a halt. Storage recovery is set by specifying SVD=(NO|YES|nn) in the SIT. (You can request the first nn dumps.) If the corrupted area cannot be restored, DFHSCR might just patch around it, so you will lose some DSA during the execution. SCR recovers SAAs, but not the user data. So the question becomes whether you want this type of recovery on a production system. What are the chances that only the 8-byte SAA was destroyed, and none of the user data on either side? Probably pretty low. On the other hand, the production system needs to stay up, and the task will probably abend with an ASRA some time later, when it encounters the bad user data.

### 14.3.5. Storage recovery logic

For recovery, DFHSCR figures out which subpool is involved, and will recover only three subpools: TP, Isolated, and Mixed (or, for later versions of CICS, just TP and Isolated). It figures out whether there was a GETMAIN or FREEMAIN performed, and thus knows whether to chase FAQEs or SAAs, and decide whether it can find the error.

For a FREEMAIN, SCR looks to see whether the address is outside the subpool, whether it is pointing to a free area (a FREEMAIN should point to an allocated area), or to an area whose SAA is invalid, and the address on the chain where the SAA is invalid. If DFHSCR can locate the

**258  Chapter Fourteen**

error, it will try to locate and use the duplicate SAA. If DFH0503 cannot find the error or use the duplicate SAA, it issues an abend. If this was a `GETMAIN`, the FAQE chain is invalid. If the error is found, DFHSCR tries to correct the chain by using the backward FAQE chains and retrying the request. Again, if it cannot locate the error, it issues a DFH0503. If a FAQE is corrupted, DFHSCR tries to take it out of circulation by giving it a length of 10 so that it will be bypassed (FAQE length field includes L'FAQE, which is 12). Or it will simply chain around the bad FAQE. If the pointer is okay, but DFHSCR has searched the entire FAQE chain, CICS abends with a DFH0503.

## 14.4. Temporary Storage Recovery

There are two kinds of temporary storage: main (TS MAIN) and auxiliary (TS AUX). There is no support for DTB or Emergency Restart for TS MAIN. User journaling is possible, through explicit Journal Control or through a Temporary Storage Program (DFHTSP) exit. TS AUX, since it resides on nonvolatile storage media, can usually be recovered, and is supported by both DTB and Emergency Restart.

### 14.4.1. Users of TS recoverable DATAIDs

To recover temporary storage, the DATAID, or the first few characters, must be defined in the TST. By coding a TST, we let CICS know about the queues we wish to protect. Most of the time the application program writes to an unprotected TS queue, and the name often consists of the four-character terminal id followed by four other characters, perhaps the transaction id.

For recoverable queues you might set up a scheme where the first two characters are AR, meaning Application Recoverable, then the next four characters could be the termid and the next two some sort of unique identifier. In the TST you can then specify that every queue name starting with AR is recoverable.

Interval Control, BMS, and Terminal Control all are users of recoverable DATAIDs. The default request id name for Interval Control is DFxxxxxx. Following is the format of the Interval Control `START` command and equivalent macro:

- `START TRANSID(tranid) FROM(data) REQID(reqidnme)`
- `DFHIC TYPE=PUT,ICDADDR=queuedata,REQID=reqidnme`

For BMS, the default request id name is \*\*xxxxxx for SEND and \$\$xxxxxx for CMSG. Here are various instances of BMS usage:

Recovery/Restart Examples    259

- SEND MAP(mapname) PAGING ACCUM REQID(reqidname)

- SEND PAGE REQID(reqidname)

- DFHBMS TYPE=(PAGEBLD,STORE),MAP=mapname,REQID=YES

- ROUTE REQID(reqidname)

- DFHBMS TYPE=ROUTE,REQID=YES

- CMSG PROTECT=YES/NO/prefix

The Terminal Control SEND and RECEIVE commands have a type of recovery, available to VTAM terminals only, which also makes use of recoverable DATAIDs: recovery of transactions that have been defined in the PCT with protection options, such as Protect or Message Integrity. The request ids are DFHZxxxx, DFHMxxxx, and DFHDxxxx.

- SEND FROM(outdata)

- DFHTC TYPE=WRITE

- RECEIVE INTO(indata)

- DFHTC TYPE=READ

The DBP also uses temporary storage. The default DATAID is x'FF',c'DTB xxx', where xxx is the task id number. The x'FF' is difficult to key, thus minimizing the possibility that a user might enter this name in the TST.

Direct user requests also take advantage of recoverable temporary storage, and this is what we are mostly concerned with as application programmers. This is the format of the command and equivalent macro:

- WRITEQ TS QUEUE(queuename) FROM(queuedata) AUXILIARY REWRITE

- DFHTS TYPE=PUT/PUTQ,DATAID=qname,TSADDR=qdata,
        TYPOPFR=REPLACE

This is an example of what a TST might look like:

```
DFHTST TYPE=INITIAL,SUFFIX=xx,TSAGE=1
DFHTST TYPE=ENTRY,DATAID=($$,**,DFHZ,DFHM,DFHD,DF)
  (BMS CMSG, BMM OTHER, VTAM, IC)
DFHTST TYPE=ENTRY,DATAID=user entries
DFHTST TYPE=FINAL
```

The TSAGE= parameter of the TYPE=INITIAL macro stands for temporary storage age, which says, in this example, to recover only those DATAIDs one day old or younger. The next entry is a multiple entry which covers every DATAID that starts with $$, **, etc. We use additional entries to specify our own queues.

Figure 14.5 contains an example of how Temporary Storage is protected by enqueue/dequeue logic. The PUTQ and GETQ in the example are the equivalents to the command-level READQ and WRITEQ. What is the difference between a TS PUT and PUTQ? When Temporary Storage first became available, it was a single-record scratchpad facility, written to with a TYPE=PUT macro. Later, when it became a collection of records, or a queue, the TYPE=PUTQ macro became available. There is no command-level equivalent to the TYPE=PUT macro for Temporary Storage.

#### 14.4.2. TS resource protection characteristics

We can see in this example that Task 1 causes an enqueue on the character string "DFHTS.queuename". During this time Task 2 can read

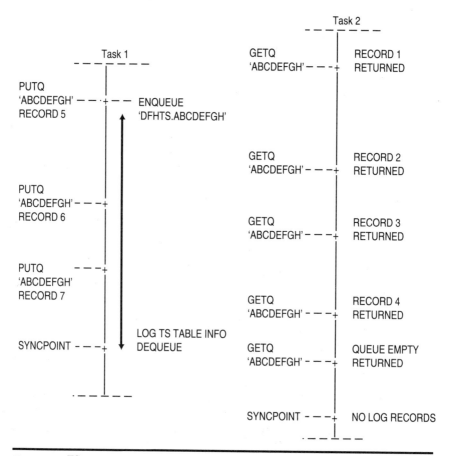

**Figure 14.5** TS resource protection.

Recovery/Restart Examples **261**

the queue and is able to get records 1 through 4, but it cannot access records 5 through 7 because these records do not exist on the queue until the Task 1 LUW takes a syncpoint. We have an enqueue on the DATAID until syncpoint, with one task able to modify the DATAID and other tasks able to read it.

When protection has been defined for an AUX DATAID in the TST, a DWE is created for the following operations:

- `WRITEQ TS QUEUE(qname) FROM(qdata)`
- `DFHTS TYPE=PUT/PUTQ,DATAID=qname`
- `DELETQ TS QUEUE(qname)`
- `DFHTS TYPE=PURGE/RELEASE,DATAID=qname`
- `DFHTS TYPE=GET,DATAID=qname,RELEASE=YES`

The DWE is processed at syncpoint time or at logical or physical EOT. At this time the VSAM buffer is written, the logical queue count is updated to the physical queue count, and a `DFHKC TYPE=DEQALL` is issued.

### 14.4.3. TS DTB and Emergency Restart

For DTB to take place, the DATAID must be defined in the TST. The DATAID is restored to its status at the start of the LUW. `PUT` or `PUTQ` records are restored, new records are deleted, pointers for replaced records are reset, and the temporary storage byte map for the CI status is reset to where it was at the start of the LUW. There are no specific exits for Temporary Storage, but at the input exit XDBINP you can examine each log record, decide whether or not it is Temporary Storage, and take whatever action is indicated. Do not modify recoverable Temporary Storage at the initial exit, or it will be backed out, of course.

Emergency Restart is similar: DFHSIP starts out with a cold start, and does not format the Temporary Storage data set. DFHRUP reads the activity keypoint and syncpoint records on the system log and creates a table of DATAIDs and queue counts. It also copies TS `REPLACE` records back to the restart data set (RDS).

Then we go to a special processing module for Temporary Storage only, DFHTSRP. This program locates RBAs for recoverable DATAIDs by scanning the Temporary Storage data set, and re-creates the Temporary Storage Utility Table (TSUT), the Temporary Storage Identification (TSID), and the byte map. It creates and chains ICEs if there is an Interval Control identifier in the TS record (DATAID DFxxxxxx, the standard for Interval Control). ICEs may have been created by IC `PUT`s which were using Temporary Storage at the time.

**262   Chapter Fourteen**

Next, DFHTBP, which has the before-image of replaced records available to it, proceeds to back out TS REPLACE records by rewriting the before-image. And those ICEs that were chained by DFHTSRP are started as they would be in normal processing: the ICE expires and becomes a task.

The chart in Fig. 14.6 shows a comparison of TS recovery. Emergency Restart contains a little extra processing of aged messages. CICS is now designed to run nonstop. The only time it should come down is during a system hit or some type of maintenance. So TSAGE allows us to get rid of things that are just lying around, that people forgot to delete. This cannot be done selectively by DATAID; it is for all the recoverable queues or none.

## 14.5. Interval Control Recovery

Figure 14.7 illustrates how Interval Control uses Temporary Storage. The Interval Control PUT to queue 'ABCDEFGH' (equivalent to the WRITEQ command) causes a TS PUT and an enqueue on 'DFHTS.ABCDEFGH'. Task initiation does not get deferred until syncpoint, which, as we will see, can cause some funny results.

In the example, as Task 2 starts, perhaps something else may be going on in Task 1, such as a File Control WAIT, thus giving Task 2 a chance to start. Task 2 does an IC GET on the DATAID, causing a TS GET with RELEASE, which means it is destroyed (no command-level

| DTB | Emergency Restart | Warm Restart |
|---|---|---|
| AUX:<br>Backout changes to recoverable DATAIDs | AUX:<br>Backout changes to recoverable DATAIDs made by in-flight tasks.<br>Committed recoverable DATAIDs are kept. | All AUX DATAIDs kept<br><br>No backout |
| MAIN:<br>No backout | MAIN:<br>No backout<br><br>Aged messages purged as per TSAGE | Main is lost<br><br>TSAGE not used |

**Figure 14.6**  TS DTB and restart comparison.

### Recovery/Restart Examples

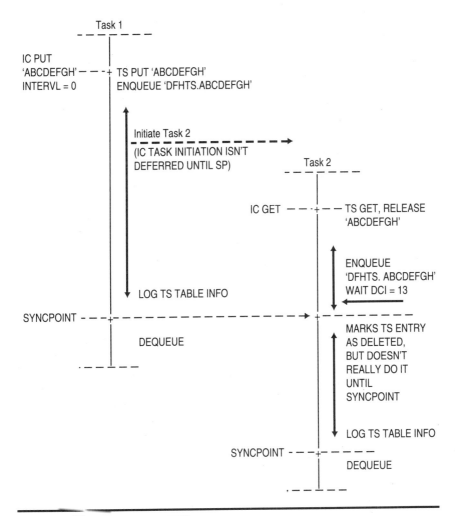

**Figure 14.7** IC PUT resource protection.

equivalent). Task 1 still has control of this piece of storage by virtue of the enqueue on it, so Task 2, as it attempts an enqueue, is forced to WAIT with DCI=13. Then Task 1 takes a syncpoint, logs information in the TST, and dequeues on the storage. At this point Task 2 logically deletes the storage. It does not actually delete it but marks it for deletion, because there are no guarantees that Task 2 will complete, and the record may have to be put back in case of an abend. When Task 2 takes a syncpoint, it really deletes the storage, dequeues on it, and logs that it was deleted. The mark which prevents access to the queue record is

**264    Chapter Fourteen**

called the logical deletion flag. This mark prevents deleted records from being presented to other tasks that may be reading the queue.

### 14.5.1. IC PUT resource protection characteristics

Protection is provided only for TS AUX defined in the TST, and extends until syncpoint for the DATAID. DWEs are created for:

- `START TRANSID(tranid) FROM(trandata) LENGTH(datalen) REQID(queuename)`

- `DFHIC TYPE=PUT,TRANSID=tranid,ICDADDR=trandata,REQID=qname`

DWE processing consists of updating the logical to physical queue counts, logging the Temporary Storage information on the system log, writing the VSAM buffer, and issuing a `DFHKC TYPE=DEQ`. If the task issuing a `START` or `DFHIC TYPE=PUT` abends, we back out the IC control data (Temporary Storage), but the ICE does not get cancelled and the task may start, although it may not have anything to read. If the started task abends, we back out normally, as we would for the task. Protected resources are backed out, and the task is not reinitiated.

### 14.5.2. Interval Control DTB and Emergency Restart

Interval Control issues temporary storage macros, both `PUT` and `PUTQ`, both `GET` and `GETQ`, and `RELEASE` and `PURGE` macros (a `PURGE` purges something created with a `PUTQ`, and a `RELEASE` purges something created with a `PUT`). For a `START` without data there is no backout, because there is no Temporary Storage involved. When do things get `START`ed?

In an earlier example we saw that the `START` gets honored before a syncpoint. Now we will see that IBM giveth and IBM taketh away. A task can `START` in the middle of an LUW, but then it will not get backed out: since it is happening independent of syncpoint, CICS loses track of it. However, if we do a `START` with data, it is a little bit different because we now may qualify for Temporary Storage recovery.

Let us look at a `START` with a recoverable DATAID, that is, a `START` with data that is recoverable. The good news is that the data gets backed out. The bad news is that the task is ready to go and CICS will not cancel it. So what happens? The new task starts and, expecting data, issues a `READ`, but gets a DATAID error, because the data has been backed out. Remember, we are talking not about the task that issued the `START`, but about the task that was started.

Things are different with Emergency Restart. For `START` requests

| DTB | Emergency Restart | Warm Restart |
|---|---|---|
| START w/recoverable DATAID: Data is backed out, task initiation isn't cancelled: new task gets DATAID error on READQ | START requests with recoverable AUX DATAIDs are backed out if the task was in flight. | All START requests with data are kept, if SIT TSP = WARM |
| No backout for START without data. | START requests without data are lost. | START requests without data are kept |
| An incomplete STARTed task w/recoverable DATAID is backed out. | Incomplete STARTed tasks w/recoverable DATAIDs are backed out and restarted | No backout or restarting of incomplete STARTed tasks |

**Figure 14.8** IC DTB and restart comparison.

with recoverable data, the request gets backed out. Tasks with no data will never be started. But an incomplete started task gets restarted. This is the opposite of what happens with DTB. We can see that there are some anomalies between DTB and Emergency Restart. Some of them are by design. Some of them are because certain resources are available for the different actions. During DTB the system is still running, whereas at Emergency Restart the system is not running, we are bringing it back. So the difference in environments can affect the manner in which recovery is performed. Figure 14.8 compares the differences by type of recovery, step by step.

## 14.6. BMS Recovery and DTB (Page Building)

BMS recovery is available in limited form to users of BMS paging. For those who use this BMS feature, Fig. 14.9 may be of some interest. CRASH means that the system goes down, and what is written after it applies to Emergency Restart. ABEND refers to a task abend and applies to DTB.

# 266 Chapter Fourteen

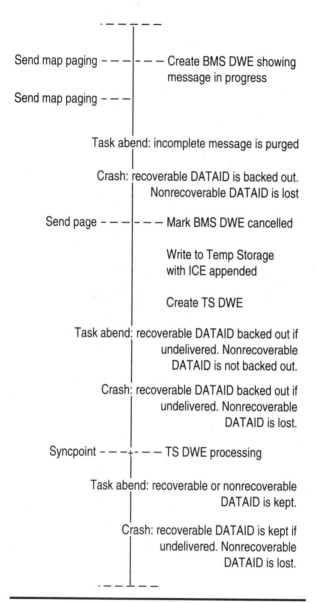

Figure 14.9  BMS recovery and DTB.

### 14.6.1. BMS DTB and Emergency Restart

Figure 14.10 shows the disposition of completed and incompleted messages written to recoverable DATAIDs during DTB, Emergency Restart, and Warm Restart.

| DTB | Emergency Restart | Warm Restart |
|---|---|---|
| Incomplete messages are purged for both recoverable and nonrecoverable DATAIDs.<br><br>If not already sent, complete messages written to recoverable DATAIDs are backed out. | All complete and syncpointed messages that were written to a recoverable DATAID are kept.<br><br>Incomplete or unsyncpointed messages written to recoverable DATAIDs are backed out. | All completed routed messages are kept if TSP = WARM and ICP = WARM.<br><br>Messages completed with RETAIN or RELEASE are lost.<br><br>No backout (PURGE) of incomplete messages. |

**Figure 14.10** BMS DTB and restart comparison.

## 14.7. Terminal Control Error Handling

There is no DTB or Emergency Restart available for BTAM, but applications can use user journaling or Terminal Control input and output exits.

Both DTB and Emergency Restart are available in VTAM for protected tasks (for nonprotected tasks, users may journal, as for BTAM). For error processing, VTAM and BTAM drive exits in CICS, routines which attempt to figure out what kind of error occurred. They pass the information on to DFHZCP or DFHTCP (Fig. 14.11), who then pass it on to the Node Abnormal Condition Program (DFHZNAC) or the Terminal Abnormal Condition Program (DFHTACP), where the error is analyzed and some sort of default action provided. DFHZNAC is associated with the transaction CSNE, DFHTACP with CSTE. User code is in the Node Error Program (DFHZNEP) or the Terminal Error Program (DFHTEP); in that code we can either accept the action or in some cases override it. The final word though, lies with DFHZNAC or DFHTACP.

### 14.7.1. User recovery strategy

In this section we will ask (and try to answer) a few questions about terminal recovery:

## 268 Chapter Fourteen

| Processing | VTAM | BTAM |
|---|---|---|
| Error detected by | VTAM | BTAM |
| Error info passed to | DFHZCP | DFHTCP |
| Error analyzed and default action set by | DFHZNAC (CSNE) | DFHTACP (CSTE) |
| User accepts defaults or changes action in | DFHZNEP | DFHTEP |
| Final error processor | DFHZNAC | DFHTACP |

**Figure 14.11** Terminal Control error handling.

- Why bother?
- What recovery makes sense?
- When and how can recovery be accomplished?

In answer to the first question, why bother, take an example of an operator who needs to know if an update took place. We might have a transaction that sends a message out to confirm that something has been done. It might not be practical or even reliable for the operator to run a confirmation transaction to see whether or not the update was successful. So we would like to be able to send a message out saying that something happened, and we would like to have confidence that this message gets through in all situations. For instances such as this, a little recovery may be in order.

If there is an error, we can either reroute the message to another terminal or send it to the same terminal later. Maybe the message is destined for a printer (CICS reroutes messages to alternative destinations such as CSTT).

The Terminal Control terminal user area (TCTUA) is a way to keep information on a terminal basis rather than a task basis. The good thing about the TCTUA is that it is still there after the task is no longer attached. The bad thing is that it requires a lot of storage. Let us say you have 20,000 terminals, each with a TCTUA of 500 bytes. This is not storage acquired when it is needed; it is there all the time, as part of the TCT. So this is not really being recommended, although it must be noted as a way to keep terminal-oriented information between tasks. The autoinstall feature helps in this regard, since the terminal is not defined if it is not in session.

You could recover a problem by issuing an IC START to start a task that will get the message out to either another terminal or a printer, or to start a task later, in case the problem clears. The VTAM resend queue and a user resend program can be used to send the message to the same terminal at the next session.

You can even have a table that keeps track of how this is going: if it has not been routed within an hour, try something different. The above can be accomplished during ZNEP/TEP processing, which is user-written error processing.

### 14.7.2. ZNAC/ZNEP interface (VTAM)

What we are really interested in is the interface between ZNEP and ZNAC during error processing. In general, ZCP issues a DFHKC TYPE=ATTACH of transaction CSNE (NE for node error). ZNAC points to the TCT and the problem TCTTE. ZNAC sets some default action flags, then LINKs to ZNEP, which addresses CSNE's TWA. There is an IBM-supplied ZNEP which you can modify to do your own processing. In ZNEP we can go into CSNE's TWA and modify whatever action bits we need to modify, and ZNAC will accept some of the modifications. The CICS Customization Guide explains what the different bits are.

### 14.7.3. ZNEP recommendations

Using the sample NEP is not recommended unless your processing needs are extremely basic: it will not do things like reroute messages to another terminal or save messages to be rerouted later. Take the sample NEP and use it as a guide. Again, the Customization Guide is pretty clear on this. You can code a NEP with subroutines for each LU type, since each LU type sends different combinations of sense information on the same error. Rather than attempting to construct some kind of giant decision table, it is easier to simply test for one kind of sense information and go to the appropriate subroutine. Once there, and this is a matter of programming style, you might want to go to a subroutine specific to the type of error.

You can look at the status analysis routine in DFHZNAC for examples of actual coding techniques for analyzing the problem. Use one NEP-CLASS in the PCT. When you specify NEPCLASS in the PCT, it says go to such and such a node error processing routine if there is a VTAM error. This is probably not such a good idea, as we again run into the problem of different LU types. Transactions do not need to be assigned to sepa-

**270    Chapter Fourteen**

rate LU types: we want them to be able to run on different types of LUs. So a good approach might be to have a common entry point, after which a branch is made to the appropriate routine based on LUTYPE, then a branch to the indicated action routine based on the error.

If it is really necessary to do specific processing for particular transactions (perhaps you get the same error on the same LUTYPE, but you want it treated differently for different transactions), use a table of transids.

### 14.7.4.  TACP/TEP interface (BTAM)

The sample TEP provided by IBM is not a general cure. It should be used as a design and coding example, and is fairly easy to modify. The TEP Table (DFHTEPT) is a table associated with TEP that holds error information for each terminal. TEPT contains a header (TETH) that points to entries within the TEP Table. The table entries are called terminal error blocks (TEBs) and are either permanent (PTEBs), temporary (TTEBs), or reusable (RTEBs). Each TEB has the termid and error status elements (ESEs) from BTAM, which contain the number of errors for each terminal.

There are two tables: one is the limits for error condition table (TEPT), and the other is the TEP default action table. This table contains default actions and threshold values for each type of error. It is indexed by an array in its prefix. If the index value is positive, the error code has a permanently defined ESE in each TEB, and the index value is the displacement to the ESE. If it is negative, an ESE must be defined dynamically from a reusable ESE (if one has not been created because of a prior occurrence). The complement of the negative index value is the displacement to the threshold limits for the error type retained in the TEP default table.

The Customization Guide provides a detailed look at this. Basically, there are ESEs that are defined permanently and also a pool of them that can be used. This is so you can cut down the size of the TEPT. Writing a TEP is a tedious chore. You must go through the Customization Guide with a fine-tooth comb, getting all the details in place. The overall flow goes like this:

- TCP puts the terminal or, if necessary, the line out of service.

- TCP then creates a new control block called the terminal abnormal condition line entry (TACLE), which is chained off the normal TCT line entry (TCTLE), for the line involved in the error.

- TCP places error information and action flags in the TACLE TCP, then attaches CSTE, the Terminal Error Program, which is associated with the Terminal Abnormal Condition Program (DFHTACP).

- TACP analyzes the error and sets default flags in the TACLE.

- TACP LINKs to TEP, passing the TACLE address.

- TEP returns to TACP, after possibly changing some of the flags.

- TACP examines the TACLE action flags, some of which may have been changed by TEP, and handles the errors as per the flags.

- CSTE terminates.

What we have talked about so far is normal terminal error processing: things that you will get no matter what you specify in the PCT. For VTAM, you can specify things in the PCT such as Protect. When you specify these things in the PCT, the Protect takes effect only for VTAM, so if you are running an all-VTAM shop you are okay, but if you are not, then you are going to get different actions—for example, we do not have DTB for BTAM. So another thing you can specify in the PCT just to be on the safe side, just as protection against the possible addition of a BTAM terminal to your network, is to protect the transaction (that is, make it DTBable), protect or define message integrity, and also only allow this transaction to run on a VTAM terminal.

## 14.8.  VTAM Message Protection Logging

Both DTB and Emergency Restart are available for message-protected, DTB=YES tasks. Message protection logging means that we specified PROTECT=YES in the PCT. The task is attached and we log the input message and the sequence numbers. We do a terminal WRITE, and indicate a deferred WRITE: the WRITE does not really happen. Rather, a DWE is created. The transaction does a RETURN, which implies a syncpoint. At syncpoint we log the output and the sequence numbers, place the message on the WAIT queue, log end of task, then do a STARTIO for the log WRITE, which forces a journal WRITE (Fig. 14.12).

There is a problem with this. We are in a VTAM shop with 37X5s all over the place, we have 20,000 terminals on-line, we are SNA, and we have got this tape drive hanging out there. Every time we send a message through our super network, we are going to force a WRITE to the tape. That's a serious drawback.

Message protection is very, very costly, and should be done only if we have really got to save that message. This is something that can be avoided with a good system design. Of course, we could be writing to disk instead of tape. But still, a STARTIO means a physical I/O. We have a block that holds maybe 42 journal records. We write one record to the block, then say WRITE it. So we have multiplied the number of

# Chapter Fourteen

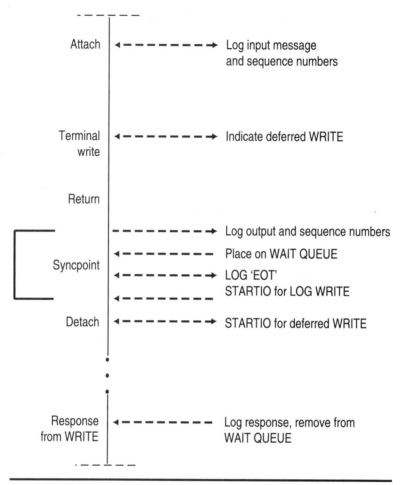

**Figure 14.12** VTAM message protection logging.

possible writes by 42. What is the biggest bottleneck in any system? I/O. So there's really not a lot to recommend this kind of processing.

To avoid this, you might do your processing in ZNAC if you really have to protect the message. You might want to do something at the TC or ZC output exit or input exit: you could determine whether this was a crucial message and then take some action. A lot of this takes place at design time, and requires a good understanding of the resources involved.

### 14.8.1. DTB for message-protected, DTB=YES tasks

What actually happens after we have done all this logging and journaling before we send out the message on VTAM? In PCP we enter the

SET EXIT (STXIT) routine and get a transaction dump. We then enter DBP if it is DTB=YES. We issue a DFHTC TYPE=RECOVER, which brings us into DFHZCP. In ZCP we reset the write request, clear the DWE, then return to DBP. DBP links to the Abnormal Condition Program (DFHACP). If it is Stall Purge, we set a sense bit. We write a message to CSMT, then return to DBP.

DBP then calls the various DWE processors (TD, FC, BMS, etc.). Then we XCTL to DFHACP. At this point either DBP has backed out the message or it hasn't. There is also the possibility that DBP failed. So DFHACP sets the sense to one of the following:

| | |
|---|---|
| Success | 0824089E (backout was ok) |
| Errors | 0824089F (backout no good) |
| DBP Abend | 082408A0 (DFHDBP failed) |

After this, DFHACP LINKs to DFHPEP, where we can do our own processing. Then we RETURN to DFHACP, where it does a TD PUT to CSMT with message DFH2206, 2207, or 2208, saying either that backout was okay, that backout was no good, or that DBP failed. We then branch to DFHPCP to issue a DFHKC TYPE=DETACH for the task.

Emergency Restart is pretty much the same for VTAM protected messages as it is for other processing. The Recovery Utility Program (DFHRUP) copies logged and journaled messages from the system log to the restart data set. It creates the Message Backout Table (MBO) from information found on the log and writes the MBO to the restart data set, then branches to the Transaction Backout Program (DFHTBP). If the message was committed but in doubt (that is, the transaction committed it, but we do not know whether it arrived), it is written to a Temporary Storage queue (DFHZtermid), which is a recoverable DATAID. It flags the TCTTE as requiring recovery. If there were messages from an active task, we write to another Temporary Storage queue (DFHMtermid) the following:

- The last output sent, if it was an output message.
- The last input, if it was an in-flight task.

Finally we set some recovery indicators. For more information on how CICS communicates with VTAM, refer to the Customization Guide and the Diagnosis Reference Guide. There is also a very good discussion in the back of the System Programmer's Reference Guide for version 1.5, if you still happen to have one lying around.

## 14.9. Summary

One more thing we must consider is what will happen when recovery fails. What happens when we get an I/O error on the system log while creating the restart data set? An important step in designing recovery procedures is to sit down and pose the tough question, "What do we do when all this stuff doesn't work?"

There are no generalizations to be made. Extended Recovery and Disaster Recovery are two current attempts to lessen the impact of failure. Disaster Recovery involves the idea of a CICS "hot" site which maintains a redundant "mirror image" of the system. So far this has not met with much success because of the tremendous costs involved in duplicating a network.

One obvious place to address the issue is in the application itself. Not only do we need to design the application to take advantage of recovery facilities in the best possible way, we also need to design it so that impact is minimal in the event recovery itself fails. It is important to design the application so that it does not rely too much on all this in the first place.

Chapter

# 15

# Advanced Recovery Topics

## 15.1. Introduction

We have seen that two main objectives of the recovery process are to ensure not only the integrity of resources, but also their availability. The demand for continuously running on-line systems is increasing, and much attention is being paid to this area, as is evidenced in some of IBM's recent product announcements.

CICS/ESA version 3.1.1 and the accompanying IMS/ESA version 3.1.1 do much to address the issue, as do the Extended Recovery Facility (XRF) and CICS VSAM Recovery (CICSVR). This chapter describes some of the new features relating to recovery and availability in the following products:

- CICS/ESA 3.1.1
- XRF
- DBCTL
- CICSVR

## 15.2. CICS/ESA

CICS/ESA 3.1.1 takes a step forward in the area of storage isolation, with a new domain-based architecture. Major parts of CICS have been restuctured into functionally separate areas called domains, which communicate through a strict standard interface called the kernel.

Management modules such as Storage Control and Task Control have been rewritten. The new CICS offers improved reliability, with domains taking responsibility for the resources they own. Domain isolation offers better protection against storage violations, and minimizes the impact of failures when they can be contained within the domain in which they occur.

275

**276   Chapter Fifteen**

For VSAM, extensions to Resource Definition On-line (RDO), backout failure control, and the CICSVR forward recovery facility offer further support for continuous operations. CICS/ESA extensions to RDO provide for the on-line definition of VSAM files and LSR pools. With backout failure control, if DTB or Emergency Restart fails while backing out a particular VSAM data set, CICS sets a backout failed switch in the catalog and base cluster, writes a journal record, and prevents further updates to the data set. Whereas previously the course of action was to abend CICS in order to preserve data integrity, this is no longer the case. For IMS databases, the new CICS–IMS interface called DBCTL isolates DL/I from CICS, in a manner similar to DB2.

## 15.3. Extended Recovery Facility

Support for the Extended Recovery Facility (XRF) was first made available to CICS with the release of CICS/MVS 2.1.1, and a CICS system running with `XRF=YES` can communicate with another CICS 1.7 or later, and with IMS 2.1 or later. For CICS, XRF automates the recovery process by providing restart after a system failure. It can also be used to keep a CICS system running during application of service or maintenance.

Over the years, fault-tolerant systems were developed that used duplication of hardware to allow graceful degradation instead of outright failure. IBM's offering for CICS involves distributing the workload across subsystems through the use of MRO and ISC, optionally in conjunction with XRF. Although its full effect and capability depend upon the underlying hardware configuration, XRF may be seen as a software approach.

XRF is not specifically a CICS product, but works for CICS in cooperation with other system products such as MVS, VTAM, and IMS. It can be used to address primarily CICS failures, primarily non-CICS failures, or any combination of major component failures (CEC, MVS, CICS, IMS). Only those system components which are duplicated can be protected. It cannot protect against communication failures of links, or channels, for example. However, products such as IBM's Netview or Network Command Control Facility (NCCF) can be used to complement XRF.

### 15.3.1.  How XRF works

XRF is accomplished with a pair of regions, both operating at the same release level. One runs as the active region, and the other, which is called the alternate, remains in a partially initialized standby state, monitoring the active. If the alternate detects a failure of the active, it is able to perform a takeover and become the new active region.

Advanced Recovery Topics **277**

XRF support is defined with XRF=YES in the SIT, along with START=AUTO for the active and START=STANDBY for the alternate. The type of takeover that will occur is determined by another SIT operand for the alternate, TAKEOVR= AUTO | COMMAND | MANUAL. If AUTO is specified, the takeover requires no intervention. COMMAND means that an operator command must be issued before takeover. MANUAL means that the operator must approve a takeover when the alternate is not sure that the active has failed.

The goal is to provide minimum disruption to the end user, while restarting CICS and recovering protected resources. Emergency Restart is still performed, but it is faster because the partially initialized alternate and VTAM backup sessions are already established.

### 15.3.2. The CAVM and the CLT

The active and alternate communicate with each other under the supervision of the CICS Availability Manager (CAVM), which is the software responsible for the integrity of the XRF system. The CAVM executes under its own TCB, making use of subtasking where needed. It oversees the activities of the alternate, and controls the sharing of resources.

The two regions share system and user data sets. The CICS system log (which for XRF must be on disk), journals, CICS system definition (CSD) data set, the Temporary Storage data set, the Restart data set, and other critical data sets are "passively" shared, which means that the alternate does not have access to them in its partially initialized state.

The CAVM ensures the integrity of access to these data sets through the Control data set, making sure that an active region has stopped using resources before an alternate starts using them. The CAVM Control and Message data sets are "actively" shared by both regions at all times. Some data sets—for example, the Extrapartition, Dump, Auxiliary Trace, and Statistics data sets—are unique and never shared. The CAVM also controls the takeover, using the Command List Table (CLT) to provide the various MVS commands and messages to the operator to be issued by the alternate. Each alternate has a CLT, although several logical CLTs can be combined in one physical load module. You can code a single CLT for all the regions involved in a multi-MVS MRO system.

During the time that the alternate is only partially initialized, the usual CICS system commands do not apply. CEBT commands are system console commands used from the time the alternate is initialized until after takeover, when CEMT becomes usable. They may be issued by the operator, by the overseer, or from a master or coordinator region to a dependent region. A CEBT command can, among other things, re-

**278 Chapter Fifteen**

quest or prevent a takeover, change takeover type as specified in the SIT, shut down an alternate, or switch alternate surveillance on or off.

Resource Definition On-line (RDO) provides local security at the level of the individual CICS system, but cannot provide the global protection needed by XRF. Instead, information for takeover is placed in the CLT, which is link-edited into an APF-authorized library. The MVS system commands coded in the CLT require MVS services that are restricted to authorized programs. CICS normally runs without MVS authorization, but the CICS SVC has been extended to allow these services to be used. For further security, the CLT is loaded only temporarily, when the alternate is initialized, and when it signs on to the CAVM.

### 15.3.3. Takeover

The active and alternate communicate with each other by continually sending surveillance signals to the CAVM control and message data sets. The alternate monitors the active and its VTAM sessions, and when it detects an absence of signals, it notifies the operator or initiates a takeover on its own.

A takeover shifts the work load and resources from the active to the alternate. CLT information is used to issue the commands. An MVS CANCEL command is sent to cancel the active CICS job. Shutdown programs in the PLT and any remaining steps in the CICS job are bypassed.

VTAM backup sessions established by the alternate during surveillance get switched at takeover. While the active and alternate each have specific APPLIDs that uniquely identify them to VTAM, they have the same generic APPLID, so they appear to be the same system to the user, who does not need to log on to VTAM again.

XRF makes use of the VTAM USERVAR facility to control the generic and specific APPLIDs. The user is only aware of the generic APPLID used at logon, known to VTAM as the USERVAR. Within CICS, the ASSIGN APPLID command returns the generic APPLID, and applications cannot determine the specific APPLID of the current system, or whether or not XRF is in effect. During takeover, the alternate issues an MVS MODIFY VTAMNAME USERVAR command to change the specific APPLID in the local VTAM USERVAR table, and the entire network is updated.

### 15.3.4. Recovery of terminals

A terminal's class determines the nature of its recovery. End users on class 1 or class 2 terminals do not have to log on to VTAM, and class 1 terminals, depending on options, do not have to sign on to CICS again,

Advanced Recovery Topics   **279**

since sign-on security may be passed from the active to the alternate. CICS does not determine the XRF capability of terminals, but when a terminal logs on, CICS is notified by VTAM whether the terminal is eligible to be switched automatically without losing its session. Logged-on terminals that are XRF-capable are automatically switched from the active to the backup session on the alternate CICS.

A terminal which is executing a transaction at takeover must have its session state recovered by CICS before continuing. After the switch, the terminal is processed by the Abnormal Condition Program (DFHZNAC), during which time the services of the Node Error Program (DFHZNEP) are available. Just as in non-XRF transaction backout, the user must reenter in-flight transactions that were backed out at failure.

Class 1 terminals are XRF-capable SNA VTAM terminals connected through a boundary network node (BNN) with the Network Control Program (NCP) in a 3745, 3725, or 3720 communications controller. These terminals have backup sessions to the alternate created by NCP. At takeover, the alternate issues the switch command for class 1 terminals, and service is almost continuous. Terminals that need high availability should be class 1.

For class 2 terminals, the alternate tries to reestablish the session, and there is a delay while the session is acquired. Class 2 terminals are not routed through a BNN 37xx communication controller and NCP, and are not XRF-capable. They do not have backup sessions to the alternate, but are tracked as they are acquired and released, and those active at takeover are recovered first. Class 2 terminals do not have to log on to VTAM, but they must sign on to CICS. A class 2 terminal with `RECOVOPTION(NONE)` specified in its RDO definition becomes a class 3 terminal.

Class 3 terminals, which include TCAM and non-VTAM terminals, are not tracked, and must log on after service has been reestablished. Class 3 terminals go through the normal CICS Emergency Restart procedures. The terminal loses service, and the operator must reestablish the session. However, class 3 terminals still benefit from faster restart under XRF.

The `FORCE` keyword, which determines which terminals remain signed on during takeover by forcing sign-off, can be used on three levels. In each case, if `FORCE` is used, the terminal is forced to sign off. The SIT option `XRFSOFF=FORCE|NOFORCE` applies to all terminals, and takes precedence. The `XRFSIGNOFF(FORCE|NOFORCE)` keyword on the `CEDA DEFINE TYPETERM` affects a group of terminals. The lowest level is the `XRFSOFF=FORCE|NOFORCE` keyword of the `TYPE=ENTRY` in the Sign-on Table (SNT), which can be used for a single terminal.

Two additional options for terminal definitions are used to control recovery. `RECOVOPTION` controls tracking of terminals and the specific

**280   Chapter Fifteen**

format of the recovery that is to occur. The default is to let CICS control this. RECOVNOTIFY is used to determine whether a message is sent to a terminal, notifying it that a takeover has occurred. If recovery is to be transparent, no message is sent. If a transaction is not specified for a customized message, then a default transaction and standard messages are provided.

### 15.3.5. Restart in place

A restart in place equates to an Emergency Restart of the failing active region. At times it can be used instead of a takeover, because it is faster and causes less disruption to end users not otherwise affected by a failure. For example, in a large MRO configuration across MVS images, a takeover involves all alternates. It might be desirable to first try a restart in place, before calling for a takeover of all regions. When an active is restarted in place, its alternate closes down automatically, and must be started again to continue XRF support. The overseer can be helpful when performing a restart in place.

### 15.3.6. The overseer

The overseer is an optional program which runs in its own address space, and is used to help plan, manage, and automate XRF procedures. It can accelerate the restart process by automating it. It allows sites to customize takeover procedures for specific situations, or to modify the recovery process based on the nature of the failure. The overseer obtains its information from the CAVM data sets. It can monitor and display the status of the actives and alternates, restart a failed active or a new alternate in place, or initiate a takeover.

IBM provides a sample overseer with basic functions, which can be modified to address specific installation requirements that are not satisfied in the standard SIT and CLT options. For example, instead of coding a user exit, you might choose to customize the overseer to make decisions about what course of action to take in the event of a VTAM failure. Or you might choose to issue commands through the overseer instead of the CLT.

The overseer is especially useful in a large MRO system with a hierarchy of master, coordinator, and dependent regions. A multi-MVS system needs multiple overseers, one for each MVS image.

### 15.3.7. Hierarchy of regions

In an MRO complex, the hierarchy of regions determines what happens after a failure. Each region is considered a master, dependent, or coordinator, based on CLT commands or SIT operands. The SIT operand TAKEOVER=AUTO defines a master, and TAKEOVER=COMMAND defines a dependent region. If there is more than one master, one of them can be designated in the CLT as the coordinator, to avoid duplication of effort on the part of the masters. The coordinator will then issue all the commands in event of the failure of any of the masters.

The failure of a master region results in a takeover by its alternate. The alternate issues `CEBT PERFORM TAKEOVER` commands from the CLT to all the other alternate regions involved.

The alternate of a dependent region does not automatically initiate a takeover of connected regions in the event of its own failure. In this case, a takeover command (`CEBT PERFORM TAKEOVER`) or, more probably, a restart in place command (`CEMT PERFORM SHUTDOWN`) is issued by the operator or the overseer.

## 15.4. XRF Configurations and Recovery Strategies

Many configurations of XRF are possible. You may have a single or multiple MVS images. An MVS image is a copy of the MVS operating system. You may run one or two CECs. CEC, which stands for central electronic complex, refers to several processors running under a single MVS image, or separate copies of MVS, in a logically partitioned machine. You may have XRF and non-XRF regions running in the same MVS image. You may have a combination of MRO and non-MRO XRF regions. MRO links can be maintained between XRF and non-XRF regions. You may have actives and alternates from different CICS systems in the same MVS image. Even though you can run XRF on two MVS images, you may, for some systems, prefer to run with active and alternate in the same MVS.

You may decide to install a communications management configuration (CMC), so that if the active or alternate MVS fails, VTAM ownership is not lost. In a CMC, VTAM is in a different CEC from the active or alternate. A CMC has three MVS images: one for the active, one for the alternate, and one for the VTAM network owner. In this environment, terminals owned by a VTAM in a different MVS image from that of the active CICS are defined as "cross-domain" terminals.

### 15.4.1. XRF with a single MVS

You may choose to have both the active and the alternate running in a single MVS image. In a single-CEC, single-MVS, single-region scenario, there is protection only for the part of the system that is duplicated, the CICS address space. There are two paths from NCP through VTAM: one to the active and one to the alternate. If the active fails, or upon request, the alternate takes over. Similarly, with MRO in a single-MVS image, when an active region fails, the alternate takes over

**282    Chapter Fifteen**

and reestablishes MRO links to the other actives. There is no need for the restart in place suggested for multi-MVS systems, as the other actives remain unaffected by the takeover.

### 15.4.2.  XRF with multiple MVS images

Multiple MVS images mean higher availability. You can operate in a single CEC (i.e., 3090), for example, which is either physically partitioned into multiple processors, where each partition is running under the control of a single MVS, or logically divided by the Processor Resource System Manager (PR/SM) feature into partitions, each of which can run its own MVS and VTAM images. Here XRF minimizes the effect of a CICS, MVS, or VTAM failure. However, you need two CECs to protect against a CEC outage. In a two-CEC configuration, XRF will minimize the effect of a CICS, MVS, VTAM, or CEC failure. Both CECs must share a single job queue (via JES2 multiaccess spooling or JES3) and have access to shared DASD.

In a multiple-MVS MRO configuration, the takeover is across MVS images. If one alternate takes over, all alternates in the MRO system must take over, since interregion communication does not operate across MVS images. Takeover would be indicated in the event of a CEC or MVS failure, but for a CICS failure, the importance of each region must be weighed against the disruption of the entire MRO complex. For example, you may want a takeover to occur if a terminal-owning region with XRF-capable terminals fails, but you may decide on a restart in place if an application-owning region fails.

### 15.5.  Forward Recovery with CICSVR

CICS VSAM Recovery (CICSVR) is an IBM-licensed program that provides forward recovery for VSAM data sets. CICSVR/MVS supports the journal format introduced in CICS/OS/VS 1.7, as well as a new format for CICS/ESA 3.1.1, which produces journal records not compatible with previous releases of CICS. CICSVR/VSE is the equivalent for CICS/DOS/VS 1.7, running under DOS/VSE.

CICSVR supports high availability because data sets can be recovered and returned to CICS without bringing CICS down. When a VSAM data set becomes unusable, CICSVR reads CICS journals forward, and applies after-images sequentially to a backup copy of the data set. The key to successful recovery consists of correctly defined journal options and established and rehearsed recovery procedures. Procedures include not only the execution of CICSVR, but also scheduled backups and archived journal data sets.

Advanced Recovery Topics  283

### 15.5.1. Journal archiving

Journals must be archived before they are rewritten, and kept for the period between the last and most recent backups. All journals needed beyond the day's operation of CICS should be archived. If you take a backup daily, you need only the journal produced the day after the backup was taken.

For releases prior to CICS/ESA, you can use a utility such as IEB-GENER or DFSUARC0 to archive journals to tape or disk. CICS/ESA improves journal archiving with a new journal option (JOUROPT=AUTOARCH), which, in conjunction with a new journal archive control data set (JACD), makes sure that CICS will not reuse a journal until it has been archived. It preserves journals in the order required for subsequent forward recovery, simplifies operations, and reduces opportunities for error.

### 15.5.2. How CICSVR works

CICSVR runs in batch mode, independent of CICS. Any VSAM KSDS, ESDS, or RRDS can be recovered. For a KSDS, the term *sphere* is used to refer to a base cluster and some or all of its paths. CICSVR will recover at minimum a KSDS base cluster and, optionally, all or some of its associated indexes defined as unique. It will not reapply updates to a VSAM sphere via a nonunique alternate index.

Journaling must be specified for each data set of the sphere to be recovered, and all members of the sphere must be journaled to the same journal id. Alternatively, after a base cluster is recovered, the alternate indexes may be rebuilt with the BLDINDEX command of the IDCAMS utility. CICSVR will not recover spheres that were updated in batch, or spheres that do not have after-images written to a journal data set.

### 15.5.3. Implementing forward recovery

The procedure for forward recovery consists of several steps. For each data set to be recovered, after-images can be journaled through either explicit or automatic journaling. For automatic journaling, the appropriate parameters (e.g., WN, WU) must be coded on the JREQ operand of the definition for each data set to be recovered. CICSVR recovers single or multiple spheres in one execution, provided that all after-images were journaled to the same journal id.

A decision must be made to write the after-images to the system log (JFILEID=SYSTEM) or a user journal (JFILEID=2 to 99). CICS/ESA uses the new CEDA DEFINE FILE parameters RECOVERY(ALL) and FWDRECOVLOG(nn) to specify forward recovery to a journal id. The performance impact of journaling to a heavily used system log must be

**284 Chapter Fifteen**

considered, along with the fact that recovery may be faster with user journals, as there are fewer records to read through. Also, user journals can be maintained for specific data sets and archived and retrieved efficiently.

Periodic backups must be performed, using the IDCAMS REPRO or EXPORT, or some other utility. If a data set becomes unusable, the latest backup copy must be restored, and all the archived journals since that backup retrieved. If the failure occurs on-line, the data set may be taken off-line to CICS and a switch performed on the current journal, which would be needed as the last input to the recovery run. This can be done if a secondary journal (TAPE2 or DISK2) has been specified. JCL is then prepared, which points to the spheres that are to be recovered. It specifies the data set names, restored backups, and journals to be used, and other recovery options.

### 15.5.4. How recovery is performed

CICSVR reads control statements from SYSIN to control its execution. When a forward-recoverable VSAM data set is opened, CICS writes a DSNAME record to the journal before the first update is performed. The DSNAME record relates the FCT file name to the VSAM data set name. During recovery, CICSVR searches sequentially through the journal for a DSNAME record for the base cluster or path to be recovered, then starts searching for after-images for the file name in the DSNAME record. It either replaces the old version of the record, deletes the old record, or inserts a new record. Records added to an ESDS cannot be backed out with a delete, and must be handled with a user-written exit. If a VSAM logic error occurs, a user exit is available to report the error, or decide whether to continue or terminate the recovery. If CICS did not abend, the recovered data set may be returned to CICS. If CICS abended, Emergency Restart must be performed.

When it is run after DTB or Emergency Restart, CICSVR reapplies all updates, including those performed by DTB and transaction backout. To avoid problems with uncommitted LUWs, it is advised to use DTB for all transactions. There is no additional overhead if no updates to protected resources are performed, and DTB=YES is the default with CICS/ESA.

If DTB or Emergency Restart fails because of an I/O error, it is not known whether all uncommitted LUWs were backed out, and after-images may or may not have been produced. In this case CICS would be abended (by coding the DTB error exit XDBFERR and the Emergency Restart error exit XRCFCER). CICSVR would then be run to recover the VSAM spheres up to that point, after which CICS would be restarted with START=AUTO, to back out the in-flight tasks.

## 15.6. IMS/ESA with DBCTL

With the release of IMS/ESA 3.1, IMS/DB and IMS/DC were unbundled into the two new products IMS/ESA Database Manager and IMS/ESA Transaction Manager. IMS/ESA Database Manager can run alone as IMS/ESA DM, providing database support through the new interface, Database Control (DBCTL). It can also run as IMS/ESA DM/TM, in conjunction with IMS/ESA Transaction Manager.

IMS/ESA 3.1 with DBCTL is available with CICS/ESA 3.1.1 as part of the pregenerated system, or for CICS/MVS 2.1.1 with an SPE. DBCTL constitutes a major change to CICS use of IMS databases. It runs as a subsystem in its own address space, independent of CICS. If you do not use DBCTL, DL/I code and its associated control blocks, including Database Recovery Control (DBRC), reside in the CICS address space. With DBCTL most of this is moved out.

The new environment results in improved failure isolation. You can start and stop CICS and DBCTL subsystems independently, and CICS can connect to or disconnect from DBCTL dynamically. Further isolation can be achieved by directing logging to the IMS log instead of the CICS system log. A DBCTL failure should not cause a CICS system to fail. Each DL/I request runs under its own MVS task control block (TCB), rather than under the TCB of CICS. This means that more concurrent DL/I requests can be processed, at less cost to CICS.

DBCTL offers better data-sharing facilities, and represents an improvement over MRO function shipping with CICS database-owning regions (DORs). It offers increased data availability by allowing successful scheduling of PSBs even if some of the requested databases are not available. Full-function databases that have been stopped or locked do not cause scheduling failures; the application is simply prevented from accessing them.

Applications running under CICS/ESA can access IMS databases through either the new DBCTL interface or the old CICS-DL/I interface, for compatibility purposes. Support for local DL/I and remote function-shipped DL/I requests remains as it was in CICS MVS 2.1 and CICS/OS/VS 1.7. Existing CICS applications with EXEC CICS DLI or call-level DL/I statements do not require any changes to run in the DBCTL environment, and the user can choose to use a combination of local DL/I and DBCTL, although all the databases in a single PSB must be managed by either one or the other.

### 15.6.1. How DBCTL works

The DBCTL subsystem is made up of three separate address spaces: DBCTL, Database Recovery Control (DBRC), and the DL/I address space (DLIAS). DBRC must be used to control DBCTL logs, and op-

## 286 Chapter Fifteen

tionally may be used to control batch logs, recovery, and data sharing. DLIAS contains DL/I code, control blocks, and buffers.

DL/I requests are no longer being serviced directly under CICS, but are routed to DBCTL through an adapter. CICS receives a DL/I request from an application program and passes it to the CICS interface module, DFHDLI, which determines whether this request is to DBCTL, local DL/I, or remote DL/I. A DBCTL request is passed to the DBCTL processor DFHDLIDP, which in turn passes it to the adapter transformer, DFHDBAT. DFHDBAT communicates with the database resource adapter DFHDRA via parameter lists, instructing the DRA to connect or disconnect to DBCTL, and to issue PSB scheduling requests, DL/I requests, and syncpoint requests.

The DRA allocates a thread for each program specification block (PSB) that it schedules, and does not release this thread until it terminates the PSB. Each thread operates under its own MVS TCB and represents a CICS transaction within DBCTL. Figure 15.1 shows where each component resides within the CICS and DBCTL subsystems.

### 15.6.2. Sharing data with DBCTL

IMS/ESA 3.1 resolves a serious issue related to the sharing of IMS databases, which is the inability of CICS and IMS to share data for update with integrity. CICS and IMS users who were previously able to read but not update IMS databases simultaneously can now have multiple IMS jobs process the data at the same time, with integrity assured by DBCTL acting as the common database manager. Now you can share databases between multiple CICS systems in the same MVS

DBCTL components within CICS

| | |
|---|---|
| DFHDLI | – CICS/DL/I call router |
| DFHDLIDP | – CICS/DL/I DBCTL processor |
| DFHDBAT | – CICS database adaptor transformer |
| DRA | – Database resource adapter |

DBCTL components within IMS/ESA

| | |
|---|---|
| DBCTL | – Database Control |
| DLIAS | – DL/I, DBRC, and program isolation (PI) |
| DBRC | – Database Recovery Control code and control blocks |
| IRLM | – IMS resource lock manager |

**Figure 15.1** DBCTL components.

image without the need for IMS data sharing and the associated overhead of DBRC and IRLM.

You can use either IMS/ESA resource lock manager (IRLM) or program isolation (PI) to control concurrent database access. PI, which is DL/I's lock manager, keeps all the activity of an application program separate from that of other programs until syncpoint, and is used for lock management unless the extra facilities of IRLM are needed. For example, you need IRLM to maintain integrity if you are sharing databases at block level (the CI for VSAM, and the physical block for other databases).

### 15.6.3. Batch sharing

If they do not use DBCTL, batch jobs can access IMS data through either IMS data sharing or CICS shared database. IMS data sharing allows multiple subsystem access to the same database, through the control of IRLM. Batch jobs can still use IMS data sharing to access databases owned by DBCTL.

Jobs that use the CICS shared database facility cannot access databases owned by DBCTL, but can be migrated to batch message processors (BMPs) that can communicate directly with the DBCTL address space. DBCTL allows concurrent access to IMS databases for batch jobs running as BMPs and CICS systems within a single MVS image, which has performance benefits over CICS shared database.

### 15.7. Recovery with DBCTL

With DBCTL there are a number of changes to the recovery process. DBCTL takes responsibility for backing out its DL/I databases after failure, using IMS backout facilities. Neither a CICS nor a DBCTL failure should cause the other subsystem to terminate. After recovery, the two address spaces must be reconnected, at which time in-doubt LUWs are resolved automatically.

CICS and DBCTL perform similar recovery functions, with some differences. Both have Cold Start, Warm Start, and Emergency Restart, with both system-level and task- (or thread-) level synchronization points. The concept of DBCTL checkpoints is the same as that for CICS keypoints, but the implementation is different. During Emergency Restart, CICS reads the keypoints on the system log backward to find the start of an LUW. DBCTL gets the last checkpoint before synchronization from the Checkpoint ID table in the restart data set (RDS), then reads the IMS log forward from that checkpoint on.

The meaning of the term *dynamic backout* also differs. While for CICS, backout is the result of a transaction failure, for DBCTL, back-

**288   Chapter Fifteen**

out is the result of a program (thread) failure. Program failures include CICS transaction abends and BMP failures.

XRF and overseer services can be used to coordinate recovery between the two subsystems. DBRC can also be used to automate much of the recovery process. It runs in the CICS address space as an MVS subtask for local DL/I, or in its own address space for DBCTL. In a data-sharing environment, each subsystem has its own copy of DBRC. DBRC records its recovery information in three related VSAM data sets known collectively as the RECON data set. It provides three types of database recovery: full forward recovery, time-stamp recovery, and track recovery. In general, DBRC does not affect backward recovery operations.

### 15.7.1. Logging

DBCTL uses IMS logging, and writes before- and after-images of only the data that were changed. This represents an improvement over local DL/I logging, which writes before- and after-images of entire segments to the CICS system log. IMS log records containing the information needed for recovery and restart are written to the on-line log data set (OLDS) or, if they are committed but still in the buffer which is not yet full, to the temporary write-ahead data set (WADS). The logged images support both backward and forward recovery. You can direct logging to the IMS log instead of a CICS journal if you use the DL/I log request instead of the EXEC CICS JOURNAL command.

### 15.7.2. Transaction backout

When a transaction terminates, its thread is released, and a record is written to the IMS log. If there is an error, a return code is passed to the application, either to the DL/I interface block (DIB) for command-level requests or to the user interface block (UIB) for call-level requests.

If a transaction fails in DBCTL, the CICS transaction is abended. If a transaction fails in CICS after issuing a DL/I request which is being processed, an error is passed to the DBCTL thread. When the transaction is abended, the thread is also terminated, and all recoverable resources, including DL/I, are backed out. The PSB is released because the transaction has completed.

DBCTL will detect transaction deadlocks, and terminate tasks where appropriate. If one resource is a DBCTL database and the other is a CICS resource, the task using the CICS resource is abended after its DTIMOUT period has elapsed (if DTIMOUT is not coded, the two tasks are suspended indefinitely). If both resources are DBCTL databases, the task with less update activity is abended.

### 15.7.3. Units of recovery and the two-phase commit

A DBCTL unit of recovery is created for each processing request. This corresponds to the CICS LUW, except that the LUW begins at the beginning of a task and the unit of recovery begins with the first DL/I request. If a program or system failure occurs, in-flight units of recovery must be backed out. Recovery tokens are passed to DBCTL from CICS, and are used to correlate work done in CICS and DBCTL for the same unit of recovery. The token is a 16-byte field containing a CICS APPLID and a unique LUW (unit of recovery) identifier. The lifetime of a recovery token is the life of the unit of recovery it represents, lasting until a database update is committed.

CICS and DBCTL coordinate the updates using a two-phase commit process. Two-phase commit consists of a prepare phase, which is initiated by CICS when it receives a syncpoint request, and a commit phase, at which time an update is committed and DBCTL locks are released.

Between the two phases lies what is known as the in-doubt period. Depending on system activity, DL/I database buffers may be written before they are committed, and may require backout. If a failure occurs while a transaction is in the process of terminating or issuing a syncpoint, DBCTL cannot determine whether CICS intended the updates to be backed out or committed, and must request this information of CICS after it is reconnected. For an in-doubt unit of recovery, a recoverable in-doubt structure (RIS) containing the recovery token and the data that were changed is constructed and written to the IMS log. IMS log records contain both phases of the commit for each unit of work.

CICS is the coordinator of the two-phase commit, making sure that all resource managers involved, including DBCTL, are in synchronization before committing. If all the resource managers indicate that a COMMIT is possible, CICS tells them all to COMMIT; otherwise CICS tells them all to ABORT. At completion of the two-phase commit, a syncpoint is recorded and changes are committed.

Normally, Emergency Restart of DBCTL followed by reconnection of CICS and DBCTL will resolve in-doubts automatically. If not, they must be resolved manually with a DBCTL operator command. If dynamic backout or Emergency Restart backout fails, the database is stopped, and backout is automatically reattempted when the database is restarted.

## 15.8. XRF Support for DBCTL

For CICS ESA 3.1.1 with DBCTL, you have the option of using either CICS XRF support or, if CICS is connected to an IMS/ESA DM/TM sub-

**290 Chapter Fifteen**

system, IMS XRF support. Whichever is used, the resulting takeover is the same, although the mechanics and some options differ slightly.

With IMS XRF, the active and alternate are standard IMS/ESA active and alternate subsystems, and you have the option of automatic switching and reconnection or operator intervention by coding or not coding `AUTO=YES` in the IMS XRF definition.

For CICS XRF, DBCTL offers the flexibility of allowing you to code several DBCTL subsystems in the Recoverable Service Table (RST). Connection can be made to any DBCTL in the same RST, which allows you to have more than one alternate to choose from. Depending on what failed, you may choose an alternate DBCTL in the same or another MVS image. For instance, if DBCTL failed, you may use an alternate in the same image. If CICS failed, you may bring up an alternate CICS and DBCTL in a second image. You can also use special DBCTL facilities of the overseer to automate restart. However, a failing DBCTL that is not connected to CICS cannot be restarted automatically.

# Index

Index note: An *f.* after a page number refers to a figure.

Abend Control Program, 67*f.*
Abend processing, 61–62
Abend recovery strategies, 225, 228*f.*, 240–241
  task abend, 225, 228*f.*, 240*f.*
Active chain, 37, 38*f.*
Active region, 276
Active tasks dispatch, 34–37
  chain, 34, 35*f.*, 37
ADABAS, 158
Addressing, BTAM, 87–89
Advanced program-to-program communi-
  cation (APPC), 173
After-images, 230
AID (automatic initiate descriptor), 216
Alternate index, 154
Alternate region, 276
APPC (advanced program-to-program
  communication), 173
Application programs, 1–3, 8–9
  preparation of, 5
  service requests, 8*f.*
  (*See also* Program Control Program)
Application request handler, 77
Assembler Language, Program Control
  Program interface and, 72–73
Asynchronous communication, 174
Asynchronous journal-writing, 235
Asynchronous Processing, 174, 178, 181
ATI (*see* Automatic task initiation)
ATTACH, 31–34
Auto list, 87
Automatic initiate descriptor (AID), 216
Automatic journaling, 230–232
  FCT parameters, 232*f.*
Automatic logging, 230–231
Automatic task initiation (ATI), 209, 213–216
  automatic initiate descriptor chains, 216

Automatic task initiation (ATI) (*Cont.*):
  printing, 213–215
  trigger levels, 215
Automatic terminal installation, 124–127
  generating, 126
  TCTU considerations, 127
  terminal naming conventions, 126
Auxiliary Temporary Storage (AUX TS), 258
  buffers, 192–195
  byte map, 196
  control areas, 190–198
  data set, 185–187
  flags, 194*f.*
  pointers, 195*f.*
  temporary storage common area, 190–192
  temporary storage queue element, 196–197
  temporary storage request element, 196–198
  TSVCA fields, 196*f.*

Backout, 228*f.*, 276
  Dynamic Backout Program, 228, 237, 287 288
  Emergency Restart tables, 241
  transaction, 288
  Transient Data Program recovery summary, 253*f.*
  (*See also* Dynamic Transaction Backout)
Backout tables, 241
Backward recovery, 4, 223, 224
  logging, 223
Basic Mapping Support (BMS), 4, 13, 129–143
  map definition, 130–131

## 292   Index

Basic Mapping Support (BMS) (*Cont.*):
partition maps, 131
recovery/restart, 265–267
temporary storage, 184
3270 data streams, 138–143
3270 device support, 131–137
Batch DL/I, 170–171
Batch forward recovery, 223
Batch job submission via internal reader, 212
Batch sharing, 287
BDAM, File Control Program and, 147–148
Before-images, 230
BMS (*see* Basic Mapping Support)
Bracket protocol, 107–108
BTAM Terminal Management, 78–90
CICS-BTAM interface, 78–79
data flow, 80–82
DFTRMLST macro, 87*f.*
error processing, 89–90
lines and terminals, 82–86
polling and addressing, 87–89
Terminal Control Table, 79–80
terminal scanning, 80
Buffers:
Auxiliary Temporary Storage, 192–195
dynamic, 236
File Control Program, 150–151
Byte maps:
Auxiliary Temporary Storage, 196
Page Allocation Maps, 11, 13, 19–21, 23

CAVM (CICS Availability Manager), 277–278
Chaining, 22–23, 26, 108–109
CICS:
components, 1–9
as multiprocessor, 1
storage layout, 9–14
CICS Availability Manager (CAVM), 277–278
CICS/ESA, 275–276
CICSVR (CICS VSAM Recovery), 223, 282–284
forward recovery, 282–284
journal archiving, 283
Class maximum match, 32*f.*
CLT (Command List Table), 277–278
CMC (communications management configuration), 281

COBOL, Program Control Program fields of, 51–52
Command-level interface, 65–72
COMMAREA, 72
DFHEIP initialization, 65–66
EXEC interface flow, 67
file control, 72
HANDLE CONDITION, 68–71
LINK, 71
Command List Table (CLT), 277–278
COMMAREA, 72
Common System Area (CSA), 7, 11, 12*f.*, 32*f.*
Common work area (CWA), 11, 12
Communications management configuration (CMC), 281
Control blocks, 1, 2, 7–8, 10–11
in Auxiliary Temporary Storage, 190–198
CICS-VTAM, 92–93
in Storage Control Program, 19–24
terminal error, 89*f.*
Control modules, 1–5
Control subpool, 17–18, 23
Cross-memory service (XMS), 160, 166, 173, 174
CSA (Common System Area), 7, 11, 12*f.*, 32*f.*
CWA (common work area), 11, 12

Data flow, BTAM, 80–82
Data sets:
Auxiliary Temporary Storage, 185–187
File Control Program, 154–155
Interval Control Program, 204, 205*f.*
Journal Control Program, 234, 235*f.*
Data sharing, DBCTL, 286–287
Data streams, 3270, 138–143
Database:
hierarchical, 157, 158
recovery/restart, 224
relational, 157, 158
Database management system (DBMS), 157–172
DB2, 157–169
IMS, 157, 158, 169–172
DATAID, 258–260
DBCTL, 285–290
batch sharing, 287
components, 286*f.*
data sharing, 286–287

**Index  293**

DBCTL (*Cont.*):
 Extended Recovery Facility support for, 289–290
 IMS/ESA with, 285–287
 logging, 288
 transaction backout, 288
 two-phase commit protocol, 289
 units of recovery, 289
DBMS (*see* Database management system)
DBO (DL/I Backout Table), 241
DBP (Dynamic Backout Program), 228, 237, 287–288
DB2, 157–169
 attachment architecture, 160, 162–165
 attachment processing, 166*f*.
 Internal Resource Lock Manager, 159, 168
 multithread connection, 160–165
 precompiler, 161–162
 security, 161, 163, 165, 167–168
 Structured Query Language, 158, 162, 163
 subsystem, 159*f*.
 transaction flow, 159, 165–168
 two-phase commit protocol, 160, 168–169
DCA (*see* Dispatch Control Area)
DCI (dispatch control indicator) values, 33, 34*f*.
DCT (Destination Control Table), 6–7
Debugging session, temporary storage and, 184–185
Deferred work element (DWE), 40, 237
DEQ (dequeue), 38–40
Destination Control Table (DCT), 6–7
DETACH, 39, 40
DFGSNEP macro, 121*f*.
DFGSNET macro, 122*f*.
DFHEIP initialization, 65–66
DFHSG macro, 112*f*.
DFTRMLST macro, 87*f*.
Disaster Recovery, 274
DISPATCH, 31–34
 of active tasks, 34–37
Dispatch Control Area (DCA), 7–8, 27, 33*f*.
 active chain, 37, 38*f*.
 suspend chain, 37, 38*f*.
Dispatch control indicator (DCI) values, 33, 34*f*.
Distributed Transaction Processing (DTP), 174, 178–179

DL/I, 169–172, 174
DL/I Backout Table (DBO), 241
Domains, 275
DSA (dynamic storage area), 2, 9, 11, 13, 16–18
DTB (*see* Dynamic Transaction Backout)
DTP (Distributed Transaction Processing), 174, 178–179
Dump management, 3
DWE (deferred work element), 40, 237
Dynamic Backout Program (DBP), 228, 237, 287–288
Dynamic buffer, 236
Dynamic storage area (DSA), 2, 9, 11, 13, 16–18
Dynamic Transaction Backout (DTB), 169, 236–238, 252
 of Basic Mapping Support, 265–267
 deferred work element, 237
 Dynamic Backout Program, 228, 237, 287–288
 dynamic buffer, 236
 exits, 237–238
 of Interval Control recovery, 264–265
 Page Building, 265–267
 of protected resources, 225
 of Temporary Storage recovery, 261–262
 of Transient Data Program recovery, 252–254
 of VTAM message protection logging, 272–273

EIB (Executive Interface Block), 41
EIS (Executive Interface Structure), 41, 66*f*.
Emergency Restart (ER), 224, 225, 227–228, 231, 241
 backout tables, 241
 of Basic Mapping Support, 265–267
 of Interval Control recovery, 264–265
 restart exits, 241
 of Temporary Storage recovery, 261–262
 of Transient Data Program recovery, 252–254
ENQ (enqueue), 38–40, 172
ENTRY macro, 115*f*.
ER (*see* Emergency Restart)
Error analysis, 225, 226*f*.
Error processing:
 BTAM, 89–90

**294  Index**

Error processing (*Cont.*):
logical errors, 119–120
physical error, 119
Program Error Program, 238–241
request error-handling routines, 225
TEP, 90, 225, 270–271
Terminal Control Program, 267–271
terminal error control blocks, 89*f.*
VTAM, 98, 106, 117–124
(*See also* Node Error Program)
EXEC, 65
interface flow, 67
Executive Interface Block (EIB), 41
Executive Interface Structure (EIS), 41,
66*f.*
Explicit journaling, 230
Extended Recovery Facility (XRF), 274,
276–282, 289–290
CICS Availability Manager, 277–278
Command List Table, 277–278
configurations, 281–282
DBCTL support, 289–290
with multiple MVS, 281–282
overseer, 280
recovery of terminals, 278–280
regions, 276, 280–281
restart in place, 280
with single MVS, 281–282
takeover, 278
Extrapartition Transient Data, 212,
245–246

FAQE (*see* Free area queue element)
FBO (File Backout Table), 241
FCP (*see* File Control Program)
FCT (File Control Table), 6, 146–147
File area addressing, 149*f.*
File Backout Table (FBO), 241
File Control Program (FCP), 3, 13, 16,
77, 145–155
alternate indexes, 154
BDAM considerations, 147–148
buffers and strings, 150–151
command-level processing, 72
data set states, 154–155
file area addressing, 149*f.*
File Control Table, 6, 146–147
file management programs, 3, 13, 146
file request areas, 148–150
FIOA addressability, 150*f.*
FWA addressing, 149*f.*
Local Shared Resources, 151–153

File Control Program (*Cont.*):
VSAM subtasking, 153–154
File Control Program (FCP) resource
protection, 242–243
exclusive control, 242*f.*
programming restrictions, 242–243
summary, 243
File Control Table (FCT), 6, 146–147
File request areas, 148–150
Files, 174, 224
FIOA addressability, 150*f.*
Flags, Auxiliary Temporary Storage,
194*f.*
Forward recovery, 4, 223, 224, 276
batch, 223
with CICSVR, 282–284
journaling, 223
on-line, 223
Free area queue element (FAQE), 19, 23
chaining, 23–24, 26
Function Request Shipping, 174–178,
181
FWA addressing, 149*f.*

HANDLE CONDITION:
Handle Condition Table, 69*f.*
label data, 70–71
processing, 68–70
response tables, 68*f.*
Hanging ICE, 201
Hierarchical database, 157, 158
High-Level Language (HLL) Interface,
41
information pointer, 55*f.*

I/O error on recovery/restart facilities,
273–274
ICE (Interval Control Element), 40
expiration analysis, 206–207
hanging ICE, 201
ICF (*see* Intercommunication facilities)
ICP (*see* Interval Control Program)
IDMS(R), 158
Implicit sync point, 226
IMS, 157, 158, 169–172
DL/I initialization, 171–172
batch DL/I, 170–171
enqueueing, 172
performance, 172
IMS/ESA, 285–287
with DBCTL, 285–287
Indirect Transient Data, 212–213

INITIAL macro, 104–106
Initialization, 5, 62
  automatic task initiation, 209,
    213–216
  DFHEIP, 65–66
  DL/I, 171–172
  LOAD, 56–58
  Program Control Program, 58, 60*f.*, 61
  Program Properties Table, 47
  START, 203–204
  task initiation, 203–204
Integrity, 245, 275
Intercommunication facilities (ICF), 4–5,
  172–182
  advantages of, 174–175
  Asynchronous Processing, 174, 178,
    181
  connections, 174
  Distributed Transaction Processing,
    174, 178–179
  Function Request Shipping, 174–178,
    181
  interregion communication, 5, 173,
    174, 181
  intersystem communication, 5, 173,
    179–181
  multiregion option, 5, 173, 174, 179,
    181
  remote resources, 173, 174
  remote tasks, 173, 174
  resource definition, 182
  Terminal Control Program and,
    179–182
  Transaction Routing, 174, 176, 177,
    181
Internal Resource Lock Manager
  (IRLM), 159, 168
Interprogram communication, 53–56
Interregion communication (IRC), 5, 173,
  174, 181
Intersystem communication (ISC), 5,
  173, 179–181
Interval Control Element (*see* ICE)
Interval Control Program (ICP), 40,
  201–207
  canceling, 204
  data sets, 204, 205*f.*
  interval control element, 40
  logic, 205–206
  task initiation, 203–204
  task synchronization, 202–203
  time of day, 201–202

Interval Control Program (ICP) recovery,
  262–265
  Dynamic Transaction Backout,
    264–265
  Emergency Restart, 264–265
  Put resource protection, 262–264
Intrapartition Transient Data, 210–211,
  245
  recovery/restart, 211–212, 224, 225,
    245–254
  uses of, 211
IRC (interregion communication), 5, 173,
  174, 181
IRLM (Internal Resource Lock
  Manager), 159, 168
ISC (intersystem communication), 5,
  173, 179–181
Isolated subpool, 18, 21, 23, 24, 26

JCT (Journal Control Table), 7
Journal archiving, 283
Journal Control Program, 230, 233–234
  data sets, 234, 235*f.*
  Journal Control request, 234–236
  recovery/restart, 224
  synchronization options, 235–236
Journal Control Table (JCT), 7
Journals, 4, 13, 223, 229–236
  automatic journaling, 230–232
  explicit journaling, 230
  forward recovery, 223
  writing to, 234–236

Kernel, 275

LIFO (last-in first-out) storage, 29–31
  stack entry, 30*f.*
Line I/O area (LIOA), 80*f.*, 82*f.*
Lines, BTAM, 82–86
LINK, 53–56, 72
  command-level processing, 71
  logic, 58
  PC LINK table, 71*f.*
LIOA (line I/O area), 81*f.*, 82*f.*
LLA (load list area), 57*f.*
LOAD, 56–58
  logic, 58
Load list area (LLA), 57*f.*
Load routines (*see* Initialization)
Local Shared Resources (LSR), 151–153
Log write-ahead protocol, 168
Logical errors, 119–120

**296    Index**

Logical recovery, 224, 227, 246–248
Logs, 223, 229–236
   automatic logging, 230–231
   DBCTL, 288
LSR (Local Shared Resources), 151–153

Macros, 8–9, 65
   DFGSNEP, 121*f.*
   DFGSNET, 122*f.*
   DFHSG, 112*f.*
   DFTRMLST, 87*f.*
   ENTRY, 115*f.*
   INITIAL, 104–106
   TERMINAL, 107–112
Magnet slot reader (MSR), 137
Main Storage recovery, 254–258
   program compression, 24–25, 51, 254–255
   recovery logic, 257–258
   short-on-storage condition, 24–26, 254,
      256–257
   storage cushion, 254
   storage violation recovery, 257
Main Temporary Storage, 258
Mapping programs (*see* Basic Mapping
   Support)
Master Terminal Support, 5
Message Backout Table (MBO), 241
Message protection, 114–116
Mirror transactions, 176
Mixed subpool, 24, 26
MRO (multiregion option) communica-
   tion, 5, 173, 174, 179, 181
MSR (magnet slot reader), 137
Multiregion option (MRO) communica-
   tion, 5, 173, 174, 179, 181

NCP definitions, 116–117
NEP (*see* Node Error Program)
NEWCOPY flag, 50*f.*
NLT (nucleus load table), 52–53
Node Error Program (NEP), 119–124,
   225
   DFGSNEP macro, 121*f.*
   DFGSNET macro, 122*f.*
   node error processor, 122*f.*
   TWA action flags, 124, 125*f.*
Non-XA flags, 48–49
Nucleus, 11
Nucleus load table (NLT), 52–53

Off-line forward recovery, 223
Off-line functions, 5

OFL (optional features list), 11, 12
On-line forward recovery, 223
On-line functions, 5
Open list, 87
Operating system storage, 9, 13–14,
   22–23
Optional features list (OFL), 11, 12
ORACLE, 158
OS/VS storage, 10*f.*
Overseer, 280

Page Allocation Map (PAM), 11, 13,
   19–20
   byte maps, 11, 13, 19–21, 23
   information area, 19, 20*f.*
   subpool header, 19, 20*f.*
Page Building, 265–267
PAM (*see* Page Allocation Map)
Partition maps, 131
Partitions, 136–137
PCP (*see* Program Control Program)
PCT (Program Control Table), 1, 6,
   114–116
PEP (Program Error Program), 238–241
Performance, 172, 245, 275
Physical errors, 119
Physical recovery, 224, 227, 246–248
PIP (Process Initialization Parameter),
   178
Pointers, Auxiliary Temporary Storage,
   195*f.*
Polling, BTAM, 87–89
PPT (*see* Program Properties Table)
Precompiler, DB2, 161–162
Printing:
   via automatic task initiation, 213–215
   3270 printers, 135, 142–143
Process Initialization Parameter (PIP),
   178
Program compression, 24–25, 51,
   254–255
Program Control Program (PCP), 3,
   41–73
   abend processing, 61–62
   assembler language interface, 72–73
   COBOL fields, 51–52
   command-level interface, 65–72
   initialization, 58, 60*f.*, 61
   interprogram communication, 53–56
   LINK, 53–56, 58
   LOAD, 56–58
   nucleus load table, 52–53

Program Control Program (PCP) (*Cont.*):
postinitialization processing, 62–63
  Program Properties Table, 6, 42–47,
    50–52
  program status flags, 48–49
  programs in core, 49–50
  RELEASE, 56–58
  RETURN, 53*f.*, 61
  services flow, 58, 59*f.*
  shutdown processing, 63–65
  SVA program counters, 51
  XA and non-XA flags, 48–49
  XCTL, 53*f.*, 58
Program Control Table (PCT), 1, 6,
  114–116
Program Error Program (PEP), 238–241
  functions of, 239
Program Properties Table (PPT), 6, 42
  COBOL fields, 51–52
  coding, 42
  command-level interface, 47
  core address, 43, 44*f.*
  DASD address, 43*f.*
  entry point address, 43, 44*f.*
  initialization, 47
  macro-level interface, 47
  MAP, 46–47
  NEWCOPY flag, 50*f.*
  program indicators, 44–47
  program use counters, 51*f.*
  reload indicator, 46*f.*
  in storage, 43
Program subpool, 18, 21, 23, 24
Programmed symbols (PS), 137
Protected resources, 224, 225
Protocols:
  bracket protocol, 107–108
  log write-ahead protocol, 168
  two-phase commit protocol, 160,
    168–169, 289
PS (programmed symbols), 137
Put resource protection, 262–264

Queue element area (QEA) chains, 38,
  39*f.*

RA (Receive Any) processing, 93–95
RAP (resident application program), 46
RCT (Resource Control Table), 160
RDO (Resource Definition On-Line), 5,
  104, 182, 276, 278
Read Modified, 138*f.*

Receive Any (RA) processing, 93–95
Recoverable resources, 224, 225
Recovery/restart facilities, 221–290
  backward recovery, 4, 223, 224
  Basic Mapping Support recovery,
    265–267
  CICS/ESA, 275–276
  CICSVR, 223, 282–284
  database, 224
  DBCTL, 285–290
  Disaster Recovery, 274
  Dynamic Transaction Backout, 169,
    236–238, 252
  Emergency Restart, 224, 225, 227–228,
    231, 241
  error analysis, 225, 226*f.*
  Extended Recovery Facility, 274,
    276–282, 289–290
  File Control Program resource protec-
    tion, 242–243
  I/O error, 273–274
  IMS/ESA, 285–287
  Interval Control Program recovery,
    262–265
  Journal Control Program, 224
  journals, 4, 13, 223, 229–236
  logical recovery, 224, 227, 246–248
  logs, 223, 229–236, 288
  Main Storage recovery, 254–258
  objectives of, 221–223
  physical recovery, 224, 227, 246–248
  recoverable resources, 224, 225
  sync points, 40, 226–228
  System Recovery Program, 224, 225
  for tasks, 225
  Temporary Storage Control recovery,
    224, 225, 258–262
  Terminal Control Program recovery,
    267–271
  transaction restart, 225
  Transient Data Program recovery,
    211–212, 224, 225, 245–254
  units of recovery, 289
  user recovery, 238–241
  VTAM message protection, 224,
    271–273
  (*See also* Forward recovery)
Recovery token, 227
Recovery Utility Program (RUP), 231
Regions, 276, 280–281
Register save area (RSA), 54–56
Relational database, 157, 158

## 298 Index

RELEASE, 56–58
Remote resources, 173, 174
Remote task, 173, 174
Request error-handling routines, 225
Request Parameter Lists (RPL) subpool, 18, 23
Resident application program (RAP), 46
Resource Control Table (RCT), 160
Resource Definition On-Line (RDO), 5, 104, 182, 276, 278
Restart (*see* Recovery/restart facilities)
Restart in place, 280
RESUME, 37–38
RETURN, 53*f.*
  logic, 61
RETURN TRABSID, 72
Reusable thread, 161
RPL (Request Parameter Lists) subpool, 18, 23
RSA (register save area), 54–56
RUP (Recovery Utility Program), 231

SAA (storage accounting area), 19, 21–23
SCP (*see* Storage Control Program)
SCR (Storage Control Recovery Program), 26
Scratchpad facility (*see* Temporary Storage Control)
Screen Definition Facility (SDF), 130–131
Security, DB2, 161, 163, 165, 167–168
Segment, 30
Shared subpool, 18, 23
Short-on-Storage (SOS) condition, 24–26, 254, 256–257
SIT options, 113–114
SOS (Short-on-Storage) condition, 24–26, 254, 256–257
Sphere, 283
SPP (*see* Sync Point Program)
SQL (Structured Query Language), 158, 162, 163
SQL/DS, 158
START, 203–204
STIMER, 37
Storage:
  OS/VS storage, 10*f.*
  system storage, 9, 13–14, 22–23
  transaction storage, 21–23, 26, 108–109
  virtual storage, 175
  VSE storage, 11*f.*
  working storage, 55, 56*f.*

Storage accounting area (SAA), 19, 21–23
Storage Control Program (SCP), 13, 15–26, 203, 275
  allocation, 18, 21
  control blocks, 19–24
  dynamic storage area organization, 16–18
  storage stress conditions, 24–26
Storage Control Recovery Program (SCR), 26
Storage cushion, 254
Storage isolation, 175, 275
Storage layout, 9–14
Storage recovery, 26, 257
Storage stress, 24–26
Strings, 150–151
Structured fields, 135–136
Structured Query Language (SQL), 158, 162, 163
Subpool header, 19, 20*f.*, 23
Subpools, 16–18
SUPRA, 158
SUSPEND, 37–38
SVA program counters, 51
Sync Point Program (SPP), 40
  recovery/restart, 226–228
Synchronous communication, 174
Synchronous journal-writing, 235
System area, 29, 31
System initialization/generation (*see* Initialization)
System Recovery Program, 224, 225
System storage, 9, 13–14, 22–23
System tables, 1, 2, 6–7
  (*See also specific table*)
System tasks (*see* Task)

TACP (Terminal Abnormal Condition Program), 89–90
  Terminal Control Program error handling interface, 270–271
Takeover, 278
Task, 1, 3, 28
  active, 34–37
  automatic task initiation, 209, 213–216
  initialization, 203–204
  recovery/restart, 225
  remote task, 173, 174
  task synchronization, 202–203
  user tasks, 28

Task abend, 228*f.*, 240*f.*
  exits, 225
Task Control (TC), 2, 7, 13, 28, 77–78,
    275
  VTAM, 100–102
Task control area (TCA), 1, 7–8, 27–40
  active tasks dispatch, 34–37
  ATTACH, 31–34
  dequeue, 38–40
  DETACH, 39, 40
  DISPATCH, 31–34
  end-of-task processing, 39–40
  enqueue, 38–40, 172
  LIFO storage, 29–31
  RESUME, 37–38
  SUSPEND, 37–38
  system area, 29, 31
  transaction work area, 29–31, 124,
    125*f.*
  user area, 29–31
Task control block (TCB), 160
Task recovery facilities, 225
Task synchronization, 202–203
TBO (Transaction Backout Table), 241
TBP (Transaction Backout Program),
    228
TC (*see* Task Control)
TCA (*see* Task control area)
TCAM ACB interface application, 117,
    118*f.*
TCB (task control block), 160
TCP(*see* Terminal Control Program)
TCT (*see* Terminal Control Table)
TD (*see* Transient Data Program)
Teleprocessing (TP) subpool, 18, 23, 26
Temporary storage common area
    (TSMAP), 190–192
Temporary Storage (TS) Control, 3, 13,
    18, 174, 176, 183–200
  Basic Mapping Support and, 184
  debugging and, 184–185
  internal uses, 184–185
  main, 258
  record, 186*f.*, 187*f.*
  Temporary Storage Table, 7, 13,
    199–200, 258–260
  WRITEQ processing, 187–190
  (*See also* Auxiliary Temporary
    Storage)
Temporary Storage (TS) Control
    recovery, 224, 225, 258–262
  DATAID, 258–260

Temporary Storage (TS) Control
    recovery (*Cont.*):
  Dynamic Transaction Backout,
    261–262
  Emergency Restart, 261–262
  resource protection, 260–261
Temporary storage queue element
    (TSQE), 196–197
  difference between transient data, 210
Temporary storage request element
    (TSRE), 196–198
Temporary Storage Table (TST), 7, 13,
    199–200, 258–260
Temporary Storage Unit Table (TSUT),
    188
Temporary Storage Unit Table entry
    (TSUTE), 188–190
TEP (Terminal Error Program), 90, 225
  Terminal Control Program error han-
    dling interface, 270–271
Terminal Abnormal Condition Program
    (*see* TACP)
Terminal access methods, 76
Terminal Control Program (TCP), 3–5, 8,
    13, 75–127
  application request handler, 77
  automatic terminal installation,
    124–127
  BTAM Terminal Management, 78–90
  DFHSG macro, 112*f.*
  generating, 112–116
  intercommunication facilities and,
    179–182
  NCP- and VTAM-related definitions,
    116–117
  Program Control Table options, 1, 6,
    114–116
  SIT options, 113–114
  Task Control, 2, 7, 13, 28, 77–78, 275
  TCAM ACB interface, 117, 118*f.*
  terminal access methods, 76
  terminal control modules, 76–77
  3270 data streams, 138–143
  3270 device support, 131–137
  VTAM Terminal Management,
    90–112
  (*See also* Terminal Control Table)
Terminal Control Program (TCP) error
    handling, 267–271
  TACP/TEP interface, 270–271
  user recovery strategies, 267–269
  ZNAC/ZNEP interface, 269–270

## 300 Index

Terminal Control Table (TCT), 6, 76
  for BTAM, 79–80
  prefix, 82*f.*
Terminal Control Table (TCT) coding,
  75, 104–112
  INITIAL macro, 104–106
  TERMINAL macro, 107–112
Terminal error control blocks, 89*f.*
Terminal Error Program (*see* TEP)
Terminal hardware (*see* Basic Mapping
  Support)
Terminal Input-Output Area (TIOA), 8,
  81*f.*
TERMINAL macro, 107–112
Terminal Management structure, 77*f.*
Terminal naming conventions, 126
Terminal scanning, 80
Terminals, 174
  automatic terminal installation,
    124–127
  BTAM and, 82–86
  Extended Recovery Facility and,
    278–280
  3270 data streams, 138–143
    input, 138–140
    output, 140–142
    printing considerations, 142–143
    Read Modified, 138*f.*
  3270 device support, 131–137
    display fields, 132–133
    extended functions, 135–137
    features, 131–134
    input options, 134–135
    printer control, 135
Time of day (TOD), 201–202
Time management, 3
TIOA (Terminal Input-Output Area), 8,
  81*f.*
TOD (time of day), 201–202
TP (Teleprocessing) subpool, 18, 23, 26
TPCP (*see* Two-phase commit protocol)
Trace management, 4
Transaction, 1, 27–28, 159, 174, 176
Transaction backout, 288
Transaction Backout Program (TBP),
  228
Transaction Backout Table (TBO), 241
Transaction flow, DB2, 159, 165–168
Transaction restart, 225
Transaction Routing, 174, 176, 177, 181
Transaction storage, 21–23
  chaining, 22–23, 108–109

Transaction storage subpool, 26
Transaction work area (TWA), 29–31,
  124, 125*f.*
Transient Data (TD) Program, 3, 6–7, 13,
  174, 176, 209–219
  automatic task initiation, 209,
    213–216
  extrapartition destinations, 212,
    245–246
  facilities, 219
  indirect destinations, 212–213
  intrapartition destinations, 210–212,
    224, 225, 245–254
  services flow, 217–219
  difference between temporary storage
    queue element, 210
  user exits, 219
Transient Data (TD) Program recovery,
  211–212, 224, 225, 245–254
  backout summary, 253*f.*
  Dynamic Transaction Backout, 252–254
  Emergency Restart, 252–254
  logical protection, 249–252
  logical recovery, 246–248
  physical protection, 248–250
  physical recovery, 246–248
  recovery logic, 248*f.*
  system components, 246–247
Translator, 5
TS (*see* Temporary Storage Control)
TSGID, 188–190
TSIOA, 187–188
TSMAP (temporary storage common
  area), 190–192
TSQE (*see* Temporary storage queue ele-
  ment)
TSRE (temporary storage request ele-
  ment), 196–198
TST (Temporary Storage Table), 7, 13,
  199–200, 258–260
TSUT (Temporary Storage Unit Table),
  188
TSUTE (Temporary Storage Unit Table
  entry), 188–190
TSVCA fields, 196*f.*
TWA (transaction work area), 29–31,
  124, 125*f.*
Two-phase commit protocol (TPCP):
  DB2, 160, 168–169
  DBCTL, 289

Units of recovery, 289

User area, 29–31
User recovery, 238–241
    abend recovery strategies, 225, 228*f*.,
       240–241
User tasks, 28

Virtual storage, 175
VSAM subtasking, 153–154
VSE storage, 11*f*.
VTAM error processing, 98, 106,
    117–124
    CICS messages, 119–120, 123*f*.
    node error program, 120–124
    non-CICS messages, 118–119
VTAM message protection logging, 224,
    271–273
    Dynamic Transaction Backout,
       272–273
VTAM Terminal Management, 90–112
    CICS application, 92
    CICS-VTAM communication, 95
    CICS-VTAM connection life cycle,
       98–99
    CICS-VTAM control blocks, 92–93
    conversation life cycle, 102–104
    definitions, 116–117
    exit routine addressing, 95, 96*f*.
    logical units, 91*f*.

message structure, 100
network, 90–92
physical units, 91*f*.
Receive Any processing, 93–95
Task Control, 100–102
Terminal Control modules, 95–98
Terminal Control Table coding,
    104–112

WAIT, 35–37
Working storage, pointers, 55, 56*f*.
Wrap list, 87
WRITEQ processing, 187–190
    TSGID, 188–190
    TSIOA, 187–188
    TSUTE, 188–190

XA flags, 48–49
XCTL, 53*f*., 72
    logic, 58
XMS (cross-memory service), 160, 166,
    173, 174
XRF (*see* Extended Recovery Facility)

ZNAC/ZNEP interface of Terminal
    Control Program error handling,
    269–270

## ABOUT THE AUTHORS

JOHN KNEILING is a consultant with Price Waterhouse.

RICHARD LEFKON works at the Equitable Insurance Company in New York and specializes in CICS programming.

PAMELA SOMERS is an independent consultant specializing in CICS programming.